CISTERCIAN FATHERS SERIES: NUMBER ELEVEN

ISAAC OF STELLA
SERMONS ON THE CHRISTIAN YEAR
VOLUME ONE

CISTERCIAN FATHERS SERIES: NUMBER ELEVEN

ISAAC OF STELLA

SERMONS ON THE CHRISTIAN YEAR

VOLUME ONE

Translated by
HUGH McCAFFERY
Monk of Mount Melleray

Introduction by
BERNARD McGINN

CISTERCIAN PUBLICATIONS
Kalamazoo, Michigan
1979

THE CISTERCIAN FATHERS SERIES
BOARD OF DIRECTORS

This translation has been made from the Latin edition of Dom Anselm Hoste OSB and G. Salet, *Isaac de l'Etoile: Sermons,* Sources chretiennes 130 (Paris: Editions du Cerf, 1967) and 207 (1974).

Available in Europe and the Commonwealth through
A. R. Mowbray & Co Ltd
St Thomas House Becket Street
Oxford OX1 1SJ

Library of Congress Cataloging in Publication Data

Isaac of Stella, d. 1169.
    Sermons on the liturgical year.

    (Cistercian Fathers series ; no. 11-   )
    Translation of the original Latin text as published
in Sermons, Paris, beginning in 1967.
        1. Church year sermons. 2. Catholic Church—
Sermons. 3. Sermons, English—Translations from Latin.
4. Sermons, Latin—Translations into English.
I. McCaffery, Hugh. II. Title.
BX1756.I176S4713   252'.6   78-868
ISBN 0-87907-611-9

Book design by Gale Akins
Typeset at Humble Hills Graphics, Kalamazoo, Michigan 49004

Printed in the United States of America

TABLE OF CONTENTS

ISAAC OF STELLA
SERMONS ON THE CHRISTIAN YEAR
VOLUME ONE

INTRODUCTION

A SUPREME LOVE for the monastic ideal lived to
the fullest, an original and powerful theological mind,
a dense and highly individual style—these are the
characteristics that make Isaac of Stella at once a
rewarding but at the same time a difficult author.
Less humane, less easy of access than the other great
contemporary English Cistercian, Aelred of Rievaulx,
Isaac surpasses him in the depth and scope of his
theological vision. Lacking the stylistic virtuosity, the
incredible range and the supreme mystical flights of
the greatest Cistercian author, Bernard, Isaac is nonetheless more the speculative theologian than the
abbot of Clairvaux. In terms of this intellectual
power he might best be compared with the fourth of
the great names among the Cistercian Fathers of the
twelfth century, the deep and subtle William of
Saint Thierry. Both men display an interest in negative theology, an anthropology open to the influence
of Gregory of Nyssa and John the Scot and an
ecclesiology in which the theme of the Mystical Body
plays a key role. But important differences remain,
not only in the way in which they developed their

common interests, but in the attitude that each took towards the theological tensions of the day. The abbot of Stella is very much his own man, however vital the themes that tie him to the other great Cistercians.

Several good general introductions to Isaac's thought exist, notably those of Fr G. Salet and Gaetano Raciti.[1] I have written at some length on important aspects of his thought,[2] and there is a respectable body of specialized literature that can be consulted with profit.[3] While still not as well known as the other major Cistercian authors, Isaac is scarcely "the great mystery among the Cistercians," as Louis Bouyer once called him.[4] Nevertheless, he remains a difficult author, one for whom some form of access (*accessus ad auctorem*) is eminently useful. Such an *accessus* need not try to rival the introductions currently available, but it should provide a perspective from which to read the abbot of Stella. The whole enterprise of the Cistercian Fathers Series is founded on the premise that there is no substitute for reading the masters of monasticism, even filtered through the distorting veil of another language. What follows is designed to set the stage for the reader's encounter with this author, not to determine the outcome beforehand.

There are, of course, many ways to read an author, especially an author dead eight hundred years. One popular approach to past theological texts is the search for relevance, the attempt to retrieve certain themes, methods and conclusions still challenging or useful for current theological tasks. In this approach the present judges the past, measuring it against contemporary consciousness, criticizing, selecting, retrieving. But it is also possible to approach classic texts in another way—to allow them to measure us rather than to attempt to fit them into the confines of our own horizons, however generous we may judge these to be. We can turn to the past not only to mine it for our own purposes, but also to be undermined. Our views, our cherished insights and conclusions, can be challenged and perhaps stretched if we are willing to hear a text speaking on its own terms. Without such a "sympathetic" reading, at least as an initial step, it is doubtful that the theological appropriation of any classic text can be more than an enlightened misreading.

Few of us are totally free of the modern prejudice that the latest is most likely the best—the newest car, entertainment or idea. It is worthwhile to reflect that exactly the opposite view formed an *a-priori* for many centuries of western intellectual history, the belief succinctly put by Richard Hooker when he said: "There are few things known to be good 'til such times as they grow to be ancient."[5] Either view, baldly put, would be disastrous as the sole criterion of judgment; but they do at least indicate the boundaries within which the delicate task of reading theological classics is to be conducted.

At its crudest, the search for relevance is nothing more than one disguise of the prejudice that the newest must be the best. The prejudice of archaism, while the lesser temptation today, can easily masquerade under the laudable desire to hear the text speaking in its own voice. Even to recognize the dangers is not always to avoid them, hermeneutics being both art and science, with both a methodical and an unmethodic moment, to borrow a phrase from Paul Ricoeur.

These difficulties do not absolve us from the obligation of making at least some general suggestions. I believe that the best way to *begin* to read an author as distant and yet as powerful as Isaac of Stella is to approach as closely as possible to the latter pole—to let the author's vision become, at least initially, the measure and norm of our own, to think of the ancient as the good and the profitable (Isaac himself was far more the witness to tradition than a conscious innovator). To do this we must be prepared to suspend, or perhaps better to bracket, our critical reactions; we must renounce our "heresy" of picking out what seems still useful and true and rejecting what seems outmoded, jejeune, even harmful. Precisely what is strange, disconcerting and distant may be most revealing when seen in the light of the whole. Without a sincere effort to appreciate this strangeness we will come away from reading the text no richer than when we began it, or perhaps at best with a few more proof texts or foreshadowings of our own cherished notions. If we do make the effort, and if the text itself is rich enough, we may be changed, our horizons widened, our world expanded. We can be converted to a new stage of life through the world unfolded by the text and thus made capable of appropriating it on a new and more vital level. Thus it is possible to make use of a text in the present, but not just for the present. Through this process of change and conversion in the encounter with the text we learn how to avoid searching the past just to serve the present and begin appropriating our own past and that of others in the service of a broader future.

Not all texts offer the proper stimulus to make such an effort worthwhile. I have no intention of attempting to analyze what constitutes such a a theological or monastic classic. I can only offer personal testimony that I have found Isaac of Stella's sermons and treatises to be of this nature and to invite others to test my reactions.

ISAAC'S WORLD

Isaac was born into a century of remarkable accomplishment in almost every area of human endeavor. A burgeoning economy and growing population provided a solid material basis for creative advances in government, religious life, law, education, science, thought, art and literature. What strikes us most about this rapidly-changing era is the youthful self-confidence with which problems were tackled, the almost effortless ease with which new ideas and new institutions were created.[6] The abbot of Stella's life and thought can only be understood against the background of two of the most significant of the new institutions of the twelfth century: the

Cistercian reform and the rise of the university.

Isaac was born in England sometime not long after 1100.[7] Nothing is directly known concerning his life until 1147, when he first appears as abbot of Stella, but the indirect evidence present in his writings allows us to make some important conjectures. Isaac's mastery of the technical vocabulary of the Schools, and the character of his speculative thought, especially as seen in his Sermons for Sexagesima and *Letter on the Soul*, clearly indicate that like so many other bright young men he had first come to France to attend the Cathedral Schools that were involved not only in the creation of a new era in the history of theology but also in the formation of a new educational institution, the university. We shall not be far wrong if we place his arrival in France about 1130, and while we cannot be sure exactly where he studied, his writings show familiarity with the thought of the Masters active in Paris and neighboring Chartres in the 1130s, such as High of St Victor, Peter Abelard, William of Conches, and Thierry of Chartres.[8] Isaac was a schoolman before he became a monk, and always, to the end of his days, remained something of a schoolman.

Sometime not long after 1140, the English scholar entered the monastic life, most likely at the great Cistercian house of Pontigny in the diocese of Auxerre.[9] In 1147 he was made abbot of Stella (Etoile) some twelve miles from Poitiers, a small reform abbey that had just been incorporated into the Cistercian order in the filiation of Pontigny.

In 1147 the Cistercian movement stood at the apogee of its success. Eugene III, a pupil of Bernard, had been raised to the papacy in 1145, the first Cistercian pope. The peerless abbot of Clairvaux was the most influential figure in Christendom. Cistercian houses had proliferated with such rapidity in just over three decades that they now numbered in the hundreds and could be found throughout Europe. The "new model" monastery established at Cîteaux in 1098 had become far more of an archetype than its founders could ever have imagined.[10]

To enter the Cistercians was a religious decision on Isaac's part, an election to turn his back on the world and to commit his future to a rigorous form of monastic life. Precisely because this decision was so total it involved an intellectual component as well. To turn one's back on the world did not mean turning one's back on the intellect and the intellect's appropriation of faith in theology, though it did mean placing intellectual appropriation in a new perspective. It is clear that this was Isaac's way; nor was he totally out of step with his fellow Cistercians. Despite Bernard's well-known opposition to Abelard and Gilbert of Poitiers, his friendship and support of Hugh of St Victor and Peter Lombard among others show that it is a gross simplification to characterize him as anti-theological or even anti-scholastic.[11] William of St Thierry shared Bernard's battles against some forms of contemporary speculation, but like Isaac he had been educated in the Schools and this remained a formative influence in his intellectual career. Guerric of Igny, a friend of Bernard and sermonist of note, had also been a schoolman before his conversion. Two of the foremost Masters of the twelfth century, men whose thought shares a number of themes with Isaac, ended their days as Cistercians— Thierry of Chartres about 1150 and Alan of Lille about 1200.[12]

In Isaac's mind the relation of these two great movements of the twelfth century, the world of the Schools and the world of Cîteaux, was complimentary, not antagonistic. It is hard not to think that his theological studies had been a contributing factor in the search that led him to Cîteaux; his sermons and treatises are evidence of the fact that his experience of the monastic life provided an ideal situation for theological meditation, while his duties as abbot saw to it that these meditations were communicated to others. Even about 1165 when the abbot of Stella found it necessary to abate temporarily the speculative cast of his public addresses, he did not turn his back on theology. An important passage in the Forty-Eighth Sermon, known in some manuscripts as "The

Apology of Isaac, Abbot of Stella", shows that while
he was aware of the problems raised by some Masters,
for him they were still " . . . men of notable intelligence and marvellous research".[13]

Our information about Isaac's life after 1146
allows us tantalizing glimpses, but not enough information for a real biographical study. Two key events
stand out as important clues for his personal commit-
ments: the first his adherence to the cause of Thomas
à Becket, the other his mysterious retirement to a
new monastery on the island of Ré.

On 22 June 1164, John Bellesmains, the English
bishop of Poitiers, wrote to his good friend Thomas à
Becket that he and their common friend Isaac of
Stella had been interceding with the great abbey of
Pontigny in the Archbishop's behalf. This intercession was not in vain, because when Becket finally fled
the power of Henry II in October of the same year it
was at Pontigny that he was received, beginning his
exile there in January of 1165. In November of 1166,
however, Becket left Pontigny at the request of no
less an authority than the General Chapter of the
Cistercian order. After a difficult struggle between
pro- and anti-Becket factions, in most un-bernardine
fashion the order had capitulated to the threats and
pressure of the implacable Henry II and retreated
from the strict reformist stance of their earliest days.[14]

It is clear that Isaac was an important member of
the party favorable to Becket, a party whose strength
lay with Pontigny and her daughters. Many English
Cistercians of note had sited with Henry; Isaac's
view of the quarrel made this impossible. Whether or
not the abbot of Stella actually suffered as a result of
the defeat of the pro-Becket forces is impossible to
tell, but we may hazard a guess that his departure
from Stella, probably in 1167, could well have been
at least partially triggered by disillusion over recent
events in the order.

A number of Isaac's surviving sermons make
reference to the desolate island situation in which
they were given. Three charters and some indirect
witnesses enable us to identify Isaac's other monastery

as Notre-Dame des Chateliers on the island of Ré
off the Atlantic port of La Rochelle. Despite the
obscurity that still surrounds the circumstances of the
founding of this house, some things seem generally
accepted. At the invitation of the noble Eble of
Mauléon, Isaac and his friend John of Trizay ap-
parently set up a small foundation on Ré and retired
there in 1167. This action, as well as the allowance
of non-Cistercian customs, was technically illegal; it
seems likely that Isaac was deposed as abbot of Stella.
Not long afterward, Eble petitioned the abbot of
Pontigny and the General Chapter to regularize the
foundation and this was duly done, the re-endowed
house being taken into the line of Pontigny. The
evidence of the sermons indicates that Isaac con-
tinued as abbot, whatever irregularities he had com-
mitted. It is difficult not to agree with G. Salet that
it was primarily for spiritual reasons,[15] the desire for
more perfect solitude and poverty, that Isaac betook
himself "... to this remote island shut in by the
ocean" where, as he put it "... naked and shipwrecked we few are able to embrace the naked cross
of the naked Christ."[16]

A late tradition has it that Isaac died in 1169, but
the considerable literary activity from the Ré period
(at least twenty-five of the surviving sermons) may
well point to a longer life. Raciti has lately argued
persuasively for a date as late as 1178.[17] An unknown
grave near the solitude of the sea seems a fitting
resting place for so great a lover of monastic peace.

ISAAC'S WORKS

The authentic works of the abbot of Stella are not
extensive: two treatises in letter form and fifty-five
sermons. During the twentieth century, two scriptural
works, a *Commentary on the Song of Songs* and a
Commentary on the Book of Ruth, have also been
attributed to the abbot of Stella, but there is no solid
reason for supporting these claims. Jean Leclercq's

discovery of a new sermon some years ago encourages hope for other surprises, but it is doubtful that any substantial additions to our knowledge are in the offing.

Isaac's two letters were more widely read than his sermons. His *Letter on the Office of the Mass,* an allegorical interpretation of the liturgy in the tradition of the Carolingian Amalarius of Metz, survives in at least twenty-five manuscripts and was used by no less an authority than Pope Innocent III; the *Letter on the Soul* addressed to Alcher of Clairvaux, one of the most important anthropological treatises of the twelfth century, is found in nine manuscripts and was influential on later medieval thought, especially through its use in the pseudo-Augustinian *On the Spirit and the Soul.*[18] Despite the fact that the manuscript tradition for the sermons is fragmentary and indicates that they were not widely known,[19] one can well argue that the surviving sermons constitute the core of Isaac's theological contribution. The broad lines of the theological anthropology found in the *Letter on the Soul* can be recovered from the sermons (e.g., Sermon Four), but many of abbot's major themes on the doctrine of God, on predestination, on Christ and the sacraments, are not present in the letter-treatises.

We must remember that the sermons of Isaac are a form of "written rhetoric", a highly conscious literary genre whose relation to actual preaching is distant and in some cases non-existant.[20] Many of them undoubtedly reflect elements of conferences given in monastic chapter; some even are related to festal sermons given to both the brothers and the *conversi.* Even those that were never preached in any way were created for monks as texts for reading, meditation and discussion. We should beware of taking the charming literary fictions that sprinkle some sermons (e.g., Sermons Nine, Eleven, Twenty-Four and Twenty-Five) as evidence of the real life situation.

The properly theological character of Isaac's sermons is enhanced by the way in which he groups them into series concentrating on specific issues or ranges of issues. By far the larger number of surviving pieces are not isolated meditations on particular feasts, but parts of treatises on theological topics that use the readings of the liturgy as starting points. Isaac's systematic view of the Christian mystery makes this way of using scripture far less arbitrary than it might seem.

Exact agreement on the breakdown of the treatises and their dating is difficult, but broad consensus exists.[21] Sermons One to Five, a tract on the stages of the spiritual life in the form of a commentary on the beatitudes, give no indication of dating. The second treatise in the present volume clearly dates from the Ré period. Sermons Seven to Twelve, Fifteen and Fourteen form a series consisting of two sermons for each of four Sundays after Epiphany.[22] The theme is soteriological: the main lines of the fall and redemption of man. Sermons Sixteen and Seventeen make up a short treatise on conversion, while Sermons Eighteen through Twenty-Six on the parable of the sower from the Gospel for Sexagesima constitute a treatise on the divine nature, the most profound expression of Isaac's speculation.[23] There are also several short groupings among the later sermons to be issued in a subsequent volume of the Cistercian Fathers Series.[24]

ISAAC'S THOUGHT

The true character of the abbot of Stella's highly synthetic theology is blurred by attempts to survey it under the heading of particular doctrines. Such a procedure can provide us with the building blocks but not the system, the way in which everything fits together. Despite the fact that the sermons in this volume contain three major treatises, the nature of the sermon genre and Isaac's special interests in each case preclude the existence of anything like a doctrinal summary or *summa* in which all the elements of his thought would appear in one place. To some degree at least, then, the presentation of his synthesis must be a matter of interpretation.

I do not think it false to Isaac's synthesis, though it certainly goes beyond anything he says in explicit fashion, to portray the coherence of his thought according to the Neoplatonic triad of God as he is in himself, God as the origin of all things, and God as the universal goal. In more Christian terms, these three moments are frequently reduced to two: *creatio* and *recreatio,* or the going forth (*exitus*) and return (*reditus*) of all things to God. Such a unified cosmic vision was common to many of the abbot's sources; the following exposition will try to show that it is central to understanding the harmonies that govern his own thought as well.[25]

By way of prolegomenon, we must first see how the abbot believes it possible for man to know anything about God. According to Sermon Nine, there are six "books" by means of which man is instructed about God: Divine Wisdom, the created spirit, the visible world, the Old Testament, the Word made flesh and the Gospel.[25a] Fallen man has been so blinded by sin that he can scarcely know anything about God through the first three books; had not God chosen to speak to him anew through Christ and the Scriptures saving knowledge would be impossible. As with other contemporary Cistercians, for Isaac theology was fundamentally biblical and Christocentric; the proper way of reading the Scriptures was the essential precondition of the theological task. The abbot of Stella does not provide a systematic introduction to biblical hermeneutics, but partial discussions scattered through the sermons (e.g., Sermons Nine, Ten, Eleven, Sixteen, Thirty-Three, Forty-Eight, Fifty-Two and Fifty-Four) allow us to reconstruct his thought.[26]

For Isaac, as for so many of his predecessors, the Scriptures are the expression of Divine Wisdom and hence are an inexhaustible source of truth. Different interpretations are not only allowed but demanded (Sermon 16:1-3).[27] The abbot adheres to the traditional scheme of four senses—historical, moral, allegorical and anagogical (e.g., Sermons 9:14; 10:14; 54), but he makes clear his own preference for the allegorical, or better, the mystical sense over the moral (Sermons 11:16; 33:11; 35:3). His Fifty-Second Sermon, a brief sketch of an interpretation of the Song of Songs, that book so dear to Cistercian authors, lays down the principle that ". . . almost everything that takes place externally in historical fashion is repeated within in mystery". Isaac's speculative bent was at one with his desire to search for the mystery revealed in the heart of God's word.

The abbot's doctrine of God in himself and God as the source of all things is set forth in detail in the Sermons for Sexagesima. Sermon Twenty-Two in this series presents his understanding of the nature and divisions of theology, a Neoplatonic one in harmony with the thought of the Pseudo-Dionysius and John the Scot.[28] The symbolic and rational theologies that make use of human words have their uses, but only within a hierarchy that gives pride of place to the divine negative theology that denies that any words can be properly applied to God and thus takes refuge in the superaffirmations (e.g., *super-substantia* or "more-than-being" of Sermon 19:19) that are positive in form but negative in meaning (22:6-12).

With this caution in mind, we can follow Isaac's explorations of the possibilities of rational theology within the limiting horizon of negation, first with regard to God as One (Sermons Nineteen to Twenty-One) and then with respect to God as Three, the Christian doctrine of the Trinity (Sermons Twenty-Three to Twenty-Six). Isaac introduces his discussion with a dense survey of general metaphysics in Sermon Nineteen. The basic reason for the introduction of this most scholastic moment in his writings is to indicate the limits of philosophical metaphysics: the analysis of substance and accident shows that God cannot be contained within these categories (Sermon Twenty). In Sermon Twenty-One a consideration of unity, simplicity and immutability, the three properties of the supersubstantial nature of God, already begins to hint at God as creator, for the unity of God is the source of the multiplicity of creation, as his simplicity and immutability are the preconditions of the composite and changeable character of the realities of the world. These contrasts are crucial to Isaac's notion of creation.

The later Sermons for Sexagesima pursue two intertwined themes: the threefold nature of the Godhead and the relation between the three Persons and the work of creation. Isaac does not claim that God is three because he creates, but he certainly indicates that it is through God's creative activity as known to us in Scripture that we come to know the Trinity. God is the source and efficient cause of all (Sermons 21:1-3; 22:8), but also the Exemplar, the "Holy Mind" that gives of itself (Sermon 24:15-20) and illumines all men that come into the world (Sermon Twenty-Six). Thus, creation reveals to us the Father and the Son. Another divine activity begins to make itself known through a consideration of creation in terms of its final cause. The profound agreement between Moses and Plato (Sermon 24:7), the joy and goodness of God mentioned by these two theologians, point to the Holy Spirit, the third Person of the Trinity. Appropriating various Augustinian analogies for the relation between the Trinity and creation in Sermons Twenty-Four and Twenty-Five, Isaac presents one of the most tightly organized theologies of creation of his time.[29]

The abbot of Stella's universe was a highly anthropocentric one: corporeal nature exists to serve rational nature whose end is to rejoice in God (Sermon 25:4-5). It is essentially in his theological anthropology then that we find the *reditus* as well as the *exitus* of creation, the return to as well as the procession from God. By means of first or creating grace,[30] man was made in the image and likeness of God (e.g., Sermons 2:13-15; 8:3; 16:15-16; 25:15). Isaac's anthropology, in conformity with the patristic and early medieval tradition, was founded on the notion of the *imago Dei*. But man was also created to be the image of the world, the microcosm for which the "great animal" of the universe was made. The homology between the five levels of the ascent of the intellective power (*sensus*) to God and the five ascending elements of the physical universe set forth in the *Letter on the Soul* underlies much in the sermons and is explicitly put forth in Sermon Four. Along with the remarkable Sermon Seventeen that provides a succinct statement of the psychology and physiology of conversion (a good example of a text that demands a bracketing of modern perspective if we would hear the message) these two pieces give us the main lines of Isaac's theological anthropology.

Man had been created with these prerogatives and powers, but he was not long to remain in this state. Through the free choice (Sermon 10:18) given by God he fell away from his first condition. Original sin and its effects play a large role in the abbot's thought, as they do in that of any medieval thinker. Isaac is not so much interested in defining original sin as he is in describing its ravages.[31] An important passage in Sermon Fifty-Four (PL 194: 1874D-75A) shows us that for Isaac what is most central in this archetypal sin was its destruction of the cosmic order, the ". . . first natural world, the golden age of Saturn and the golden chain of the poet". As a result of this corruption of the created order man now labors under ignorance and difficulty (Sermon 4:2), beset by the seven deadly sins that can only be cured by the infusion of the seven gifts of the Holy Spirit (Sermon Six). Adam's voluntary descent placed him under the control of the devil and assured that his descendents would be born as much sons of Satan as of God (Sermon 6:10).[32]

Isaac's cosmic vision, however, is not ultimately perverted by original sin. God is not only the source of all things, but also their final goal, and nothing can negate the movement by which he draws things back to himself. The cosmic harmony that Adam destroyed is restored in Christ; what first grace failed to achieve, second grace brings to perfection.

The doctrine of the return brings us to the Christological heart of the abbot's thought. Isaac's

interest in the metaphysical constitution of the
person of Christ is not pronounced;[33] his concern
rests rather upon the redemptive incarnation, the
work by which Christ restores man to God. Christ
the Redeemer is portrayed by means of a wide series
of metaphors—as Divine Physician (Sermon Six),
Exemplar of Virtues (Sermon Eight), the Strong One
who frees us from the devil (Sermon Thirty-Nine);
the role of the mysteries of the Passion and Resurrection is also stressed (Sermon Fifteen). What is
central to Isaac's theology of redemption is the
solidarity that exists between the God–Man and the
rest of the human race. The theme is a traditional
one, but few authors have developed it with the
power that Isaac does.[34] Again and again he returns
to the motif: Sermons 5; 6:10; 10:3-4; 29; 33; and
especially 51.

This solidarity, the reestablishment of cosmic
harmony in Christ, is at the root of Isaac's conception of the Church as the Body of Christ. Since the
investigations of E. Mersch he has been noted as one
of the foremost exponents of the doctrine of the total
Christ in the twelfth century.[35] Among the sermons
found in this volume, numbers Nine, Fifteen, and
particularly Eleven, are rich sources for this teaching;
Sermon Forty-One stands out among the later ones.
The intimate union of Christ and the Church in one
body is the presupposition for the details of Isaac's
ecclesiology. The notion of obedience to authority in
Sermon Thirteen is founded on the humble example
of Christ, and the doctrine of penance in Sermon
Eleven is also rooted in this solidarity.

If the work of return is archetypically accom-
plished in the God–Man, its realization in fallen men
still requires considerable attention on the part of a
writer who is also fundamentally a guide of souls. As
Jean Leclercq has pointed out,[36] monastic theology
is always directly oriented to the experience of faith,
so we should not be surprised at the preponderant
role that Isaac's teaching on the return of the soul
takes in his surviving works. Several useful surveys of
his teaching on the stages of spiritual ascent already

exist, most notably that of G. Raciti;[37] what follows
here is only the merest introduction.

A preliminary remark is necessary at the outset.
Isaac was a Cistercian abbot writing for monks. While
it is tempting to try to make a division in his spiritual
teaching between general requirements incumbent on
all Christians and those particularly directed to monks,
such a division is not easy to work out in detail.
Unlike the wider-ranging Bernard who gives us advice
suited to various orders in the Church, especially in
his *Letters,* Isaac always speaks directly to his charges.
It would be foolish to think that the abbot of Stella
did not allow for the possibility of ascent to God
outside the monastic state, but the sermons do not
give us direct witness for his ideas on non-monastic
spirituality.

From the viewpoint of the individual monk, the
return to God has an existential starting point, the
desire for self-knowledge (Sermons 2:11-13; 17:5;
Letter on the Soul 20).[38] This desire is the precondition for the *reditus* or return, a dynamic movement
described under a variety of metaphors, the two
most popular being those of the ascent of the soul
(*ascensus*; especially Sermons Five, Ten and Twelve)
and the conversion of the soul (*conversio;* see
Sermons Sixteen and Seventeen). These metaphors
and their related themes, such as the communion of
truth and charity (Sermons 5:20-21; 16:16), the
notion of virtue (Sermons 3:1-2; 17:10-13),[39] and the
purification of regard (Sermon 4:1-5), are so wide-
spread in Isaac's sermons that to attempt a more
specific treatment would be to go beyond the confines of this introduction. No commentary is a substitute for the reading of the text.

The dialectic of the return of the soul to God
through Christ and in the Holy Spirit (see Sermon
Twenty-Four for the work of the Spirit) cannot be
separated from the abbot's teaching on the meaning
of monasticism. Poverty (Sermon Two), chastity
(Sermon Five), obedience (Sermon Thirteen), fasting
(Sermon Thirty-One), and separation from the world
(Sermon One) are necessary virtues; but Isaac's

teaching goes deeper. As central as his stress on the life of contemplation is (e.g., Sermon Fourteen), the abbot never forgets the monk's duty of mercy and love of neighbor (Sermons 3:12-16; 12:6; 25:10), another trait that finds him at one with Bernard of Clairvaux and the other Cistercian masters of his time.

The goal of conversion and ascent is union with God. Isaac is not chary, here or in later sermons, of attempts to describe this indescribable condition, both in terms of the traditional language of marriage (Sermon 5:17-22), or in the more metaphysical accents of the illumination of the highest power of the soul, the understanding (Sermon 26:7-10).[40] There are few sermons of the abbot of Stella which do not touch upon the ultimate goal of the return in some way.

These brief remarks have been intended to highlight the density and profundity of Isaac's thought, but also the reward that awaits those who read him with attention and care. Anyone who has ever wrestled with the abbot's text in the original Latin will be aware of the considerable problems faced by the translator and will salute Father Hugh McCaffery for the ability and verve with which he has rendered Isaac's sermons into English. In the presence of the text itself, both translator and commentator assume their rightful positions—"We are merely servants: we have done no more than our duty." (Lk 17:10)

BERNARD McGINN
University of Chicago

NOTES TO INTRODUCTION

1. *Isaac de L'Étoile. Sermons I* (Paris: Editions du Cerf, 1967. *Sources Chrétiennes* 130). G. Salet, "Introduction," 7-63. (Hereafter this volume will be abbreviated as Sermons I.) G. Raciti, "Isaac de L'Étoile," *Dictionnaire de spiritualité* VII: cc.2011-38 (Paris: Letouzey et Ane, 1971).

2. B. McGinn, *The Golden Chain. A Study in the Theological Anthropology of Isaac of Stella,* CF 15 (Washington, D.C.: Cistercian Publications, 1972); *"Theologia* in Isaac of Stella," *Cîteaux* 31 (1970) 219-35; "Isaac of Stella on the Divine Nature," *Analecta Cisterciensia* 29 (1973) 3-56.

3. This earlier literature can be found in the bibliographies attached to the general works already mentioned: Special mention should be made of the articles and translations published in *Cistercian Studies* in recent years.

4. *The Cistercian Heritage* (Westminster, Md.: Newman, 1958) 161.

5. *Ecclesiastical Polity* V, vii, 3.

6. Two key works on twelfth-century culture and thought are R. W. Southern, *The Making of the Middle Ages* (New Haven: Yale, 1963) especially chaps. IV and V; and M.-D. Chenu, *La théologie au douzième siècle* (Paris: Vrin, 1957). A partial English translation of the latter is found in *Nature, Man and Society in the Twelfth Century* (Chicago: University of Chicago, 1968).

7. The three most recent biographical studies may be found in *Sermons I,* 7-25; *The Golden Chain,* 7-23; and DS 7:2011-16.

8. *The Golden Chain,* 8-9.

9. Agreeing with Raciti (DS 7:2013) against my earlier supposition that he entered Stella directly (*Golden Chain,* 10-12).

10. For the flourishing of the Cistercian reform, see *The Cistercian Spirit,* CS 3 (Spencer: Cistercian Publications, 1970); and L. Lekai, *The Cistercians. Ideals and Reality* (Kent State: Kent State University Press, 1977).

11. See J. Châtillon, "L'influence de S. Bernard sur la pensée scolastique au xiie et au xiiie siècle," *Saint Bernard Théologien* (Rome: Editiones Cistercienses, 1954) 268-88.

12. Lekai, *The Cistercians,* 46-7, 77, 229, emphasizes the attraction of the order to the intellectuals of the twelfth century.

13. See the detailed study of this Sermon and its implications for Isaac's biography by Raciti in "Isaac de l'Étoile et son siècle," *Cîteaux* 12 (1961) 281-306; and 13 (1962) 18-34, 133-45, 205-16. Raciti's later study in the DS appears to have abandoned some of the positions adopted in these articles.

14. For a more detailed study of these events, see *The Golden Chain*, 34-50; L. A. Desmond, "Becket and the Cistercians," *Canadian Catholic Historical Association Reports* 25 (1968) 9-29; and M. Preiss, *Die politische Tätigkeit und Stellung der Cistercienser im Schisma von 1159–1177* (Berlin–Halle: Historische Studien 248, 1934).

15. *Sermons I*, 23.

16. Sermon 18:1. Cf. Jerome, Ep 52.4.

17. DS 7:2013, 2017-18.

18. Both works are translated in *Three Treatises on Man. A Cistercian Anthropology*, CF 24 (Kalamazoo, Mich.: Cistercian Publications, 1977). For a detailed study of the *Letter,* see *The Golden Chain*, chaps. 3-4.

19. The sermons survive in eight manuscripts, but no single witness contains all fifty-five. Indeed, we are dependent on early printings for the texts of six sermons, the manuscripts having perished. The fullest study of the state of the text is by A. Hoste (*Sermons I*, 69-81) who was responsible for the edition found in the *Sources chrétiennes* series. Vol. I (1967) contains Sermons 1-17; Vol. II (1974) Sermons 18-39. This edition has been used as the basis for this translation, unless otherwise noted.

20. See J. Leclercq, *The Love of Learning and the Desire for God* (New York: Fordham, 1961), 155, 168-70, for general remarks on the sermon as "written rhetoric"; and Salet, *Sermons I*, 31-5, for application to Isaac.

21. See *The Golden Chain*, 27, note 119; and DS 7:2018-19.

22. Raciti demonstrates that Sermon Thirteen does not belong to the series and that Fifteen and Fourteen should be reversed. He argues from internal evidence that the series dates from 1173 (DS 7:2017).

23. This group of sermons definitely dates from the Ré period. I have studied it in detail in my article "Isaac of Stella on the Divine Nature".

24. E.g., Sermons Twenty-Seven to Twenty-Nine for Quinquagesima Sunday, a tract on asceticism; and Sermons Thirty-Three to Thirty-Seven on salvation and predestination.

25. For a superb brief characterization of the cosmic dimensions of Isaac's theology, see L. Merton's introduction in *Cistercian Studies* 2 (1967) 245.

25A. I shall restrict references where possible to the twenty-six sermons translated in this volume. Because of our concentration on the sermons available here, some aspects of Isaac's thought that are strong in the later sermons will be slighted. Among the most important of these are his treatment of the Blessed Virgin, aspects of his doctrine of the sacraments, and especially his teaching on predestination.

26. See "Note complémentaire 12. Les sens de l'Écriture," in *Sermons I*, 343-44.

27. For the history of this theme, see H. deLubac, *Exégèse médiévale* (Paris: Aubier, 1959-64) Part I, Vol. 1, chap. 2, "Mira profunditas".

28. For a more detailed study of his teaching and its sources, see my "*Theologia* in Isaac of Stella".

29. Sermon Twenty-Six even contains a brief theology of history, though it cannot be said that Isaac's main interests are here.

30. The distinction between first (creating) grace and second (helping) grace is of central importance in Isaac, e.g., *Letter on the Soul* 21, and Sermon 26:4-6. See *The Golden Chain*, 186-88, for this theme and notes on its interpretation.

31. There is a brief scholastic discussion of evil as a *passio* in Sermon 16:10. See *Sermons I*, 338-39, for a useful note on original sin in Isaac.

32. Isaac is not much concerned with the contemporary question in the Schools of the manner of the transmission of original sin. For other treatments, see Sermons 7, 17, 26, 35, and the *Letter on the Soul* 19-20.

33. He repeats traditional formulas regarding the three "substances" (flesh, soul and the Word), two natures, and one Person in Christ (e.g., Sermons 9:14; 29:5; 42), but is not interested in exploring the manner of the union.

34. See G. Salet, *Sermons I*, 44-47; and L. Gaggero, "Isaac of Stella and the Theology of Redemption," *Collectanea OCR* 22 (1960) 21-36.

35. E. Mersch, *Le corps mystique du Christ* (Paris, 1933) Vol 2, 142-48. See also "Note complémentaire 13. Le Corps mystique du Christ" in *Sermons I*, 344-45.

36. *The Love of Learning*, 213-18.

37. DS 7:2026-35.

38. See *The Golden Chain*, 109-12; and the classic study of E. Gilson on this theme in chap. 11 of *The Spirit of Mediaeval Philosophy* (New York: Scribner, 1940).

39. See *The Golden Chain*, 143-49; and R. Javelet, "La vertu dans l'oeuvre d'Isaac de l'Étoile," *Cîteaux* 11 (1960) 252-67.

40. For Isaac's doctrine of union, see Raciti, DS, 2029-31.

ISAAC OF STELLA
SERMONS ON THE CHRISTIAN YEAR
THE TEXT

SERMON ONE
For the Feast of All Saints

"JESUS, seeing the crowds, went up into a mountain."* If only we could sometimes do the same; see the crowds, dismiss them, and then "place ascending steps in our hearts"!* But it is difficult in a crowd to see the crowd.[1] Inevitably there is some confusion in a crowd and confusion makes clear vision and discernment and sound judgment impossible. The crowd must be sent away if it is to be seen and judged. And anyone who really sees the crowd has no further time for it, he longs to escape and gladly sends it away.

2. If a man has never seen light he will not recognize darkness either.[2] It was only after "he commanded light to shine out of darkness"* that the Almighty "separated light from darkness".[3] Then it was that he discerned and judged and "he called the light Day and the darkness Night".[4] And God saw, says Genesis,* as though he had not seen before. In the same way a man who has scarcely got above the level of the crowd, has not yet seen the crowd. Furthermore, if he has never known the silence of solitude,

*Mt 5:1

*Ps 83:6

*2 Co 4:6

*Gn 1:4

4

he will not hear the crowd's clamor, he will not realize the commotion it is making.[5]

3. My Lord Jesus[6] and perhaps he alone, could be in a crowd and yet be undisturbed by it and so could see it. Yet he, "when he saw"* it, dismissed it, and "withdrew"* "into a mountain",† where it could not follow him. How sad it is, brothers, that many nowadays resolve to leave the crowds yet settle down where they are certain to be found by them again. Then they are even more harrassed than before and the "final" disturbance from the crowd "is worse than the first".*

4. So, brother, "escape far away" do not run back to the crowd but "stay in solitude"*, "follow" Jesus, climb the mountain, tell the crowd: "Where I am going, you cannot come."*

Although the literal sense, beloved, makes reference to an earthly mountain and an exterior crowd, it is upon the allegorical sense that I wish to focus attention, especially upon that which will most teach us how to live and "build" us "up on the one foundation".*

5. For though it is difficult, if not impossible, that a real crowd should be without accompanying clamor, yet with still greater reason do I distrust that interior crowd, so to speak, which is all the more troublesome as it is inward.[7] So, "because of this" crowd, "climb high",* follow Jesus. He has descended into you, so that you, after him and through him, may ascend above yourself, even up to him who is within you.[8]

6. Here is deep mystery indeed! Leaving the crowds, Jesus "climbs up the mountain".* The disciples—all of them and only they—follow him. Surely all the disciples were not physically stronger than all the others in the crowd! Was it not, rather, that they were "spiritually more fervent, so that they went wherever the Spirit urged them"?* But why then, at another time, when the disciples were just as willing and eager, just as strong and ardent, did Jesus leave nearly all of them behind and with only a few climbed another mountain which was, as Scripture testifies, "very

*Mt 5:1
*Lk 5:16, 9:10
†Mt 14:23,
  Mk 6:46

*Mt 27:64

*Ps 54:8

*Jn 8:21

*1 Co 3:12

*Ps 7:8

*Mt 5:1

*Ezk 1:12

Mt 17:1

high?"* And indeed, brothers, what of that further occasion, when Jesus left behind even these disciples, and all the others, indeed he left behind all men and "alone he went up the mountain to pray?"[9]

7. What do these mountains signify? He climbs the first in order to teach, the second to reveal his glory, the third to pray to his Father.[10] Surely here is "the mountain of the house of the Lord, set on the summit of the mountains"?* It is perhaps in this sense "that He comes, leaping upon the mountains, skipping over the hills."* Skipping first over all the crowds, he leaps up the mountain with his disciples; then skipping over the other disciples to prefer the three he leaps with his crowd upon the "very high" mountain; finally, overleaping the whole of creation, where no one can follow him he leaps alone, the Equal to the Equal, the Son to the Father. On the first mountain the Son alone is heard; on the second the Son is seen and the Father heard; but here on the third no one sees or hears "the Father except the Son," nor "the Son except the Father."*

Is 2:2

Sg 2:8

Mt 11:27

8. Are these, perhaps, the "ineffable things which man may not utter"?* Or may we perhaps interpret these three mountains as three heavens? In the first, man's spiritual life is formed, in the second the angelic life is manifested and in the third the life of God himself lies hidden. The first designates holiness in our present existence, the second discloses the glory that is to come. The third is as it were "the heaven of heavens", to which "he climbs upon the sunset", rising even to his Source; his name is the Lord."[11] Here dwells the glorious Trinity, known only to itself and to the Man who was "taken up to"* God and who "dwells in unapproachable light."[12]

2 Co 12:4

Mk 16:19

9. Though abiding in "peace surpassing all our thinking,"* that Man prays to the Father for us; as the apostle says: "He stands in the presence of his Father and intercedes for us."* See how hiddenly he prays, who taught us to "pray in secret to the Father."* So, brother, make for yourself a hidden place within yourself, in which you can flee away from yourself and pray in secret to the Father.

Ph 4:7

Heb 7:25; Rm 8:34

Mt 6:6

10. "And now let us hear what the Lord God will speak"* about this first hidden or secret place, this first chamber, this first heaven or mountain. He tells us: "Happy are the poor in spirit."* The crowd has been left behind. No mention now of the day's troubles, of human weakness and sin; his discourse is wholly of goodness of life, happiness in glory, the kingdom of heaven.

11. "Happy," he says, "are the poor in spirit." Wisdom always acts and speaks wisely. Wishing to draw the weak, he opens seven cases of ointments for them, so that delighted by the fragrance, they may hasten after him, as it is written: "Draw me after you, we will run in the fragrance of your perfumes."[13]

12. "And when he had sat down, he opened his mouth."* May it be granted me to sit with Jesus, to sit at his feet on the mountainside and partake of his instruction. When he is in the crowd he is standing and walking, occupied and wearied, and so hard pressed that neither he nor his disciples are, as it were, allowed to eat bread, "the bread of life and understanding",* and to drink "the water of wisdom."† For this water can only be drunk in a time of leisure, and it is drawn by those who have little to do. For "the well is deep".*

13. "And he opened his mouth".* The mouth, from which the Bride implores "a kiss".* That mouth so infinitely rich, "in which are hidden all the treasures of wisdom and knowledge."* The mouth, by which "day to day pours forth speech."* Many have searched for wisdom, and for happiness, but because they did not hear this divine Mouth nor see his day, they stumbled in the palpable darkness of error, and thus night to night declares knowledge, that is knowledge only in name.

14. Opening his mouth Jesus speaks to the heart of Jerusalem, talking to her in solitude or on the mountain, and this is what he says: "Happy are the poor in spirit."* He who is Happiness speaks of happiness, he who became poor of poverty, Bread speaks of repletion, Mercy of mercifulness, he who is the Purity of hearts speaks of purification of heart, the truly Peaceful of peace-making, the Son by nature speaks of

*Ps 84:9
*Mt 5:3
*Mt 5:2
*Mk 6:31
†Si 15:3
*Jn 4:11
*Mt 5:2
*Sg 1:1
*Col 2:3
*Ps 18:3
*Mt 5:3

sonship. The true Word of the Father speaks that which he is, divine Wisdom teaches what he is and says: "Blessed are the poor in spirit." Wisely indeed he puts first, giving it precedence over everything else, what every man seeks, every man craves and desires, though almost all go astray in their search for it.

15. For who does not want to be happy? Why do men universally quarrel and fight, bargain, resort to flattery, and inflict injuries on one another? It is not simply in order to obtain, by fair means or foul, what seems good to them, something that promises to make them happy? For everyone imagines himself the happier the more he obtains what he desires.

Men agree, then in their desire for happiness, but their conceptions of it differ widely. For one it consists in physical pleasure and fleeting enjoyment, for another in strength of character, for yet another in knowledge of truth.[14]

16. So the Teacher of all men, who by love alone has become "a debtor to the unwise as well as to the wise,"* begins by redirecting those who have lost the way, then he gives guidance to those who are making good progress, and finally he gives admittance to those knocking at the door, just as he says: "Knock and the door will be opened to you."* In the name of the wanderers the Prophet prays: "Guide me, Lord, in your way;"* for those on the way: "Let me walk in your truth;"* for those who are knocking: "Make my heart rejoice to reverence your name."* And in another psalm again he prays for the wanderers: "Lead me, Lord in your justice;"* for those on the journey: "Make my path straight in your sight;"* and for those who are knocking: "May all those that trust in you have joy, they will rejoice for ever and you will dwell in them; all those that love your name will glory in you,"* and so on.

17. So he who is "the Way, the Truth and the Life",* he who corrects, guides and welcomes, begins with the words: "Happy are the poor in spirit". The false wisdom of this world, which is true stupidity, not understanding what it is saying nor of what it is speaking, has its own scale of values. In its estimation

*Rm 1:14

*Lk 11:9

*Ps 85:11
*Ibid.
*Ibid.

*Ps 5:9
*Ibid.

*Ps 5:12

*Jn 14:6

the happy are those aliens "whose right hand is the right hand of falsehood and whose mouth speaks lies",* because their "barns are full to overflowing," their "flocks are increasing" and their "cattle fat."* In a word, they have everything that relates to wealth that may fail, and to peace that is no peace, and to empty gladness. In direct contradiction, the Wisdom of God, the Right Hand of the Father, his own Son, the Mouth that speaks truth, declares that the happy people are the poor, they will be the kings of a kingdom that is everlasting.

*Ps 143:8,11
*Ps 143:13-14

18. As if he were to say: "You seek happiness but it is not where you think it is. You are running hard, but off the track. Here is the right road, here is the way to happiness. Poverty is the way, poverty willingly embraced for my sake. Happiness is the kingdom of heaven in me. You run energetically but not profitably, for the faster you run, the further you are from the track. Poverty is the way to happiness. Keep to the way and you will arrive."

19. Courage, then, brothers; it is for us who are poor to listen to the Poor Man commending poverty to the poor. Someone speaking from experience is to be believed; Christ was born poor, lived poor and died poor. He willed to die; certainly he did not will to become rich. Let us believe Truth when he tells us of the way to life. If it is hard, it is brief, while happiness is eternal. It is narrow but it leads to life and brings us out into freedom; it will "set our feet in an open place".* It is steep, of course it is, for it goes uphill, it reaches to heaven! So we must be lightly equipped, not heavily encumbered, for the climb.

*Ps 30:9

20. What are we seeking? Is it happiness? The Truth shows us true happiness. Is it wealth? The king shares his kingdom and makes kings. Men are plagued with a restless desire for novelty. Though they can obtain a sufficiency without difficulty, they must sweat for more. Some make five yoke of oxen a pretext for not coming to the heavenly wedding feast,* the feast in which poverty becomes plentitude, want becomes satiety, and the last place becomes the first. There lowliness is transformed into greatness and

*Lk 14:19

1 K 19:19 labour into repose.[15] Elisha slaughtered just such oxen that he might follow Elijah the more readily.* Taking this as model and type, let us follow Christ.

We will end here for today, brothers. Tomorrow the second sermon will be devoted to the second virtue, through the help of him who is the "Sermon of the Father" through whom and because of whom we speak, who lives and reigns eternally.

NOTES

1. St Augustine, *In Joan* 17, 11.
2. This agrees with St Gregory, Mor Bk. 24, 8, 15; PL 76:295.
3. Genesis 1:4; literally "he divided between light" etc. which the Septuagint, and is used, e.g., by J. S. Eriugena, *De Divisione Naturae*, 3:24; PL 122:691.
4. Genesis 1:5. As in St Ambrose, *Hexaemeron*, 2, 9, 35; PL 14: 143. St Augustine *Conf.* 13, 14, 2.
5. Rather like St Augustine, *In Joan* 17, 11; 51, 3.
6. "My Lord Jesus" found also in Serm 12, 2. This phrase links Isaac with St Bernard, *Miss* 4, 2; and St Aelred, *Iesu* 1, 3; PL 184:851.
7. On the "interior crowd," and need of interior solitude compare St Gregory, *Mor* 4, 30, 57; PL 75:667; and 30, 16, 52; PL 76:553. Notice the parallel: literal sense and real crowd vs allegorical sense and interior crowd.
8. See St Augustine, *Enarr. in Ps 1*, 2.
9. Matthew 14:23. This text is found, significantly, in John Cassian *Conferences X*, 6; PL 49:827.
10. Bernard *Asc* 4:7, discusses these "mountains" though in a different order.
11. Psalms 67:5-34, accommodated to context. For Christ's - climbing "upon the sunset" see St Gregory, *In Evang* 17:2, PL 76:1139.
12. 1 Timothy 6:16. This is a frequent text in Eriugena, *Div Nat*, 1:76; 5, 36 (PL 122:522c; 963c).
13. Song of Songs 1:3. The Beatitudes are here regarded as seven. See Augustine, *Contra Faustum* 22:52.
14. As reference to St Augustine shows (*Trin* 13:4; *Sermon* 150:8), the three conceptions of happiness are those of Epicureans, Stoics and Christians.
15. The heavenly banquet has *five* things to "compensate" for the "five oxen".

SERMON TWO
A Second Sermon for the Feast of All Saints

*Mt 5:4

"HAPPY are the meek, they shall possess the earth."* The disease of desire for gain[1] closely accompanies the vice of pride. For the wisdom that is not from above is earthly, sensual, of the devil,* full of

*Jm 3:15

jealousy and contention. It equates domination with happiness and buys a farm so that it can dominate others and quarrel endlessly. This wisdom is truly of the devil, it is the firstborn of him who sought to set

*Is 14:13. Cf.
Bernard, Hum.
10:31

his throne above the other stars.* But the disciples, leaving behind that disordered and disordering wisdom together with the crowd, were privileged to hear the words: "Happy are the meek, they shall possess the earth."

2.   He does not say this or that or any section of earth, however large, but simply "the earth." Did ever a man, for all his sweat and toil, his money and his fists, gain more than a part of the earth? Even in this, few have succeeded and many failed. And who has been able to keep possession of what he has won? What profit is there in working hard and long to gain something that of necessity must quickly be lost?

Heaven is for the poor, the earth for the meek, what is left for the contentious? What else do they want, in their desire of riches?

3. If heaven and earth do not suffice them, what then? "O men, how long will you be dull of heart, will you love what is futile and seek what is false?"* Earthly dominion is but an illusion of power, dignity and happiness. Why be content with only a part? Why covet so little and aim so low? The whole is promised and the way is shown. By voluntary poverty we go and by meekness we move still more speedily. The truly poor man has the happiness of heaven, the meek man the happiness of earth.

*Ps 4:3

4. What remains then for those restless with ambition except the misery of hell? You who are wealthy and powerful, what will you do? Think carefully. You have wealth on the one hand and meekness on the other and a thief is approaching. If you defend your property, you will lose your meekness. If you hold fast to meekness, you will be throwing away your money. I am caught on either side, for at one and the same time the thief may take my money and the devil my patience.

5. Indeed, brothers, would that money had never existed, for in these evil times it cannot be possessed together with meekness, nor may it be carried on the road by the disciples of Jesus.* Perhaps that is why the Wisdom which is from above and is pure and peaceable,* instructed us to carry neither purse nor money on the journey, to go to law with no one, to give even more than what is robbed, and not to ask for the return of what has been taken;* in short, to hold fast to meekness which is the way to happiness. The Apostle praises this when he says: "You gladly bear with fools, being wise yourselves. Why, you let others prey upon you, take advantage of you!"*

*Lk 9:3

*Jm 3:17

*Cf. Lk 10:4, 9:3, Mt 5:40; Lk 6: 29-30

*2 Co 11:20

6. Lord Jesus, is there anyone today "who believes what we have heard?"* Is there anyone to whom your way is revealed in the way he lives? How very narrow is your way and how few tread it!* This was "you way through the mighty sea" of this present world, but in our times "your footprints

*Is 53:1

*Mt 7:14

are unheeded."* The Apostle named your way
"wisdom"* but today it is called the greatest folly,
idleness, inertia. Alas, my brothers, these footprints
are read of everywhere, but how often disregarded!

7.   To a certain extent indeed the Carthusians
have listened with attentive ears and therefore they
willingly have but little, in order that they may not
be much involved with lawsuits. Their possessions are
meager, lest they invite the world's interest towards
themselves. The Order of Grandmont has listened
more attentively still, for it possesses nothing at all. A
Grandmont monk, journeying penniless to heaven, can
if faced by any of this world's thieves, sing light-
heartedly;[2] good for him! Some say in criticism that
the monks of Grandmont are much given to greetings
on the road. Let them see to it!

8.   Who are we to pass judgment on the servant of
another?* No need to mention those others, whose
"hands are the hands of Esau", though their "voice
is the voice of Jacob,"* who are "against every man
and every man against" them.* But happy are the
meek; with facility and felicity they will possess for
eternity the land of the living, while we, so strong and
daring for the sake of God, go against God's counsel
and command, and in this fleeting moment strive for
the land of the dying. "The meek," the Psalm says,
"shall inherit the earth and dwell there for ever,"*
that is, they shall dwell in the presence of God who
alone remains ever immovable while all else is in
movement, as the earth around which all else revolves.[3]
A generation comes and a generation goes, but the
earth stands.*

9.   The discourse then continues: "Happy are
those who mourn."* What had been said before of
poverty and meekness might have sufficed to redirect
those who had strayed, had not the malice of the
devil extended still further and the cancerous evil
penetrated deeper, even to the marrow. The three-
headed beast Cerberus is still barking and the Lord
here shatters the third head, that is, "prudence of the
flesh" which is hostile to God* and cares solely for
itself, "which glories in its shame,"* the belly its

domain.[4] He who makes his home there cannot please God.

*Ps 72:25
10. "What are heaven or earth to me?"* he says to himself; what are hoarded riches that harm their very owners? What do I care for the powers that fear, and are always to be feared? All these are outside of me. I care only for myself. He reassures himself: "You have ample goods, so feast and drink".* "What more does a man gain from all his labor under the sun".* "Let us eat and drink, for tomorrow we die."* "You fool!" You hoard wealth, not knowing who will possess it.* A rich man owns money and does not own himself.

*Lk 12:19
*Qo 1:3
*1 Co 15:32

*Cf. Ps 38:7

11. Live, while you are still alive! Why lose yourself before the time? You are in a torpor and have forgotten about yourself. Begin to recognize yourself, to love and possess yourself, to be kind to yourself, and you will be happy. Here, brothers, we have the "final error which is worse than the first,"* the "desolate pit, the miry bog."* The "joy which turns too late to sorrow,"* when perhaps, there can be no comfort no matter what the sorrow.

*Mt 27:64
*Ps 39:2

*Pr 14:13

12. But these wretched wanderers are lovingly called back to the way by that infinite Wisdom, and he who is pleased to save those who believe through the folly of preaching,* says: "Happy are those who mourn, they shall be comforted." It is as if he were saying: The way to joy is through sorrow, desolation leads to comfort; by losing your life you find it,* by making little of it you possess it, by hating it you love it and by despising it you save it.

*1 Co 1:21

*Mt 10:39

13. If you desire to know yourself and to possess yourself, go into yourself, and do not search for yourself outside.[5] Distinguish between what is around you, what belongs to you, and your self! The world surrounds you, your body belongs to you, and you yourself are within, made to the image and likeness of God.[6] Return then, "transgressor, to you heart, within, where are truly yourself."* Outwardly you are an animal, fashioned as the world is fashioned,[7] and that is why man is called a miniature world.[8] But inwardly you are made in the image of God and so are capable

*Is 46:8

of being deified.[9]

Now when a man comes to himself as did that
young prodigal son,* where does he find himself? Is it
not in a far country, in the Land of Unlikeness,[10] and
"in a strange land,"* where he sits down and weeps as
he remembers his father and his home.* And does he
not find cause for sorrow in himself, feeding pigs
while he himself is starving? If the many hired men in
his father's house have bread enough and to spare,
while he, the son, in exile and dire poverty, cannot
find even husks with which to fill his stomach, will
not his tears flow readily enough?

14. O "Adam, where are you?"* Still in the
shadows perhaps, so that you cannot see yourself?
Sewing together foolish fig leaves to cover your
shame? Your eyes are only too open to what is
around you and what belongs to you. But look
within, see yourself; there you will find things which
are much more shameful than those external things of
which you are so ashamed. Turn inward, sinner, to
your soul. Look at it dominated by vanity and ill-will,
so fettered that it cannot break loose; and mourn
for it.

15. Turn outward to your body and look at it,
subjected to corruption and death,* so weak that it
cannot raise itself. To summarize then, brothers, we
may say that man has only to probe the depths of his
own wretchedness, ignorance, neediness and unbridled
passions and make an honest reckoning with his
conscience, and he will mourn, weep and lament
more deeply for himself than at the funeral of anyone
else, however dear. His own plight is so much the
closer to him as it is within him. Why have sympathy
for others, but none for yourself?

16. It must be acknowledged, brothers, that we
are truly outside of ourselves (and "behind" rather
than in front), and that we forget, or even do not
know ourselves, whenever we indulge in scoffing,
jesting and idleness, whenever we feed on gossip or
empty talk that merely excites laughter,[11] and become
"inebriated with revelling and drunkenness",* or
succumb to the other weak inclinations of the body.

*Lk 15:17

*Ps 136:4
*Lk 15:13

*Gn 3:9

*Rm 8:21

*Rm 13:13

So it has ever been prudent Wisdom's intention to invite to a house of mourning rather than to a house of feasting,* that is, to call back into himself the man who had been outside himself, saying: "Happy are those who mourn;" and in another passage: "Woe to you that laugh now."*

*Qo 7:3

*Lk 6:25

17. For he himself wept, who now admonishes us to weep; the Gospel does not tell us that he laughed. The tears of Lazarus' sisters obtained the raising to life of their brother. The tears of the sisters made the Life-giver himself weep,* and this was so that you, by weeping over yourself, may yourself rise to life. Come now, brothers, our responsibility is not a light one, we have undertaken a task worthy of grown men. When Elijah entered the desert, he dismissed his servant.* And no boyish levity must be allowed to accompany or follow us, nor, least of all, may we ever turn back to what is childish. "For the body," as the Apostle says, "is dead because of sin, but the spirit is living because you have been justified."* That which is alive in us weeps and prays so that one day that which lies paralysed and is fetid may rise up again.

*Jn 11:33-5

*1 K 19:3

*Rm 8:10

18. "Unhappy man that I am," said one who was mourning for his own dead body, "who will deliver me from the body of this death?" But immediately there is a consolation: "The grace of God through Jesus Christ."* Think of the holy Patriarchs and Prophets, with whom almost all that happened did so symbolically; think of all their striving and suffering, their earnestness in weeping for their dead and in keeping solemn days of mourning, often extending them as became seven-day symbolism to seven days. And we, over whom they were weeping, we laugh derisively and die, or rather, we are dead long since and putrifying. We neglect ourselves and are neglected by God. There is no one who laments his sorrow before he goes to the place of no return* no one who moves Jesus our friend to tears.

*Rm 7:24

*Jb 10:21

19. O sisters, what are you doing? Where are you, the active one? Why are you not working and weeping? And you, the contemplative, why are you not praying and weeping?[12] Why is there not desolation within

the house and out in the street until Jesus sighs
Jn 11:33 and distresses himself, and says, not to the dead but
Jn 11:43 to Death itself: "Go out" so that this dying state of
1 Co 5:4 ours may be swallowed up by life?

20. Accordingly, brothers, let us accept the
correction, the teaching of divine Wisdom, and
whether we are occupied or at leisure, let us recognize
our wretchedness and mourn. "Let us weep before
Ps 94:6 the Lord" who is bounteous in pardon, turning to
Jl 2:12 him "was fasting and tears," mourning over ourselves, so that "as the sorrow weighs down our hearts,
Ps 93:19 his consolation will give joy to our souls." For he
says: "Happy are those who mourn". Happy, not
because they mourn, but because "they shall be comforted." Sorrow is the road and happiness the comfort.

21. This is how God "has ordered the world, he
Ps 95:10, 13 who judges the peoples with equity." In God's Wisdom and kindness it is truly equitable to correct the
wayward, to guide those who have been corrected,
and to receive those whom he has guided. Notice
three pairs of opposites balanced against one another.
For there are three things which lure us away from
God to the world and three which call us back from
the world to God. "All that is in the world is the lust
1 Jn 2:16 of the flesh, the lust of the eyes and the pride of life."
The first marries a wife; the second is obsessed with
Lk 14:18-20 oxen; the third buys a farm. In other words, here are
sensuality, avarice and pride or "carnal desires,
worldly appetites, and malign influences in the high
Ep 6:12 places."

22. So the disciples, leaving the crowd behind,
stride on and climb up the mountain, leaping over,
as it were, from the lower to the higher, from the outward to the inward, from the bodily to the spiritual
plane. And they hear the words: Happy are the poor,
the meek, the repentant, "for theirs is the kingdom of
heaven;" the earth too, and contentment, power,
kindliness, kingship, authority and peace. These are
all within, where the gentle and settled man is at
home, while the hairy man of the open country hunts
in the woods and is supplanted from the birthright of
Gn 25:27, 27:11 the firstborn, that birthright which has been passed

on by him who is the eldest born among many

*Rm 8:29

brethren,* the Only-begotten who with the Father reigns eternally. Amen.

NOTES

1. "The disease of desire for gain", literally, "the evil of curiosity."
2. "Journeying penniless," etc. is a very apt use of Juvenal, *Satires*, 10:22.
3. Some sources of this idea of the cosmos: Cicero's *Somnium scipionis* 4:5; Macrobius' *Comm.* 1, 19, 10 and 11; and William of Conches' *De philosophia mundi* 4:1; PL 172:85.
4. Tissier, and Migne (PL 194:1695A) who follows him, both have "wind" (*ventus*) instead of "belly" (*venter*), as has Dom Hoste; yet the latter word alone seems to belong in the context of Ph 3:19.
5. Self-knowledge, virtue, and not going outside of oneself is in line with Macrobius *Comm* 1, 9, 203.
6. This agrees with St Ambrose, *Hex* 6, 7, 42; PL 14:258.
7. "An animal", literally, "a dumb beast" (*pecus*). Cf. St Augustine, *Civ Dei* 1, 11, 2; et al.
8. "A miniature world," supplied by Boethius, *Diff* (PL 64:907). See also Macrobius, *Comm* 2, 12, 11.
9. Genesis 1:27. From what immediately follows our author, it seems, would agree with St Bernard, *SC* 80:2, and his sources, that being "in the image" refers to mere *capacity*.
10. "Land of Unlikeness", a term borrowed from platonists and found in Augustine, *Conf* 7, 10, 16. Bernard uses it frequently, e.g., *Div* 42:2, *Ep* 8:2, *SC* 27:6, 36, 5, *Gra* 10:32.
11. The sort of conduct condemned by St Benedict, RB 6, 43, and 48. See also Bernard, *Adv* 4:5, *Ann* 3:9, *Hum* 12:40.
12. The spiritual life is seen as including "the active life" i.e., Martha, and "the contemplative life," i.e., Mary (Jn 11:11 ff). E.g., in St Gregory, *Mor.* 6, 37, 61; PL 75:764; and *In Ezech* 2, 2, 11; PL 76: 954-55; and St Bernard, *Ass.* 2: 2; 3: 4; 5: 1-9; and *SC* 57:10-11.

SERMON THREE
A Third Sermon for the Feast of All Saints

*Mt 5:6
*Ezk 2:9

"HAPPY are those who hunger and thirst for justice."* The book of Wisdom, brothers, is written within and without.* It speaks from the "outside" as it were, when it re-directs those who have strayed, and it speaks from the inside when it guides those who are on the right road.[1] Here now is Wisdom's counsel to those who place their happiness not in physical pleasure nor in material possessions, but in virtue of soul.[2] Virtue has been defined as the disposition of a well-ordered soul.[3] We must therefore so unify, order, and govern the desires of the soul, in a manner befitting their true function and purpose, that they may become virtues.

2. It is these desires which qualify every external action; they are capable of degenerating into vices or of developing into virtues. If we rule them prudently and moderately, valiantly and justly, they grow steadily into the virtues of prudence, temperance, fortitude and justice. These are said to be the root of all the virtues, the hinges upon which all the others turn. And of these four, justice like an apex or crown

seems to hold the highest point and pre-eminently bears the name of virtue.[4] Happy indeed are those who choose the direct route to all virtue and hunger and thirst for justice.

3. We are told that the light radiating from all the stars above creates in the highest part of the heavens a wondrous zone of brightness which is called a Galaxy.[5] So too in the spiritual sky, we may say that it is the bright shining of all the virtues which creates the surpassing splendor of justice. And therefore justice is said to be a certain equilibrium, a due measure, a determined limit, above or below which rightness cannot be maintained. It is justice that establishes a balance between all other things and renders to each his due. The natural law contains this virtue, Scripture commands it, the Gospel fulfills it: not only must we not do to others what we would not wish to endure from them, but we should do to others all that we would wish them to do to us.[6]

4. The man who seeks happiness cannot withdraw from this obligation of justice, but must be recalled to it and be guided by it. He must not rest content with the natural law, as does the philosopher, nor build upon the justice of the law, as did the Jew;* *Rm 10:3* but as a Christian he must subject himself to the justice that is based upon faith,* *Ph 3:9* and, as a humble self-accuser press on "towards the prize of the heavenly call . . . in Christ Jesus".* *Ph 3:14* Here below, we can possess justice only in part, but there we shall possess it in its perfection,* *1 Co 13:9-10* in part on the way, in perfection in the plenitude of happiness.

5. Press on then, brother, from part to part, "from virtue to virtue,"* *Ps 83:8* until you make your own him who has made you his own.* *Ph 3:12* Be watchful that justice never leaves your hand, your mouth or your heart, for only "if a man holds firmly to justice will he fully obtain it",* *Si 15:1* a justice that is complete, mature, final, no longer preserved through great effort, but a justice possessing its possessor easily and joyously. "Happy are those who hunger and thirst for justice."

6. And the same Master tells us: "First seek the kingdom of God and his justice."* *Mt 6:33* This is what you

must seek, that is what your God asks of you, so that you might ask of him. As for what to eat or drink or wear, the pagans seek these things. But your "heavenly Father knows that you need them all",* so "cast upon him the burden of all your anxiety";* your concern is to labor. "He takes care of you,"* as long as you do not fail to take care of justice.

*Mt 6:32
*1 P 5:7
*Ibid.

7. Make that your concern, seek that before all else, and seek all else for the sake of it. Seek even the kingdom of God for the sake of justice, and not justice for the sake of the kingdom, or you will return to working as a hired man, all bothered with business. And so you will not experience the Lord's power, because you are not mindful of the justice which belongs to him alone.* All other things are subsidiary, without substance, as it were, unworthy of our search. "All these other things," he assures us, "will be given to you."*

*Ps 70:16

*Mt 6:33

8. In these days we see many men directing all their effort to the search of things that should not be sought. So little do they seek the things that should be sought, that when a man does give full and trusting belief to the word of the Word and sure of a sufficiency for his earthly needs aims toward higher justice, he is ridiculed and held in contempt.

The Master, however, is not speaking of those who seek but of those who "hunger for justice". How should we interpret that? Surely we are to understand that justice is to the soul what food and drink are to the body. In its partial state it is food on the journey, in its perfection it will be our feast when we come Home. Milk for babes here, there it will be meat for grown-ups.* And so the prophet exclaims in horror: "A weaned child on its mother's lap, will you so reward my soul?"* "Happy are those who hunger and thirst for justice, they shall be satisfied."†

*1 Co 3:2

*Ps 130:2
adapted to
context

†Mt 5:6

9. There will be complete happiness when there is full satiety. Then I will be fully satisfied with the fullness of justice, which now I enjoy only in part. Now it is as a medicine, then it will be as a delight; now as a discipline which for the moment seems hard and painful, but afterwards as glory, when it yields, for

those who have been well-trained by it, the peaceful
fruit of justice itself.* For here on earth we see but
the flower of justice and of all the virtues, but there
we will gather the ripened fruit.

Hb 12:11

10. It is evident then, that those who seek happiness in virtue need guidance both in the rudiments of
justice and in its growth towards perfection. The first
element of justice consists in not injuring anyone, its
progress consists in bearing patiently the injuries done
to us, and its perfection is to do good to all men in so
far as we are able, and where we are unable, at least to
desire to do good.[7]

The text continues: "Happy are the merciful, they
shall obtain mercy."* Even a just man cannot safely
contend with sovereign Justice, for "he could not
answer him once in a thousand times".* It would be
foolish to go out with ten thousand men to meet the
onset of one with twenty thousand.*

Mt 5:7

Jb 9:3

Lk 14:31

11. The wiser course is to send an embassy to
negotiate peace while the other is still at a distance.
And its terms will be: "Lord, do not call your servant
to judgment,"* not even him whom you recognize as
just, the man after your own heart, whom you
anointed with your holy oil, "for no man living is
just before you."* Now what is this embassy that
wins peace? It is Mercy. For only mercy obtains
mercy. Mercy is like a crown of gold engraved with
the sign of holiness on the head of a just man.* By
this shall the just man be saved, and even he with
difficulty;* justice without mercy is cruel and will
never obtain salvation.

Ps 142:2

Ibid.

Si 45:14

1 P 4:18

12. Mercy need not fear evil news, nor a severe
sentence when "a thousand", who were just but not
merciful, "fall at God's side and ten thousand at his
right hand."* But the merciful will have the "joy and
gladness of hearing"* the words: "Come, O blessed of
my Father, take the Kingdom for your heritage". And
why? "For I was hungry and you gave me food."* In
other words; because you showed mercy you will
receive mercy. "Happy are the merciful, they shall
obtain mercy." Some of you, I see groan at this, your
sighs are quite perceptible. You tell yourselves,

Ps 90:3,7

Ps 50:10

Mt 25:34

*Ps 4:5

"Grieve as you lie upon your beds."*

13. Woe to us, since mercy alone obtains mercy! We know that this is undeniable, certain and true. But what can we do? For as we do to others, so shall it be done to us. How can we help the hungry, the thirsty, the naked, the homeless, those who are sick or im-

*Mt 25:37-45
*RB 33,55, etc.

prisoned?* We have left everything; we have nothing. Private ownership is strictly forbidden to us.* How can we show that mercy which alone wins praise, salvation and acceptance? This is the sorrow which thrives within you, and makes, I know, your heart

*Ps 38:3,4

burn. This is the fire which blazed up in your minds.*

14. But you were humble and held your peace. Because of the weight of holding still and the great good of silence which is the service of justice you are silent even from good words. And we to whom a commission in the Lord's word and not our own has been entrusted must speak out; we must help you to understand the purpose of all this and to know what is yet lacking to you. David, you remember,

*Ps 100:1

sang to the Lord a song of "mercy and judgment,"* but he placed mercy first, then judgment, or his song would have ended with tears, because "to the man who has shown no mercy there will be judgment

*Jm 2:3

without mercy".*

15. Mercy has a two-fold expression, it gives and forgives, and therefore Scripture says: "Give, and it

*Lk 6:37

will be given to you; forgive and you will be forgiven".* This is according to a proportion. That is why we

†Mt 6:12

pray: "Forgive us as we forgive others".† Elsewhere we read: "The measure you give will be the measure

*Mt 7:2

you receive".* Moreover, in each of these forms of mercy there are three degrees, great, greater and greatest, or if you wish, infancy, adolescence and maturity. So it will be measure for measure. If a man possesses no degree of mercy, he need expect no indulgence for himself. In the first degree of mercy a person gives to others some of his own possessions. As the Saviour reminds us: "Give alms, and everything is

*Lk 11:41

clean for you".*

16. In the second degree he gives the whole of his possessions and he can say: "See, we have left every-

*Mt 19:27

thing. What then, shall we have?"* In the third degree
he gives himself, saying: "I will most gladly spend and
be spent for your souls." "No one can have greater

*2 Co 12:15,
Jn 15:13

love than this,"* and he who possesses it makes a
return to the Lord. He takes as far as he may, the
chalice from the Saviour's hand and trustingly calls
on the Lord's name.

It is the same with the second expression of mercy,
forgiveness. We can remit part of the debt that another
owes us. We can go further and remit the whole debt.
Finally we can give back the debtor's very self to him,
making him a free man.

17. Nor is the expression of mercy to be confined
merely to external, material things. We can forgive
injuries, give our prayers and advice, offer a good

*Cf. St Bernard
Adv. 3:5

example and sound teaching;* in fact, there fifty
times twelve[8] ways of giving and forgiving. It is true
that at times such mercy if offered to one who is not
willing to receive it, though it would always benefit
him; kindness after all, is often not welcome. What
now have you to fear, brothers? If you have left everything, you will be made the judges even of those who
shall obtain mercy.

18. If, every day, over and above the possessions
you have relinquished, you spend yourself owning
neither your own body nor your will nor freedom but
saying: "Abba, Father, not what I will, but what you

*Mk 14:36

will,"* then indeed you shall sit on twelve thrones
and judge, with authority and preparation, the twelve

*Mt 19:28

tribes of Israel.*

19. "Happy indeed, are the merciful, they shall
obtain mercy." The culmination of all ascetical
effort is fittingly placed on this mountain's summit,
for higher than this you cannot climb. Would you
renew your strength and soar in contemplation, then

*Is 40:31

you must "grant wings as an eagle's."* And if this is as
yet beyond your power, you must pray: "Who will

*Ps 54:7

give me wings like a dove to fly away and be at rest."*

20. But as a man among men, in this mortal life,
or rather, this living death[9] what more can he do to
help either himself or others, than to freely scorn

*Lk 16:9

"base wealth,"* and remains moderate and strong? It is

meekness which gives him a gentle and calm manner
towards others; compunction that makes him watchful and faithful; justice that gives him a certain
refinement and perfection[10] both within and without, while mercy urges him to do good to many and
to wish well to all. By his love of poverty he spurns
the laughing world; with the strength of his meekness he despises its anger; through the gift of compunction he regains himself; in striving for justice he
surrenders himself to God, and with mercy he gains
his neighbor. Because of his love for poverty he is
content with little; in his habitual gentleness he is
troublesome to none; his deep compunction makes
him alert to himself; in the firmness of his justice
he is acceptable to God and in the sweetness of his
1 Co 9:22   mercy he is all things to all men.

21. So, brothers, now you know what is was they
heard, those who left the crowd and climbed up the
mountain with Jesus. You know too their destiny,
for what they heard, they themselves were to become.
And of what did they hear, but of virtue and happiness? This is why, they are now on the way to both
virtue and happiness. There on the mountain, the
virtues were taught, the beatitudes proclaimed. The
vices were only indirectly indicated and their conse-
quent miseries pointed out, and how and where and
who are those who lose all—heaven, earth, themselves,
God and their neighbour. But apart from that, such
Ep 5:3   things are not even named, as is fitting among saints;
saints, such as it may be our lot to become thanks to
our Lord. Amen.

NOTES

1. Isaac's *Ep off mis;* PL 194:1892B, uses identical language.
2. In other words this refers to those who have achieved the first Beatitudes.
3. Our author's Ep an has this very definition; PL 194:1878D.
4. So teach Cicero, *De officiis*, 1, 7, 20; and St Ambrose, *Off*, 1, 20; PL 16:136.
5. "Galaxy", *galaxia* from Macrobius, *Comm*, 1, 4, 5; 1, 9, 10. Cicero's *Somnium Scipionis* and, as a result, Macrobius' *Comm* both connect "galaxy" with justice.
6. Cf. Matthew 7:12.
7. These degrees are rather like those of St Bernard in *Conv* 18,31.
8. Literally "six hundred", which is a latin phrase for a very great number, e.g., Cicero, *De divinatione*, 2, 14, 34.
9. The most likely source is Cicero, *Somnium Scipionis*, 3:14.
10. *Teres atque rotundus*, Horace, *Satires*, 2, 7, 86. Cf. Augustine, *Quan an* 16, 27.

SERMON FOUR
A Fourth Sermon for the Feast of All Saints

*Mt 5:8

"HAPPY are the pure in heart, they shall see God."* Once love is present there too is longing to see what is loved. And so the next beatitude fittingly follows: "Happy are the pure in heart, they shall see God." Those alone who have purified their hearts shall see him, because it is solely by a pure heart that God can be seen. And I ask you frankly, brothers, of what use are all our years of such effort if we have not made our hearts clean? Perhaps we have indeed purified our hearts for the sake of virtue? Well, now they must be purified for the sake of truth. And if we have already cleansed them for loving, now they must be made clean for seeing.[1]

*Lk 14:13

2. We may have healed a lame man, but there is still a blind man waiting to receive his sight.* For every son of Adam bears the twofold punishment of ignorance and infirmity. The first shuts the eyes of reason, the second shackles the soul's feet, that is, its willing.[2] It is of these sufferings common to all men that the Prophet is speaking when he laments: "My

*Ps 37:11

virtue is spent, the very light has gone from my eyes."*

Virtue, we must remember, is formed by desire, or more accurately, desire itself is formed by virtue.[3] Certainly truth is presented to the reason, but truth can be perceived only by the light which truth itself radiates.

3. When the Lord purifies the eye of a man's mind, enabling him to perceive truth, he is indeed giving a blind man his sight. It must be clearly understood, then, that when we speak of purity of heart, we do not mean simply that the heart is to be purified from vices, call them disordered desire or perverted love, but that it must be purified from the phantasies that are absorbed by the corporeal senses and remain in the imagination,[4] for these become an obstruction that prevents our seeing the sun's clear light.[5] They either cut us off from that solar body, the very source of light itself (they are so unlike it) or at least they reduce the sun's brightness.

4. Suppose that a man had the power to fly into the sky above us. He would have to leave the earth behind, and the waters that are said to be above the earth, and finally those lighter waters that hang in such wondrous fashion and are called clouds.[6] So too the man who raises his mind's eye[7] to see that which is purely incorporeal, must not only rise above every corporeal substance and image of corporeal substance, he must also rise above the whole seething complexity of his own thoughts.[8] Don't let this discourage you! Once you have passed through all these clouds by vigilance of mind and purity of heart, once your every thought is silent, or, rather, left far behind then, at last, brothers, there will appear before you a shining cloud, "a cloud filled with light",* not stormy now nor dense, a cloud of wisdom, not of ignorance.[9]

*Mt 17:5

5. For there is darkness in light, darkness all the deeper in much light,[10] until finally, when the light reaches the threshold of its own incomprehensibility and enters that unapproachability in which dwells "that peace which passes all understanding,"* it is taken from our eyes so that any further knowledge of the Light is obtained not through speculation but

*Ph 4:7

*Ac 1:9-10
through revelation, just as the apostles gazing
heavenward, learned from the men who stood beside
them in white garments.*

6. The visible world extends upwards by five
distinct strata or steps, which ascend in the order:
earth, water, air, the ether or firmament, and finally
the highest heaven or empyrean.[11] For the soul too,
while on pilgrimage in the world of its body, there
are five steps toward wisdom: sense-perception,
imagination, reason, intelligence and understanding.[12]

7. Through sense-perception the soul apprehends
corporeal objects and in imagination it forms images
of corporeal things. Through reason it perceives the
dimensions of corporeal objects and the like: here we
first meet the incorporeal, but it is dependent for
subsistence upon a body and therefore requires both
time and space. By intelligence the soul perceives that
which is above the corporeal or above created spirit
united to a body. It does not need a body to subsist
and is therefore independent of space, but it cannot
exist outside of time because it is by nature mutable.

8. Understanding, in so far as is permitted to a
created nature which has nothing above it but the
Creator, has immediate sight of the Being who is
supremely and purely incorporeal, the One who has
no need of a body in which to exist, nor of a place in
which to be present, nor of time in which to continue
existence.[13]

9. Our heart, then, does need purification, that
leaving earth and water far behind, it may ascend into
the tranquil region of the reason, there to catch sight
of the lowest incorporeal objects. Rising still higher, it
reaches the firmament of intelligence, where the second
order of the incorporeal comes into view. Finally, it
soars into the fiery brightness of understanding, as if on
to Mount Tabor, that exceedingly high mountain,
and there it sees the third order of the incorporeal—
the Unseen. There it gazes upon Jesus, Jesus trans-
figured, glorified, the glory of his flesh making his
very garments such as no fuller on earth could make
them.* But our heart is overwhelmed by the glory of
his Face, because of that pure form of Incomprehen-

*Mk 9:2

sibility, Incorporeity and Invisibility in which he remains always equal to the Father. Reason, intellect and understanding fall on their faces.*

Mt 17:5

10. Peter, James and John are permitted to hear the Father, but not to see him. And when they have come down from the mountain they may tell no one what they have seen and heard. For undoubtedly, dearest brothers, those who see and taste and feel many wonderful, sweet radiant, and joyous things when they are in prayer and contemplation and are for an instant, as though beyond themselves,[14] are wholly incapable of speaking of these things when they return to themselves, indeed they can scarcely remember them, spiritual men though they be, whose faculties have been trained by exercise.*

Hb 5:14

11. So now you know from what things the heart must be purified and to what extent, and for what purpose, namely, to be able to gaze upon the Being who is Perfection unlimited, who is Beauty without quality, Greatness without extension, Presence uncircumscribed by place, Existence beyond time.[15] But without this purification it is impossible to see God and so he tells us: "Happy are the pure in heart, they shall see God."* Here, "a confused reflection; there, as he is."†

1 Co 13:12
†1 Jn 3:2*

12. The heart that is pure may be compared to that beautiful woman with the bright eyes who was chosen and desired by that exiled fugitive. To win her as his wife he worked seven years, enduring heat and frost, and this time seemed to him but short and light because of the hope which gladdened him.* Rachel, as you know, means sheep or sight of the Beginning,[16] and stands for purity of heart.

Gn 29:17-30

13. And this, brothers, it has ever been my desire to win—the power to discover in each visible object its properties and differences, its nature and form, its Cause and its very Essence, until I see its efficient, formal, final principle—that is to say: from whence it is, and how and why. For all created things possess nature, form, purpose, or "number, measure and weight."[17] But their source and beginning? The sight of this is what I seek and do not easily find. To win

this, I willingly work and patiently bear all things.
Yet because of the custom of the country, it is the
dull-eyed, labor-ridden sister who is deceptively
given to me, though I have never sought her.[18]

14. "With us, it is not the custom," says Laban,
Gn 29:26   "to give or marry off the younger before the elder."*
You know, of course, that by the elder sister is meant
the affective or appetitive tendency of the soul,[19] of
which we have already spoken much. Desire must be
married to Reason and be ruled and ordered by him
and always kept at home, so that with a tranquil mind
he can go out in the heat of the day and meet the
Gn 18:9   three Angels as did Abraham, leaving Sarah at home.*

15. To speak plainly, brothers, no man can be
fully and perfectly spiritual nor can he be ready to go
out with tranquil mind from his tent in the leisure of
contemplation, unless he has first rid his home of vice,
that is, of all perverted and disordered love, and has
furnished and decorated it with good habits, and left
it fortified with a strong guard of virtues. Otherwise,
the adulterous unclean spirit, who lies in wait for the
first opportunity of seducing the wedded wife, if he
find "the house swept clean and put in order," but
empty of virtues, may make his way in by force or
favor and take possession, protecting himself with a
Mt 12:44-45   bodyguard of seven associates more evil than himself.*
How keen he is to Desire, the very mistress of the
house! Then indeed, "the last state of this type of
Ibid.   spiritual a man is worse than the first".* He who
began in the Spirit is now ending with the flesh, or
Ga 3:3   rather, is ended by the flesh.*

16. So, to conclude briefly: Desire must be ruled
prudently, moderately, valiantly and justly, so that
she may possess the disposition of a well-ordered soul,
which is virtue. She must be so formed and prepared
for love that, as the Song of Songs puts it, she can say,
Sg 2:4   "He has ordered charity in me."* If a man desires to
be truly spiritual, let him first pay attention to his
desires rather than to his ideas, to his way of life rather
than his form of meditation. For he must first use his
feet to walk before soaring into flight. And since he
cannot always be in flight, let him go about sensibly

on foot lest he suddenly crash down. In other words, Desire must never be precipitate, for she has the care of the whole house and of all the furnishings and the management of the household servants.

17.   Anxious and concerned about everything, it is she who gives name and purpose to every action and movement of the body. If she is good and rightly-ordered, so are they; but if she is evil, perverse or corrupt, they will be too. It follows then, that just as external action is subject to will, will or desire should be subject to reason, and reason to the Wisdom and Word of God.[20] Man then will be truly wise and will contemplate God with unveiled face, for he himself is the image of God. His head will not be covered because he is directly subject to God alone.

18.   But his wife veils her head to show that she is subject to her husband whose image she is.* She should be prudent, never quarrelsome, and so there will be peace in the house and she will deserve to be blessed abundantly, and her cattle will not decrease.* They will have sons and daughters, that is to say, the fruits of spiritual meditation, a very large household of virtues;[21] and they will have sheep fruitful in young, which mean simple and pleasant manners, and many asses and oxen—the reward of bodily effort. The whole house should be governed wisely and prudently, grow rich and plentiful. Finally it must be well-protected, for as scripture says, Adam was "to cultivate and keep it."* Then all their possessions will be in peace.

19.   And when they have peace within their borders, a peace between the husband and his Lord, that is, between Reason, the mind and God, peace between the wife and her husband, that is, between Desire and the rational mind, and finally peace between the Woman and those subject to her rule, they deserve to hear the words: "Happy are the peace-makers." But what the Lord of virtues may be pleased to reveal about this final, supreme virtue, we will leave to another time. Meanwhile, today let us rest in Christ. Amen.

*1 Co 11:7

*Ps 106:38

*Gn 2:15

NOTES

1. This need of virtue and knowledge, of love and contemplation is a commonplace in Eriugena, *Super IC* 3, 1; PL 122:174-5, and *Div Nat* 5:38; PL 122:1017-18.

2. For "reason" as the "eye" of the soul, see Augustine, *Lib Arb* 2, 6, 13. "Willing" (*affectus*) is seen as the soul's "feet" by Augustine in *In Ps* 9:15 and *In Ps* 94:1.

3. Isaac's teaching is in line with St Augustine, *Musica* 6, 11, 29 and St Bernard, *Gra* 6:17, and *SC* 50:5.

4. The reference to phantasies (*phantasiae*) recalls Eriugena, *Div Nat* 1:27; PL 122:474. In *Div nat* 5:38; PL 122:963, Eriugena insists that it is *attachment* to such phantasies that does the harm.

5. Close to the *nebula interposita* of Eriugena, *Div nat* 5:38; PL 122:1018.

6. Cf. Plato, *Timaeus* 326 and 55e, as well as the *Commentary* of Chalcidius, 318, 323-24.

7. *Acies mentis,* a much used phrase; Cf. Cicero, *De natura deorum* 2, 17, 45; and Eriugena, *Div nat* 3:16, 5:36; PL 122:669, 978. See also Augustine, *Conf* 7:1, 2, and Bernard *SC* 62:3.

8. God alone is purely incorporeal according to John Cassian, *Conf* 7, 13; PL 49:685. Rising above "one's own thoughts" is the very meaning of mystical contemplation according to St Bernard SC 52:4.

9. This cloud "of wisdom" is Christ; see Eriugena, *Div nat* 5:20; PL 122:595.

10. This reproduces Eriugena's version of Pseudo-Denis, *Epistola* in PL 122:1177.

11. These five steps are found together and in the order here given in Eriugena, *Prol. Joan;* PL 122:291BC.

12. See the more extended description of these five steps in *Ep an,* PL 194:1880-86. For the sources and meaning of Isaac's teaching here, see B. McGinn, *The Golden Chain* (Washington, D.C.: Cistercian Publications, 1972).

13. Cf. Augustine, *Gen litt* 8:20, as quoted by Eriugena, *Div nat* 1:62; PL 122:504.

14. Literally "in excess of mind". On the brief duration of ecstasy, see Bernard *Dil* 10:27; SC 18:6; 23, 15; and 41:2; as well as William of St Thierry, *Golden Epistle* II, 3, 18; PL 184:345, 350.

15. "Perfection unlimited", literally "subsisting without a body". These five paradoxes about the nature of God recall the *Summa Sententiarum,* PL 176:48-49.

16. Jerome, *Nom hebr;* PL 23:783.

17. Ws 11:21, in the form that Isaac prefers. For this form see Origen, *De principiis* 2, 9 and Ambrose, Hex 1:9, and Eriugena *Div nat* 2:28; 3:16.

18. Labor-ridden (*laborsa*) is the meaning of Leah according to Jerome, *Nom hebr;* PL 23:781.

19. "Appetitive tendency," literally, "concupiscibility". Ambrose *In Ps 37 Enarratio;* PL 14:1028; and Augustine, *In Ps 118,* 3 agree that "concupiscence" can have a good sense.

20. So Eriugena, *Comm in Evang Joan;* PL 122:336B, where 1 Co 11:3 is quoted.

21. Job 1:3. Isaac's interpretation is in line with Gregory, *Mor* 2, 30, 42; 1, 15, 21 (PL 75:31, 23). For "sons and daughters of virtues", see *Mor* 1, 27, 38.

SERMON FIVE
A Fifth Sermon for the Feast of All Saints

*Mt 5:9

"BLESSED are the peacemakers; they shall be counted the children of God."* Could a servant of God seek anything greater than to become a son of God? Why brothers, we could not even dare dream of such a privilege did not God's kindness permit and promise it to us! We were sinners, enemies of God, salvation was simply beyond both our calculations and expectations; Christ's coming changed all that. His astounding intervention has truly proved "he loved us first",* when "he underwent death for us sinners."*

*1 Jn 4:10
*Rm 5:6

2. What amazes the Apostle is precisely that Christ should undergo death for sinners, when it is well-nigh impossible to "find anyone who will die for a just man."* He hastens to admit, of course, that for a particularly "deserving man", some dearly cherished friend, "there may be those who will face death."* You remember the Pylades and Orectes story.[1] Such was not our case; we were enemies of of God, the text leaves us in no doubt: "Enemies of God, we were reconciled to him through his Son's

*Rm 5:7

*Ibid.

*Rm 5:10

death; reconciled to him, we are surer than ever,"*
and so on. "Surer than ever" of what? Of being,
thanks to the Son, God's sons. Note the various
stages in the process.

3. We were enemies of God, "slaves of sin, right-

*Rm 6:20
doing had no claims upon us."* The Son set us free,
*Rm 6:22
so that we are really "free from the claims of sin"*
and from the devil, and have become "slaves of right-
*Rm 6:18
doing".* This is the first stage, the one the Psalmist
*Ps 114:4
craves and calls for in the words: "Save me, Lord."*
Once his prayer has been granted he rejoices thus:
"O Lord, you have freed me from peril, I, your
servant and the son, not yet of you, but of your
*Ps 115:16
handmaid."* "You have broken the chains that
*Ps 115:7
bound me."* The chains, he means, with which the
devil had controlled him as though he were no better
than a four-footed beast. Kept from doing and
from moving as he should, man was no longer the
*Ps 103:23
"man who went abroad to toil and drudge".*

4. Set free, man can use his feet, is able to, at
*Mt 12:13
least, stretch out his withered hand.* The crooked
has come straight, the enemy has become a willing
servant. Though utterly worthless he would be of
*Lk 17:10
service to him who has "no need of his services."*
The service of God is profitable to such as would
*Ph 2:12
"earn salvation in anxious fears,"* to those who
remembered the words, "And you, when you have
done all that was commanded you, are to say, we are
*Lk 17:10
servants and worthless."* One who does evil with a
bad intention or good with an evil intention is
reckoned an enemy. One who does everything with a
good intention ranks as a servant, but not yet as a
friend.

5. It is for a servant of God to do good, to perform
the works of virtue, of justice and of mercy; to know
his plans and be involved in his secrets is for God's
friends. They had reached this second stage, those
one-time enemies of God become his servants, to
whom were addressed the words "I do not speak of
*Jn 15:15
you anymore as my servants but as my friends."* Is
there a further stage? Yes, none other than the third
stage where Christ's friends become his brothers,

become children of God and thereby finally his heirs, for if we are his children then we are also made his heirs".* "Blessed," says our Lord, "are the peacemakers! they shall be counted the children of God." In other words, the clean of heart have through contemplation, come to know all that the Son has heard from the Father, and because they are pacified they are counted the children of God.

*Rm 8:17

6. For the love of Christ tell me, my dear brothers, I beg you, tell me what is this satisfying peace, so worth loving and desiring, so precious that it ranks higher than all the virtues, is beyond all deserving, surpasses all else, obtains the highest and greatest happiness? Let us question our fellowmen, let us question those companions and intercessors of awe, the holy angels. Let us especially ask God for this wisdom we need so much, for "he gives freely and ungrudgingly".*

*Jm 1:5

7. Let us seek it through prayer, meditation and reading, and never be discouraged. If only our seeking is in good earnest, the gift will be ours; the truth itself that we seek has guaranteed it to me in the words, "Seek and you shall find".* This is the treasure hidden in the field, the rare pearl that repays the most unwearied search.* Cheap at any price, no miser could hoard it too closely. This is that highest of mountains upon which the Son alone had access to the Father as a natural right. Yet having no mind to be the Father's only heir, he freely chose to have adopted brothers. We should, you will agree, spare no effort to achieve whatever is necessary to become brothers of Christ and sons of God, "heirs of God and coheirs with Christ".*

*Lk 11:9

*Mt 13:44-45

*Rm 8:17

8. And here one of the seraphim cries out, one of those creatures whose love is perfect (could not this love be precisely what we are looking for?), calling out to us: "All those who welcomed him, he empowered to become the children of God".* You will notice he does not say, "All those who saw him." No, the clean of heart see; it is for the peacemakers to welcome. Should we say, rather must we not say, that the peacemakers are the field where the treasure is

*Jn 1:12

hidden? Yes, hidden in "all those who welcomed him." Some did not; they were told, "I have come in my Father's name, and you gave me no welcome".* To welcome the Word of God is really something, something so vital that the misfortune of not seeing the Word is as nothing compared to the wretchedness of seeing and not welcoming the Word. But how is the Word to be welcomed and into what kind of a house?

*/Jn 5:43

9. There are two things involved in taking care of a house: working and cherishing. When we are told that the first man was "to cultivate and care for" the garden,* we are meant to understand that the effort was divided between man and woman. Man, bound to drudgery, goes out to toil* and brings home his earnings. His wife remains at home, waits for her husband, expecting his return. From what he had brought her she prepares the feast at which on his return they may "rejoice" and refresh themselves, "glad and content".* Not so the many who labor much and whose gains are minimal. With the sweat of their brow they amass the riches that leak out at the purse's bottom, fall to the ground and get lost.

*Gn 2:25

*Jb 5:7,
Ps 103:23

*Ps 67:4

10. Should I put all this more plainly? Have you grasped all this? There is no need to tell you who heard it before what is meant by the husband we are discussing, what by the wife and her toil, and what the feast and other details stand for.[2] After all it is quite common to find those whose vigorous and lively minds, joined to earnest and perservering effort, have enabled them to so search the depths and pierce the heights that the knowledge of God is clear to their minds, as is his eternal power and divinity. For this very reason there is no excuse for them.*

*Rm 1:19-20

11. Because they have not sought Wisdom for its own sake, their thoughts have vanished away.* While enjoying the worthless credit and opinion or advantage of their fellow-men, they do not welcome the Wisdom they have caught sight of with the whole-hearted love which comes from the Father. Not they! In the desire of their soul they have snuffed up the wind,* duped slaves of self-conceit, their fall has been

*Rm 1:21

*Jr 2:24

proportionate to their pretensions; fornicators, they prodigally squander every share of the priceless substance. It is not for them to keep peace with the legitimate marriage bed; how could they deserve to hear the words, "Blessed are the peacemakers?" They are the sort of people so lost in self-admiration that they become dizzy at the prospect, lose their footing and fall headlong.

12. The Lord, for his own deep reasons, has sent upon them a spirit of dizziness; their fuddled brains are no better than those of a drunkard who staggers and vomits.*Is 19:14* Out they spew, what should, if kept, have nourished them. Their senseless heart is benighted, their show of wisdom proves them fools. Preferring darkness to the light that enlightened *Jn 3:19* them, their darkness becomes all the greater.*

13. No wonder, brothers, that that holy and truly God–seeking person who "betook himself to *Ps 72:17* God's sanctuary"* finally understood (you remember how Jacob preferred Rachel from the first). No wonder, I say, that holy person, as he pondered over *Col 1:5* "what was stored up for him in Heaven," rebuked himself for desiring anything on earth, all that wasting away of flesh and heart of his, and exclaimed, "God is the meditation of my heart and my inheri-*Ps 72:26* tance,"* that I await, long for and delight in. He is the objective I have set myself, the whole reason for my efforts. He, God himself, is the inheritance I plan to bring to a home of right-ordered love, that he may *Rv 3:20* sup with me and I with him.* He is ever in my thoughts, he is my heart's delight. I seek him, the transcendent, for his own sake. By him, the immanent, I feed on him. He is both the field I work and the food I work for. He is both reason and reward of all I do, my beginning and end without end. Forever he is mine; "eternally my inheritance," as the Psalm-*Ps 72:26* ist says.*

14. Not so those who desert your cause and will not listen to you, or, if they listen, refuse to see you, or, if they see you, refuse you welcome. They may go on listening and seeking, seeing and preaching you, though not for your sake, yet because they break

42

*Ps 72:27
their truth with you, "they will perish."* In your
hidden judgment you have already doomed all such.
How different with the Psalmist! "I know no other
good," he declares, "but clinging to my God" con-
*Ps 72:28
tinually.* I would ascend to him by no other way
than through him. Once I attain to him that good will
prevent me from falling from him. Knowing well
that for the present we have hope to guide our steps,
not the clear view that gives rest, he added, that he
*Ibid.
places his "hope in the Lord God."*

15. Here you have, then, my dear brothers, the
field, the hands and the hope to toil with. You have
not come merely into a solitary place, but into a
solitude of spirit, even of God, where he left the
*Lk 15:4
ninety-nine sheep.* Here you have pointed out to you
the fruits you have received, the place at which and
the companion with whom you are to eat "the bread
of life and understanding" and drink "the refreshing
*Si 15:3
draught of wisdom."* It is only right that the first
share of the harvest should go to the laborer who
*2 Tm 2:6
has toiled for it.* "Who would plant a vineyard and
*1 Co 9:7 .
not live on its fruits?"*

16. You must, dear brothers, keep unceasing
vigilance over the intimate marriage within you no
matter what the place or time. The husband must not
become listless and idle. He must not work where he
has no business nor should his gains be for any but his
lawful wife. She, in her turn, must not make even the
least arrangement in her household without consulting
her husband. What I mean is that zeal for good
observance should proceed from a well-ordered
interior.[3] Training of the body avails but little and
should be fully subject to holy love. Love and desire,
moreover, should be at the disposal of reason and the
rational mind should be governed by God's Word and
never stray from its teaching. What reason hears and
sees in Scripture should control, temper and direct all
things below it. It should learn from Scripture what
*Jn 7:16
it is to teach, saying, "my learning is not my own,"*
but belongs to him to whom I am subject.

17. Reason should ever cling to God with un-
wearying love, delighted to gaze on him, able to say,

*Ps 72:28

*1 Co 6:17

*Gn 2:24; Mt 19:
5

*Jn 17:11, 22

*Ps 72:26

"I know no other good but clinging to God,"* for the man who unites himself to God becomes one spirit with him,* and no wonder. Carnal union with its unmanning, enervating pleasure almost turns the very spirit into flesh, so that those so joined become one flesh, "they are no longer two but one flesh."* Is it then surprising that a person should become one spirit with God when with manly heart and virile mind, with a love all the greater for its chastity and purity, he pours himself into God as he clings to him in totally unreserved self-surrender? Is the affliction of carnal love to prove itself a greater source of harm, enslavement, destruction and change than the virtue of divine love a source of help, freedom, union and transformation?

18. The Word Omnipotent, such the power at his disposal that for him willing and doing are all one, declares: "This, Father, is my desire, that as we are one, these may be one in us."* How loving-kind the divine desire, worthy of God, full of gracious charity, a truly valid assurance of Truth! "That as we are one, these may be one in us." What heights for a slave to reach, what forgiveness for an enemy! From enemy to slave, slave to friend, friend to son, son to heir, from heir to one spirit or even one thing with the inheritance itself! You would have to annihilate him to deprive him of this inheritance that is none other than God himself. Well might such a one say, "God is eternally my inheritance."* This is the meaning of that prayer, "that they may be one in us."

19. What unity is more true, more uniquely needful than this It is a unity for whose sake all the pleasure of this world to be left behind, all bitterness withstood, all vice avoided and virtue embraced. It demands a thousand efforts, but once attained its peace and joy can never be lost. Bear with me if my terms are too daring. If I stress the resemblance between what is filthy, shameful, the lowest point of the flesh, and what is splendid, holy, the high point of the spirit. The sacred, spiritual, divine union was never expressed better, never made more clear and manifest amid the gloom of our present life than by a union that is at

once similar to it and its very opposite.

20. Nothing is more unlike it and nothing compares so well with it![4] In the passion of carnal intercourse a man's whole soul becomes flesh; defenceless his surrender is complete; his friends are forgotten; and all his anxious cares cease; the miser forgets all about money; fame means nothing to the ambitious; the vain man does not care a fig for his reputation; gladness, grief, desire, dread are each and all swallowed up by one all-absorbing delight. So it will be, only more so, when a man's whole mind is so drunk with discernment[5] and swoons away, that in God it finds nothing beyond its powers, finds joy in everything, thanks to God to whom it clings in fullest truth, virtue, and love, God the all to all his friends.*

1 Co 15:28

21. Then will a man look to God without ulterior motive, will love him for his own sake; he will find delight in nothing save what reveals his Beloved; will, consequently, love nothing but him whom he sees. What he sees will light his way to love; what he loves will enkindle his desire to see. So shall seeing and loving stimulate each other that they will form the infinite round of blessedness that only the godly deserve. This seeing and knowing is the result of love; this love and longing the fruit of knowledge.

22. It is impossible to see God and not love him; impossible to love him and not deserve to see him: has he not said, "I will reveal myself to him"?*

Jn 14:21

Knowing and loving, dear friends, are the wings that keep the blessed seraphim poised in flight before "the Lord sitting on his throne,"* him on whom "the angels satisfy their eager gaze,"* ever gazing with longing and longing to gaze. So, brothers, to bring an unusually long sermon to a close, let me stress that knowing and loving God is the religious life in a nutshell, the target of our spiritual exercise.

Is 6:1-2
1 P 1:12

23. For just as the cheribim and seraphim hold the very highest place in the hierarchy of heaven's angels, so in our heaven—I mean the soul of the just man where wisdom sits enthroned—since the same orders and grades can exist there, degrees of virtues, like angels, ought also be there, lest our heaven be

without angels. Knowing and loving God should, like the cherubim and seraphim, be preeminent and obtain obedient service from virtues of all ranks. (You may recall my teaching this at another time, or have you forgotten?)[6]

24. So, my brothers, let your exhausing toil, the snags of your solitude, the effort you put into both external observance and internal striving, I beg of you, have no other purpose save to rid you of bad habits and by regulating your behavior clothe you in virtue. As good ascetics, may you live in this present world a life of order, justice, and of holiness.* With cleansed hearts you will have sight of, with flaming hearts you will love, "the blessed hope," "the vision of God,"* love it in the full peace that is none other than the high state of divine sonship. May the infinitely living, all-ruling God graciously bestow this upon us through the Son and in the Holy Spirit. Amen.

*Tt 2:12

*Tt 2:13, Ezk 8:3

NOTES

1. See, e.g., Cicero *De amicitia* 7:24; Augustine, *Conf* 4:6.
2. See Sermon 4, Section 14 ff.
3. Cf. Bernard, *SC* 49:5; *Circ* 3:11; *Pasc* 2:6.
4. Isaac's daring comparison is, of course, a commonplace of mystical writing and has scriptural warrant in the Song of Songs and many other texts.
5. Literally, "soberly drunk". Commenting on 1 S 1:14-15, Philo, *De ebrietate*, 36, 37, remarks on the spontaneous self-giving of contemplative prayer. For "sober drunkenness", (*sobria ebrietas*), cf. Augustine *Conf* 5:13; *Sermo* 34:2; Bernard *Dil* 11:30; and, not least, the hymn "Splendor paternae gloriae" in the Cistercian Office.
6. Refers to Sermon 4, Section 14 ff.

SERMON SIX
A Sixth Sermon for the Feast of All Saints

Mt 5:1

"JESUS when he saw how great was their number, went up to the mountainside."* Today, dear friends, we see our heaven-sent Physician unsealing the precious perfumes that he has brought with him from the bosom of the Father; brought to heal the wounds of the man who, on his way down from Jerusalem

Lk 10:30

to Jericho, fell in with robbers.* This unnamed man on his way down represents Adam and all his descendants.[1] It was only right that he should fall in with robbers, he was but paying for the freely chosen folly of his journey. Had he but chosen it, Adam could have remained in the happy state[2] bestowed on him at his creation, in that wealth of good things safe from all loss. He freely fell because he chose to do so, and because he journeyed down, he fell into the grip of the ruthless. He had to endure what he did not wish precisely because he refused to stay where suffering could never have touched him.[3]

2. These malicious robbers are not only the evil spirits, but also the many passions of our bodies and spirit that wounded the Psalmist and made him groan,

48

*Ps 70:20

"Oh, how often you have burdened me with bitter trouble."* Yes, he suffers unwillingly although deservedly; the price (I beg to repeat) of his freely deciding to descend was his meeting robbers and suffering at their hands. Never would the Lord of mercy have allowed man to fall into such cruel hands had not man by his own personal and conscious wickedness first deserted him to whom he should have looked for strength. Man forsook God, man went his way down, and because he went down, he was forsaken by him who did not go down.[4]

3. Forsaken by God, man fell into the power of him to whom such power was permitted, the devil. He showed no pity, but robbed, wounded, and left him half-dead. He who is altogether dying left man half-dead, in other words half-alive. And such is the life of mortal man: a living dying.* The devil's dying, on the other hand, is completely deadly, leaving no room for recall to life. The angels' living in its turn, is fully vital, having no tendency toward death.

*See Sermon 3:20

4. Mortal man, then, is left half-dead—though alive, he tends inevitably towards death, though dead, he is open to cure. "They wounded him,"* the Gospel tells us. We must look into this, see what these wounds are, even if our situation teaches us what it means far better than any explanation. In addition to the weaknesses and afflictions of the body, themselves "past all numbering",* the wounds inflicted on and infecting mankind, in and from our first parent, are of seven kinds, of many species, and beyond all counting. The infections that stem from Original Sin and afflict us all are only seven, but they beget a wayward, viper-like brood that caters to all sorts of sinful tendencies.

*Lk 10:30

*Ps 39:6

5. These are "poisonous shoots that spring up" in great profusion,* incentives to sin, demon's lairs, cradles of death. The very first of these infections, first in the number of vices, first in degree of wickedness, first to be met with on the downward road is pride. Pride is an infatuation with one's own importance. As far as it may, it covets equality with the most High."* Disdaining to share the credit for its good deeds with anyone else, it gives birth

*Hb 12:15

*Ph 2:6

to its firstborn, envy.[7] The self-complacent cannot help
being envious. What is envy but dread of another's
success?

6. This in its turn, is followed by anger, a kind of
mental derangement; you just cannot quietly consider
the person you envy. Once anger establishes itself it
produces deep depression, which once it has really
taken hold of its dependent victim, plunges him into
the depths of despair. There he is welcomed by avarice which is another name for love of this world.
When you have no better world to hope for, the
blandishments of avarice bring calm and comfort.
Avarice soon shares its conquest with gluttony to the
tune of: "Come now, you have goods in plenty laid
up for many years to come, eat and drink."* Gluttony devours him and then lust digests him; priceless
man becomes filthiest dung; his story summed up in
the caption, "Once richly fed, now they clutch at
dung,"* or "The beasts rot on the dung heap."†

7. Behold how the man who does not understand
his true honor is compared to brute beasts, even
unclean beasts, and becomes like them. Pride stole
him from God, envy from his neighbor, anger from
himself. Sadness threw him to the ground; avarice
bound him; gluttony devoured him; lust made him
dung. Such the vices that besiege the soul, that lie in
ambush for the poor fool. The robbers that await
such a downward traveller, the hands into which he
falls, are the flesh, the world and the devil. The desires
of the flesh lead to voiding and filling, to lust and
gluttony; worldliness leads to avarice and sadness;
anger, envy and pride come from the devil.

8. When scripture speaks of "fleshly" and
"worldly appetites" and of "malign influences in a
world higher than ours,"* it is referring to all these
vices. Pride brought down the angels, envy drove
them to ruin men. Anger achieved Cain's primal
fratricide, and, when sadness drove him to despair,
avarice first enabled him found the earthly city.*
Since "Venus becomes cold once Ceres and Bacchus
fail",[8] it took gluttony and lust together to break
down the proper separation between the sons of God

*Lk 12:19

*Lm 4:5
†Jl 1:17

*E.g., 1 P 2:11;
Ep 6:12

*Gn 4:13-17

and the daughters of men and so brought on God's repentance for creating man, brought in the deluge and brought man to annihilation.*

*Gn 6:1-7

9. Such is the man who was destroyed by man and changed into a brute beast, except for the fact that beasts are such by nature, man by vice. These common wounds of Adam and his posterity, what are they but disorders that come to our nature from its origins, born at our beginning and burgeoning as we grow? Such is our condition thanks to "the Amorean that begot" us and "the Hethile that bore us" and forsook us.* Truly we are "the seed of Canaan, and not of Juda."* Born of such stock there was "no water to wash us, no salt to harden us, none would wrap us in swaddling-clothes, our navel-string was left uncut."*

*Ps 26:10;
Ezk 16:3
*Dn 13:56

*Ezk 16:4

10. None showed us the pity such cases are in need of.* No, not even those First Parents of ours, so truly of the earth, earthly did they prove. Parents at once of our nature and our guilt, they gave us death at the very time that they gave us life. They sowed what was indeed theirs to bestow; they freely donated what they had themselves sadly discovered. They begot us into their own confused condition, children in every way like their fathers. Just as our First Parents reaped variously from different sources, so did they sow in different ways, implanting in us nature from God and guilt from the devil. No wonder our origins condition us so that we are children of God and children of the devil.* We are good, well-endowed creatures of God, and also wickedly and woefully ruined by the devil. On the one hand, we have a nature that makes us something; on the other, we bear the guilt that brings us to nothing.

*Lk 10:37

*1 Jn 3:1, 10

11. This last, this nothingness of ours, is all the devil's doing and is precisely that from which the Son of God at his coming, would loose and free us, and so rescue that something that we really are. He came to restore what is his in us to destroy what another has done to us. He would re-link his friend to himself (hence the word "religion"),[9] and so undo the harm the devil caused. He would separate the

good from the evil in us, the evil from the good, the precious from the vile. The Prophet, you remember, tells us, "When you learn to separate worth from worthlessness, you shall be as my own mouth."* Christ is, in this sense, the Father's mouth.

*Jr 15:19

12. We have but to listen to Isaiah would we learn how resolutely and how ready Christ came to the task of our redemption, "From the root of Jesse," he says, "a rod shall burgeon"—it could not do so from the branches—"and out of its root a flower shall spring."* This should kindle hope in me: flowers are sure harbingers of fruit. "On him the spirit of the Lord will rest."* No wonder the Fruit is so Good. Where else could Christ be conceived if not in Nazareth, where born save in Bethlehem?[10] On him had rested "a spirit wise and discerning."* His soul was indeed rich in virtue, abounding in divine gifts; and not for nothing. Having to measure up to and vanquish seven forms of concupiscence, the Gifts of the Spirit are seven; Adam's cravings are countered by seven Gifts in Christ. Seven wounds call for seven medicines, one against the other." Though nature in Adam is one thing and guilt is another, yet both are in him together.

*Is 11:1

*Is 11:2

*Is 11:2

13. Were a single fountain to supply, even if by different pipes, wine and water together, the result would mean drawing watered wine or wine-filled water. This is our case, "sons of Adam!"* Our "wine has grown watery;"* our native guilt and our guilty nature, both, come to be simultaneously. Your nature is no sooner a good gift of the Good God than it is guilt infected by the Wicked One. Child begotten to man is by that very fact sinner begotten to sinner. Our nature, for all its goodness, is never without evil or guilt; this very evil guilt has no foothold except in a nature that is good.

*Gn 11:5

*Is 1:22

14. Therefore, brothers, there are three things to consider within us, three things you must be careful about: carnal craving, sensual enjoyment and reason's judgment.

This trinity goes to make up the serpent, the woman and the man in the paradise that each of us

52

is.[11] Carnal craving itches, sensual enjoyment gives pleasure, and sin is complete once rational will consents; as a result, the sinner is driven out of his true self.* And this, bı others, is exactly what a man does to himself should he sin, even this very day. A man is tempted when he is drawn away by the lure of one of the seven forms of carnal craving; then, his sensual enjoyment is affected and sin is conceived. Should the rational will consent to some degree, sin is being born. Once it has reached its full growth, through complete consent, sin kills both of its parents and so brings death.

*Gn 3:24

15. Our First Parents were warned that if ever they ate of the forbidden fruit their doom was death. St James says: "When a man is tempted, it is always because he is being drawn away by the lure of his own carnal craving." When carnal craving conceives through delight, "it gives birth to sin; and when sin has reached its full growth," (thanks to consent) "it breeds death,"* death, that is, to consent and delight, to man and woman. This is a breed of false aim and rebellious will,* when at their common source is the poisonous root, the ever-burgeoning, never failing seed of the venomous viper; every child of Adam is conceived, is born, lives and dies a victim of this infected seed. Conceived in corruption,* born amid pain, life is spent in weariness. As for death, it is full of danger. No doubt of it, a remedy was essential, one so sick did need a physician.

*Jm 1:14-15

*Dt 32:5

*Ps 50:7

16. Right welcome is our Samaritan, he and the wine of contrition and repentance, the oil of consolation and pardon he brings.[12] Our Physician must not merely go into the house of sick mankind, he must enter into mankind. Our Physician, while having no part in man's guilt, must take on himself man's whole nature. So he fits himself to suffer whatever is for man's benefit and to succour mankind in all its needs with his grace. This gracious assistance enables our otherwise disabled nature to vanquish every tendency towards sinful gratification. As it says, "With the lonely it goes hard, when he falls there is no one to raise him."*

*Qo 4:10

17. That the Lord entered into mankind means nothing less than that mankind has clothed itself with God. As St Paul says, "All you who have been baptized have put on the person of Christ."* It follows that those who have put on the person of Christ have put off the old Adam. Carnal craving can now merely besiege from the outside, and is met by the grace that comes to the rescue from within. Our rebirth has made grace every bit as natural to us as our birth made our guilt original. Without the old man in the likeness of sinful flesh shows his filthy face; within, God's image should shine out all the more in true newness.* Our nature, then is the battleground where grace and carnal craving contend. Carnal craving with its itching, its incitement and insinuations is on one side; nature is in the middle. For nature to find pleasure in evil desire, to go along with it, is to conceive and give birth and, consequently, to die, for the birth of such a viper-breed tears its parent asunder.

18. Grace, in its turn, makes suggestions to nature, advises and offers it help. If nature delights in it, she conceives; if she consents, she brings forth virtue. Mature virtue opens the door of beatitude, earns the right to the welcome words, "Blessed are the poor in spirit."* Poverty of spirit and the Kingdom of Heaven stand for virtue and beatitude respectively, the latter being the offspring of the former. Grace, through whose delight nature conceives and with the help of consent brings forth virtue, is the spirit of fear. As Isaiah puts it, "We have conceived of your fear, O Lord, and have brought forth the spirit of your salvation."* So true is it that the beginnings of the ascent to wisdom is the Fear of the Lord.*

19. The charisms or graces or gifts of the Spirit that come to us through Christ are seven in kind, of many species, past all counting. Each of these begets and forms in the soul that welcomes it, whose very welcome it brings about, some particular virtue that itself, in turn, merits its own proper beatitude. But always and in every case the gift, called grace precisely

*Ga 3:27

*2 Co 4:4

*Mt 5:3

*Is 26:18

*Ps 110:10, Si 1:16

because freely given, comes from God, the virtue and merit come from grace, the reward which is beatitude comes for the sake of merit, and God himself is in the reward.

20. We see then, that every gift of grace comes from God and that all merit is God's gift and that the ultimate reward of merit is God himself; in other words, all these things find in him their origin, their impulse, the goal of their being.* Grace goes before us that we may begin to desire; its gracious help makes our desire effectual; it welcomes us at last and crowns our efforts with success. Seven graces, then, are set over against seven ailments. From these seven graces come seven virtues and seven beatitudes, remedies for the seven sins and their corresponding penalties. Not only has each group of seven to face another group of seven, but each of the seven has its opposite. And let us not forget the seven petitions of the Lord's prayer, each one of which pleads for a particular grace.

21. One has but to "ask and the gift will come,"* the gift that wins the victory. So the seven times seven of the seven gifts and seven petitions will be the accomplishment of our christian warfare during the ever-recuring seven days of life on earth. I leave it to you, brothers, to work out the proper sequences of graces and vices and the exact opposition between each member of the contrary groups. While we may be sure that it is true, both now and in the future, that good, evil, wretchedness, blessedness are born of one set or other of seven and included in their total sweep, yet when it comes to naming or differentiating sins we are at a loss for terms and are by no means clear as to how exactly one vice springs from another. We are only too apt to use the same terms for different things, especially for different kinds of punishment. Blessed be God for making us richer in the better part through Jesus Christ our Lord.

*Rm 11:36

*Mt 7:7

NOTES

1. Lk 10:30 is applied to the fall of man by Ambrose, *Expos Luc* 7:73; PL 15:1718; Augustine, *In Ps.* 60:8; Eriugena, *Div. nat.* 4:15; PL 122:811, who quotes Gregory of Nyssa. See also Bernard, Asc 4:4; and SC 44:3; 60:10.

2. "In the happy state", literally, "in the peace", a reference to Jerusalem, meaning "vision of peace", according to St Jerome, *Nom hebr;* PL 23:829.

3. Cf. Augustine, *Corr gra* 10:30; and Bernard, *Gra* 7:21.

4. Augustine, *Corr gra* 11:31; *Civ Dei* 13:15.

5. This list and succession of vices follows St Gregory, *Mor,* 31:87-89; PL 76:620-22. "Deep depression" and "despair" are synonymous.

6. The definition of Augustine, *Gen litt* 11, 14, 18; etc.

7. That envy follows immediately on pride is St Augustine's teaching in *Gen litt* 11, 14, 18. See also Gregory, *Mor,* 18, 32, 51; PL 76:65.

8. A quotation from Terence, *Eunuchus,* 4, 5, 6, quoted by Cicero in *De natura deorum* 2, 23, 60.

9. So writes St Augustine, *De vera religione* 55:111.

10. "Nazareth" means "bright flower" according to Jerome, *Nom hebr;* PL 23:842. Cf. Bernard, *Dil* 3:8. "House of Bread" is St Gregory's etymology for Bethlehem in *In Evang* 8:1.

11. This trinity appears in Eriugena, *Div nat* 4:23; PL 122:847; following Ambrose, Ep 45, who follows Philo, *De mundi opificio* 59.

12. Lk 10:33-34. For Our Lord as the Samaritan, see Ambrose, *Expos Luc* 7:74; PL 15:1718; Augustine, *In Ps* 30:8; and Gregory, *In Evang* 1, 18, 2.

SERMON SEVEN

*Lk 2:42
"WHEN JESUS was twelve years old . . . "* The
canonical Scriptures, if I remember rightly, tell us
little of the Lord Jesus' doings in youth and prior to
his Baptism, or, rather, give us only this incident.
Which makes us wonder all the more what it means
and why we are told this much and no more. It were
madness to think that he spent all that time, nearly
the whole of his earthly life, idly doing nothing.
Anyhow, the text in hand is enough, in my opinion,
to tell us what he did and how he did it, how wisely
and well. Ten, as you know, stands for wisdom, two
for charity; no need to prove it.[1]

2. Twelve in this sense shows the sufficiency of
the twelve holy Apostles, those dazzlingly bright
lamps of wisdom, all aglow with charity, sent out
into the world. We may take it, then, that what Jesus
did at one time he does all the time. In contrast to
this, what the holy Gospels reveal of his infancy
deals more with what was done to him or about him
than what he did.

*Lk 2:42
"As the custom . . . "* Duty demands, if you
would avoid giving or receiving offence, that you

keep to the ways of those with whom you live; at very least, you must spare them your reproaches. The options are that you must change your ways or change your whereabouts.

3. For an even greater reason, a child must follow the ways and wishes of its parents. That Jesus stayed on though his parents had left is consequently symbolically significant, a delightful mystery. They went a day's journey without him, a day in which no infant on earth is free from guilt.* Jesus, however, is holy and "not reckoned among sinners,"* essentially holy, not merely sanctified at his conception; he made no such day's journey. His parents took the road down, "Jesus alone stayed on."* "All alike are on the wrong course, all wasted lives, an innocent man is nowhere to be found,"* except only Jesus.

4. He never took the wrong road, never went down as all others did; there was no waste in his life, he did nothing but good. His parents left him, they went down, from where? From Jerusalem, whence that poor fool went down who "fell in with robbers."* Adam, had you but been content with the peace and the vision[2] that was your Creator's gift,[3] we, your heirs, would not be what and where we are, blind beggars at the roadside near Jericho!*

5. Nor is that all, my brothers. Not only natural necessity, but willing culpability prove us day after day our First Father's heirs. Not one of us holds his ground, not one remains as he ought. Jesus alone is true to what was given him, true to his origins. We go down, fall, pitch headlong. Had we not come back to him, to him who alone stood fast, "Hell would soon have been our resting place."*

6. When our foothold seemed lost,† when startled and terrified we realized that we were walking through the world without God, we had only to turn again to Jesus. Without doubt "his mercy will come to our aid"* so that we will find him, at least after three days—the day of departure through sin, the day of return through penance, and the day of seeking through attentiveness.

Now the temple or Jerusalem stands for reason-

*Jb 14:4-5
*Hb 7:26

*Jn 8:9

*Ps 13:3

*Lk 10:30

*Cf Mt 20:30;
Mk 10:46;
Lk 18:35.

†Ps 93:17

*Ibid.

endowed beings created to have sight of God, the true peace, and to become the temple in which God dwells.* Our first step in this direction is taken when we pass from non-existence to existence, from not being to being something. Sin, on the other hand, means going back, means falling from existence to non-existence, from being something to not being anything. If sin spells nothingness, as indeed it does, to go the way of sin is to step back into nothingness and non-being.

*1 Co 3:16

7. To put it another way, creation means that man has been "taken from the dust."* Founding grace raises him immeasurably above his earthly nature; through sin he returns to the dust, and is told, "Dust you are and unto dust you shall return."* Yet return from this return is made possible through the fruitful repentance that results in finding Jesus. Jesus alone remains at the level to which he has been raised, he stays on in the Temple; far from falling back, he "advanced in wisdom with the years."* His holy and saving flesh never fell into any excess or intemperance; never soiled, it never "went down to corruption."*

*Gn 3:19

*Ibid.

*Lk 2:52

*Ps 39:10

8. Conceived of the Holy Spirit and the Virgin, this flesh's birth, its life, its suffering and death were holy and virginal. Christ's blessed soul, though joined to his flesh, did not cling to his flesh, as Adam mourned: "Deep lies my soul in the dust."* Not so Christ. His soul could love his flesh according to the law of natural affection; it could not become stuck to it with the birdlime of concupiscence. Created good by the Good God, joined to good flesh, that also was created good by the Good God, Christ's soul so kept good the goodness of his soul and body that, though being creatures, they had passed from non-being to existence and never looked back, but made ever greater progress forward.

*Ps 118:25

9. No other man can boast as he can, that his heart is pure. "Who is there among the clouds to rival the Lord Jesus; where is the Lord's like among all the sons of God?"* John the Baptist was a cloud, Jeremiah was a cloud;[4] both were holy, both had

*Ps 88:6

been made holy: "I claimed you for my own before
ever I fashioned you in your mother's womb."* Both
were born holy, but had they been conceived holy?
If so, when and from where came their holiness? If
they were sanctified, they must have been sometime
sinners. No doubt, yet when and whence?

10. Not one of us is qualified to answer!* The
Good God creates flesh that is good and into it im-
parts a soul that is good. Nonetheless, I find that
each of them is bad, both are tainted. Both need to
be made holy since neither is good before being bad
nor clean before being tainted, so that our guilt
appears as original rather than actual.

11. In other words, neither soul nor body keeps
true, no, not for an instant, to the state of its call to
being; Original Sin means that it returns to non-being
at the very moment it begins to be. Here is mystery,
here is misery! It is a case of all at once coming
forth and turning back, of rising and falling. The
wretched soul suffers death as soon as it gives life; the
unfortunate flesh simultaneously welcomes life and
confers death. The flesh kills at the very moment it is
given life; the soul is slain as soon as it bestows life.

We are reminded of Raguel's daughter and her
seven murdered husbands, and of how Tobias' son
Tobias could safely marry her because he had as
companion or, rather, guide, an angel for whom the
demon was no match.* 12. These two Tobiases,
father and son, old and young, blind and with sight
restored, represent Adam, First and Second,* father
and son, Old and New, and man and the Son of
Man.[5] When we speak of the Son of Man, we at one
time refer to his flesh, at another to his soul, and yet
again to both his body and his soul. For our present
purpose Tobias stands for the soul of the Son of
Man, Sara means the flesh of man in general, while
the Angel, Tobias' guide and companion, is to be
understood as the Lord himself, God's Word, the
wise guide, loyal companion, strong helper, prudent
counsellor of the soul he took once for all to himself.
13. As for the seven husbands who married death in
place of a wife, they symbolize the souls of all men,

*Jr 1:5

*2 Co 2:16

*Tb 3:7-8; 6:14;
8:3; 9:7; etc.

*1 Co 15:45, 47

except Christ's unique soul, joined in personal marriage to the flesh of the First Adam. All these, as already said, have simultaneously linked their lot with flesh and with death in such a way that they are joined to death because they are flesh and lost to flesh because they are dead. As for the deadly demon, he is none other than the concupiscence, so natural to our fallen nature, that haunts Raguel's house and Sara's bed-chamber as long as a more powerful spirit does not prevail.*

Lk 11:22

14. Strong as the demon might be, he was no match for the still stronger divine Word. Cast out, driven away, bound, the demon is forced to hand over the goods, that nature of ours he once held captive. "Captivity led captive,"* the marriage chamber is cleansed, the house is liberated. Sara's successful marriage amazes her father. He recognizes the mystery and thanks the angel. He prepares a banquet and invites the neighbours.* All this, brothers, is shot through with mysteries, bursting with hidden meanings! Which explains why the angel goes away just as Tobias' marriage feast gets under way,* so that like Tobias the bridegroom, he should appear as a true man by being born, crying, feeding at the breast and not speaking. 15. After a time the angel comes back far from empty handed, having delivered the bond of the precious deposit,[6] so suggesting the divineness of him who is so human.

Ep 4:8

Tb 7:11-14, 8:17-22; 12:4

Tb 9:6

Now you see why it was useless on that day of departure and forgetfulness to seek the Child Jesus among relatives and acquaintances.* He is left in the Temple, he remains in Jerusalem; would you find him you must return and seek him in the Temple.* Happy the soul that never forgets, never lets go of Jesus the Child! Happier still the soul that thinks on Jesus the grown Man! Happiest of all the soul that contemplates Jesus the "ever-Infinite."

Lk 2:44

Lk 2:45-46

16. Ever greater grew Abraham's son (whose name Isaac means "Laughter") "until he became a very great man,"* the Scriptures tell us. Let God's Son grow ever greater in each of you, brothers. He has, to be sure, been formed in you, but he must

Gn 26:13

grow infinite in you if your laughter, gladness and joy are to be so full that nobody can take it away from you.* Should you forget him for a time and carelessly let the thought of him slip from you, you have but to recall him if you would reach him. Such remembrance, the very opposite of forgetfulness leads to repentance, this in its turn achieves the conversion that makes amends for your desertion, turning-back cancelling turning-away. As the seer puts it, "Come back, return to the extent to which you have sunk and strayed."*

*See Jn 16:22

*Is 31:6

17. And yet you will turn in vain from your evil way, where you walked without Jesus, if your conversion does not become a search for Jesus. The joy of finding him is earned by assiduously seeking him. "If you seek," Isaiah tells you, "seek" that is, seek earnestly, and as the Gospel says, "you will find."* And, sure enough, "they found him in the Temple."*

*Is 21:12; Mt 7:7
*Lk 2:46

Now, dear friends, we must leave off these words at this point and finish what remains of today's work. There too we may, perhaps, find Jesus. Rebecca, you remember, found Isaac, found laughter out in the open.[7] May it be given us to find, both within and without, the true Isaac,[8] very joy, thanks to him who lives and rules as God. Amen.

NOTES

1. For the symbolical meaning of ten and two see Augustine, *Sermo* 264:5; and *In Joan* 17:6.

2. Jerusalem as the "vision of peace".

3. "That was your Creator's gift": literally, "where you were placed by creating grace". Isaac agrees with Augustine, *Sermo* 26:5-6; *Ep* 177:7; and Bernard, *Gra* 16:6; *Dil* 5:15, that our being created is, in the total perspective, the basic grace.

4. On John and Jeremiah as "clouds", see Augustine, *In Ps* 88:7.

5. This symbolical application of the text of Tobias follows Bede, *In librum Tobiae allegorica interpretatio;* PL 91:923 ff.

6. 2 Tm 12:14, is cited in Ambrose, *Tob* 19:67; PL 14:786, as evidence that "the deposit" is the Holy Spirit; hence "the divineness" of Christ.

7. "Laughter", which is the meaning of "Isaac" given by Ambrose, *De Isaac* 1:1, PL 14:502; and by Augustine, *Civ Dei* 16:31. Migne, following Tissier, and Dom Hoste have "Sara" instead of "Rebecca", but our author seems to refer to Gn 24:63-64. Indeed St Ambrose, in the very paragraph just referred to, mentions the encounter of Isaac with Rebecca.

8. On Christ as the true Isaac, see Ambrose, *De Abraham* 1:9; *De Isaac* 1:1-2: PL 14:452, 501-503.

SERMON EIGHT

WORK, my brothers, has wearied us. While we give ourselves a little breathing space and prepare for further effort, let us regale ourselves somewhat on the left-overs from yesterday's feast.

Luke tells us, "They found Him [Jesus] in the Temple in the midst of those who taught there" and other learned folk. As you know, brothers, duty demands that a youngster listen to his elders and ask them for explanations. Our text continues, "They were in amazement at his quick understanding and at the answers he gave."* There is nothing undutiful if a child answers the questions put to him.

*Lk 2:46

*Lk 2:47

Let us, however, stick to the approach adopted in yesterday's sermon. And so, as Jerome says, note that Christ was a mature man from his birth,[1] indeed, according to Jeremiah, even in the womb: "Here is a new order of things the Lord has established on earth; woman shall surround man,"* meaning that Mary shall have Christ in her womb.

*Jr 31:22

2. He was, in this view, mentally mature, wise, strong and magnanimous, though his body was that of a tender tiny infant. Why, if it comes to that,

other men's minds are not in every way conditioned
by the qualities and dimensions of their bodies.
Deformity, beauty, size of body do not necessarily
result in defect of mind or charming personality, in
either magnanimity or pettiness. Such bodily
characteristics are remote indeed from the nature of
the soul possessing the image of God—a soul,
brothers, that color, be it black, white or any other,
cannot directly affect; a soul independent of quality,
neither long nor short, unconfined as such to this
place or that; a soul that does not, in itself, move in
space, does not go up or down, backwards or forwards,
to right or left.[2]

3. Bodily natures are all bound up with qualities
and quantities, measures, motions. Rational souls are
purely spiritual, second only to God,[3] the Spirit
whose image they bear, whose being they cannot
equal. Yet such souls are somehow subject to quality
and quantity, to place and motion. In this sense
they are white, black; long, wide, tall; they have
summit and base, fore and aft, right and left; yes,
they have all these, but in their own way, not as the
body has them.[4]

4. Wisdom gives them dazzling beauty, folly
makes them ugly and gloomy. A good conscience is
all brightness, buoyancy, mirth; a bad one is nothing
but discouragement, weariness and sadness. Faith
lengthens the soul, charity widens it, hope gives it
height.[5] Fear, on the other hand, chills it, covetousness makes it narrow, halfheartedness leaves it petty.
To one side of the soul lies virtue, to the other vice.
It has before it what it seeks, behind it what it forgets.
Above it is the Unattainable, below it is the unsatisfy-
ing. At the right of it are delights, to its left distress.

Amid all these options the boy Jesus proves the
maturity of his created mind,[6] a mind divinely
taught by both the fellowship and the guidance of
God to be prudent, temperate, strong and just, knowing in every case how to "reject evil and choose the
good," thanks to his thriving on "honey" and
"butter."*

5. We too have reason to be "amazed at his quick

Lk 2:47 understanding and at the answers he gave." Was he
not the only child of his years able so to value virtue
and reject vice? "My son, why have you treated us
Lk 2:48 so?" Should we not say to her: "Mother, why have
you treated your son in this fashion?" While Joseph
might well forget the child he had not begotten, she
had no right to forget the child of her womb. "Can a
woman," says the Prophet, "forget her child, pity no
Is 49:15 longer the son she bore in her womb?" Surely you,
whatever another woman might do, ought not to
have forgotten!

6. What, did you not pray to God during all that
dark and gloomy day? Could you not think of God,
did you forget him? This is past belief! How could
you, when your Son is God? You prayed, perhaps, to
the Father and forgot the Son. But how could this
be if to name the Father is to imply the Son? And, on
the other hand, to disown the Son is to have no claim
to the Father. Or was it that well aware that your
Son's behavior had a symbolic meaning you were
drawing attention to the mystery? Yes, I would prefer
to read her words as an expression of her amazement,
rather than as a query or rebuke. Such amazement
implies a desire for investigation that is worthy of
enlightenment.

7. So, although aware of his purpose, she is
amazed. But remember, her amazement should lead
you to full attention as you exclaim with reverence
and wonder: "Child, well did you treat us as you did;
your remaining on when all of us departed is a lesson
for us full of instruction." Should you, nonetheless,
insist on reading her words as a query, the sense
remains exactly the same.

Someone may object with, "It is quite unbecoming
to find fault with Jesus' Mother as though she had
forgotten him. She had done no such thing; she
thought of him when she could not see him, thought
Lk 2:44 that he was among their travelling companions."
Quite so, let us not argue. It remains true that he, who
is lost sight of through neglect or, to put it more
mildly, inattention, is found by such as are in earnest.
This should encourage you to seek him assiduously,

even as you sorrow whole-heartedly for needlessly losing him.

8. "I and your father," she says, "what anguish and mind we have endured, searching for you."* "Could you not tell," he replies, "that I must needs be in what belongs to my Father."* Here you have where the Son desires to be sought, namely "in what belongs to his Father." How clear he makes it that at this address he is really the Son! This explains why she who sought him among the dead was told, "Do not cling to me thus" in your heart; "I have not yet gone up to my Father's side."* It seems, you do not make search for me "in what belongs to my Father." You are not yet aware that I must needs be found in what belongs to him who is whatever belongs to his nature.[7] I am not he but his, and, nonetheless, I am not other than what he is.

9. Prescinding from this uniqueness of nature, is this oneness of the Father and the Son from which neither the Father nor the Son ever departs, even as man the Son did not withdraw from the Father but remained constantly true to him in obedience and will. This explains and justifies that rebuke Christ directed to some of his hearers: "You belong to your father the devil, and are eager to gratify the appetites which are your father's."* As though he said, "You are and remain where your father would have you."

10. Adam's children, then, have three fathers: God, man and the devil. They owe God their nature, man their kind, the devil their wickedness. Their human acts make them Adam's children; virtue and vice locate them, respectively, with God or the devil. Would you dwell in what belongs to God your Father and not leave Jerusalem, you have but to love, watch over and direct to the purposes of its Creator that nature of yours so well made good by the Good God and for the good. This will have those very tempters of yours, the evil spirits, amazed at your prudence and at the answers you give,* as you respond to the thousand temptations, the extremely clever and captious questions, put you by flesh, world and devil,

*Lk 2:48

*Lk 2:49

*Jn 20:17

*Jn 8:44

*Lk 2:47

as they test you.

11. On the other hand, if you do not understand where the excellence bestowed on your nature dwells, the fact that "you were made beautiful among women," and if "you fall into step with the herd,"[8] *Ps 48:13* as though "no better than the brute beasts;"* and if, infecting the very best that is in you with wickedness begotten of the wicked one, you become swollen with pride, sick with envy, convulsed with anger, cast down with sadness, anxious with avarice, greedy with gluttony and filthy with lust, then, you are living in what belongs to your father the devil; you have proved so beyond all doubt.

As to what we owe man as our father and the animal body that is still ours, let us seek only the food and clothing that our present or, rather, passing needs demand; content with that, "no temptation *1 Co 10:13* beyond man's strength will come upon us."*

12. Those who would be rich are being fooled by the devil; they are sure to fall into the traps he sets. They yield to one temptation after another, their many iniquities earn for them that sentence of the *Jn 8:44* Son of God: "You belong to your father, the devil."* They are no exception to the rule true everywhere, "Like father, like son." A son of the devil is himself a devil, we have Christ's word for it: "Have I not chosen *Jn 6:70* all twelve of you? And one of you is a devil."* Those born of God are pronounced divine in the words, *Ps 81:6* "Gods you are, I myself have declared it."* Man is born of man, yet mortal man may, through what belongs essentially to his nature, shun the devil and his works lest he be there forever, and go over wholly *Ps 127:2* to God, with whom alone "it shall be well with him."* In other words, man must shun the devil and what is the devil's; man must return to himself and be content with his limitations; man's destiny is to ascend to God and grow divinely rich.

13. The devil's children are, indeed, all of them *Ws 2:21* blind. "Their malice has so darkened their minds"* that even when prosperous they regard themselves as paupers. They simply cannot see how readily their bodily needs are satisfied. They are deaf also, deaf to

God's voice, even when it promises that "those who fear him never go wanting."* They are deaf and therefore they keep toiling for what is useless! It is for you, dear friends, to keep your eyes on your heaven-sent Teacher. He not only became man for man's salvation, he became man for man's instruction. He would strip man of the devil's livery and clothe him with divineness.

*Ps 33:10

14. We ought to live as he lived, he whose birth, whose life, whose death were those of one truly poor. The worth of our confidence, after all, depends on whether our life in this world is like his, on whether we behave as he behaved and so make good our claim to be dwelling in him.*

*1 Jn 2:6

The spirit of Fear made him so lowly that, though he was God, he subjected himself to men. "He lived in subjection to them,"* the text says.[9] He was so meek, owing to the spirit of Piety, as to be undisturbed amid the wrongs he suffered. He had good reason to refer most specially to these two virtues of his in the words, "Learn from me; I am meek and humble of heart."* Thanks to the spirit of knowledge he was so compassionate and largehearted that "when he caught sight of the city," the city that would have none of him, "he wept over it."* His enemies were unable to disturb his meekness, but for a friend of his he lovingly distressed himself, he sighed deeply and wept over him.*

*Ph 2:6

*Mt 11:29

*Lk 19:41

*Jn 11:33-35

15. The spirit of Fortitude gave him such love for justice that for its sake, though it cost him his life, he spoke out, he made no exceptions, he pronounced woe after woe on Scribe and Pharisee, and on Lawyer as well. Full of the mercy that comes the spirit of Counsel, he did not spare himself, "but gave his life as a ransom for the lives of many,"* gave proof of love than which there is no greater.* The spirit of Understanding bestowed on him a heart so clean that his holy soul, more clearly than any other creature, perceived him to whom it was joined, God. Such peace is his, through the spirit of Wisdom, that in his person all are established in peace with God. He is the only begotten Son by his very nature; his spiritual union

*Mt 20:28

*Jn 15:13

with God makes him "the first-born among many
brethren."*

*Rm 8:29

16. Let this man, my brethren, be "your one
teacher, Christ,"* this man who is, for your sake, "a
scroll written on the inside of the page and on the
outside."* Read of this man by reading him, learn
from him by learning him. Copy from this pattern the
pattern both on the inside and on the outside of
yourselves, in your interior and in your behavior.
Your lives should teach others to live as he lived.
That is why we are told, "Glorify and carry God
about in your bodies."* May he himself make us
this very gift. Amen.

*Mt 23:10

*Rv 5:1

*1 Co 6:20

NOTES

1. Jerome, *Commentarium In Jeremiam* 6:31; PL 24:880.
2. No color, size or local motion in soul: see Augustine, *Gen litt.* 10, 25, 41; *Quant an* 3:4; *De diversis quaestionibus* 8.
3. An Augustinian theme, e.g. *Quant an* 33:70; 34:77-78.
4. See Isaac's *Ep an* for a more detailed treatment of this.
5. On enlarging the soul through love in particular, see Bernard, *SC* 27:10-11. Regarding the soul's length, width and depth, see Eriugena *Div nat* 1:15; PL 122:464.
6. Lk 2:43. "Proves the maturity of his created mind": literally, "he had the mind of a grown man" (*virilem animum habuit*). St Bernard, incidentally, uses the very same terms in his *Miss* 2:10. Judging by Augustine's definition of *animus* in his *Quant an* 13:22, and by Isaac's context, it seems that there is question not of Christ's knowledge, but of his freedom from original guilt and its effects, his fulness of the Holy Spirit. Bernard in *Miss* 2:9 says as much.
7. Literally, "who is all that is hiw own", meaning, as Bernard put it in *Csi* 5, 7, 17, that "he has nothing in himself but himself". See also Augustine *Trin* 11:10.
8. Sg 1:7. Bernard uses this text in similar fashion in *SC* 38:4.
9. For linking seven gifts of the Spirit and seven of the Beatitudes—Isaac suggested it in Sermon 6, Section 18—see St Augustine, *Sermo* 347:2-3; and Bernard *Gra* 5:18.

SERMON NINE
The First Sermon for the First Sunday after the Octave of the Epiphany

*Jn 2:1

"THERE WAS a wedding-feast at Cana, in Galilee."* As I reflect on this wedding-feast, brothers, I am captivated not so much by the great and obvious miracle as by the hidden meaning of the miracle. The

*Eph 4:29

former goes to the building-up of one's faith,* the latter does something even greater. While the first is a sign for unbelievers, the other has a mysterious mes-

*1 Co 14:22

sage for believers.* Both help our spiritual life and delight us; each is great, each is divine.

The "Book" of Wisdom "written on the inside of

*Ezk 2:9, Rv 5:1

the page and the outside"* enables both those who seek within and those content with what is without

*Jn 10:9

to find pasture.* On the outside you find the story, the secret moral meaning is inside.[1]

The primal Book of Wisdom is written all of it within the Deity. Those to whom it has been given to have sight of it, the Blessed, read there all that the Father has once and for all written there from eternity.[2] From this text, so to say, has been copied whatever can be read in that secondary Book of

Wisdom, the rational mind. 2. In other words, the autograph is Wisdom himself, God's very Word; created minds have copies of this first text and all that is written in them is written on the inside. In the first Book all things are present together;* the second is the likeness of all things, since the image of God is found in this second Book.[3] Matter is susceptible of all sorts of shapes, as he finds who has the skill to produce them; just so, a reason-endowed mind made in the image of the all-wise, has a capacity for all manner of wisdom. Had such minds not become darkened within, they would have no need to look elsewhere for information. 3. The holy angels were satisfied with these two Books of Wisdom; not for them to grow old and their eyes become dim.* The sight they have of themselves and of God, their so to say "evening and morning" vision,[4] makes up their perfect day.

Next comes the third Book, material and visible creation, it too written on the inside and on the outside. Visible creation once understood makes clear what divine Wisdom has done.* Yet this is a difficult book to read; far from dazzling the eye with an excess of brightness, its readers are like men who need a lamp if they would see the sun!

4. Man, grown old in sin, blind within, grieves that his sins have so overtaken him* that he is unable to see God within with the eyes of intelligence or see his own mind with the eye of the intellect.[5] As for the eye of reason, grievous concupiscence has so dimmed it that he can see nothing within and only a little without. Yet Wisdom far from forsaking him, has by God's mercy, with God's very finger,* written a fourth Book for him, a message that reaches man's ear. Hence the words of one who had sight to a blind people, blind Israel: "Who is so blind as my servant?"* You who have eyes, but only for coveting, listen, at least, to what comes from another outside of you, what you should have seen written inside of you: "The Lord your God is one."*

5. Even this trumpet blast was wasted on blind Israel. Having spurned the one true God, Israel set

*Si 18:1

*Gn 27:1

*Rm 1:20

*Ps 39:13

*Ex 31:18;
Dt 9:10

*Is 42:19

*Dt 6:5

itself on a course of infidelity. Worshipping many deceitful demons, it went its own blind and deaf way, "unwitting as the ox that goes to the slaughter."* *Pr 7:22 Good reason had incarnate Wisdom to reproach Israel with the words, "Was it not Moses gave you the Laws, yet none of you keeps the Laws?"* This *Jn 7:19 reference to Wisdom incarnate points to a further fifth Book provided for blind man, a book that man might handle, in which Wisdom itself is made palpable so that Wisdom's disciples were made proof against all traducers and Wisdom would ever have right on his side if called in question. 6. "The Word was made flesh and came to dwell among us."* "What we have *Jn 1:14 heard and seen of him, what it was met the touch of our hands," says the Apostle, "concerns that Word who is life."* What more could he have done, brothers, *1 Jn 1:1 for his beloved people? God's very Word becomes flesh, the Lord Jesus himself, that unique Teacher of ours, brothers, the Christ, becomes a book for our sake. His life as man would teach men how to live.

7. The holy Word himself whom the blessed Apostles saw in the flesh with their eyes touched with their hands, that very Word is with us today visible in the Scriptures, palpable in his mysteries. Though he has withdrawn his visible body, he is still at our side in writing that we can see. What the Seer foretold has come to stay: "You shall have a true counsellor in sight; he shall be no bird of passage, *Is 30:20 the man given you for your teacher."* A sixth Book, the gracious gift of the holy Gospel, makes the Word present and perceptible to us.

8. So now let us try to grasp what the Word of God has said to us through the external miracle we read about in the sixth Book. This particular work of the Word is itself a word. We can see him in his work as he was in his bodily nature; his work is a kind of cloak. It seems to me at the moment that there are three kinds of wedding feast—an outer, an inner and a higher. The first takes place externally, the second internally, and the third most intimately; the first between human beings, the second in human beings, and the third above human beings. The first kind of

union is of the flesh; the second, of flesh and spirit, the third, of spirit and spirit. The first unites two distinct persons; "they are no longer two, but one flesh,"* Scripture tells us. The second achieves an even closer union between rational soul and flesh, two things so opposite in nature, and results in a single person. The third results in the highest possible union of incorporeal beings: "The man who unites himself to God becomes one spirit with him."*

*Mt 19:6

*1 Co 6:17

9. In the first case, flesh joined to flesh becomes one flesh. In the second, call it flesh united to spirit or spirit united to flesh, the outcome is neither one flesh nor one spirit, but an individual human being. In the third case, spirit clinging to God becomes one with God, becomes what God is. This is precisely what the Son prays his Father grant to his brothers: "This Father, is my desire that they may be one with us as we are one."* This unity precedes, surpasses and outlives every other; it is both source and purpose of all that is. Two in one flesh is union so close as to be no longer two but one flesh. Greater still is the unity that results in a single person from the two substances that go to make man. The greatest union of all, however, comes about when a person clings to God and two spirits are no longer two but become one.

*Jn 17:21

10. The first kind of union begets existence; the second specifically determines a being's mode of existence; the third is the everlasting glory of existence itself. In the first man is begun, in the second he is formed, in the third he is completed. First, he comes to be, then he subsists and naturally tends to union. To be one with God: that is the meaning of his coming to be, of his subsisting. Man comes from men that he may go to God.

That this built-in bent towards God should in due time and through God's grace find fulfilment, there took place a mysterious marriage, intermediate between the second and third kinds and far distant from the first, a marriage whereby the Word and our nature, Christ and the Church were joined.[6]

11. God might be distant from the soul, but apart from God, man could not be virtuous, could not really

fulfil himself. "To guilt such as yours," says the
prophet, "blessings are denied,"* that is, God has
been denied us because our sins have come between
us and God* as between a wife and her husband. This
gave the violent adulterer his chance to lead the soul
to conceive spite and give birth to empty promise.*
But God, without any help from us, provided us with
the means of being reunited to him in the person in
whom God and man are so closely joined as to leave
no room for a rival: too narrow a bed and the adulterous one must fall out; a short cloak is no covering
for two.* 12. Having broken down the wall of
sin through which the adulterer had stolen in, he
made the two one, "reconciling in his own person"
both wife and husband, man and God.* He has swept
the old enmities out of the way by nailing them to
the cross.

This, dear friends, is the mystery of our Mediator.
What more fitting intercessor between God and man
than one who is both God and man? How could his
mediation lack for anything, how could he fail to
reconcile all to the all, who, being all that God is,
took upon himself all that man is? In order to faithfully fulfill his task, he mixed in nothing else.

13. He is only God and man; is not this everything? It follows that only through him can the wife
that has been put away by her husband and has
played the wanton with many lovers obtain access,
and, through grace more powerful than the laws, be
at liberty to return to her husband. And was this not
what the Prophet had promised? "You with many
lovers have played the wanton yet come back to me,
the Lord says."* This is the mystery-marriage already
mentioned that takes place after the second and third
kind of wedding, although in the order of excellence
its place is between the second and third. This gives us
four kinds of marriage: that between flesh and flesh,
that between spirit and flesh, that between the Word
and man; that between God and the mind of man.

14. The first is historical; the second, moral; the
third, allegorical; the fourth, anagogical.[7] Jesus
neither came from the first kind of wedding nor used

*Jr 5:25
*Is 59:2
*Ps 7:15
*Is 28:20
*Ep 2:14, 16
*Jr 2:1

it, for he was not born from it not did he generate
by means of it. Yet, when invited, he came to such
a kind of wedding. He consecrated it by his presence
and upheld it against its detractors by his miraculous
power. His chief motive, however, was to stress its
significance as a sign of the wedding that is his Incarnation and also the wedding that is the purpose of his
Incarnation. For in the second and third kinds of
marriage flesh and soul and the Word are all involved:
three substances, two natures, God and man in one
person. His coming was for the sake of the fourth sort
of wedding, a wedding he had himself already achieved
in a manner surpassing that of any other man.

15. No soul could obey God more humbly, could
submit to God more fully or could cling to God more
firmly than Christ's soul. Man without God was
divided in his duality; God without man was united in
his trinity. Man's duality being all that he was, there
was no stopping the duel within him; God being the
Trinity and nothing more, meant that no one could
trouble his tranquillity. The tranquillity of trinity
excludes a fourth. Our duel had no remedy as long as
our duality kept out a third party. A duel would start
in the Trinity were a person to depart and leave only
two Persons; the duel within us would never have
stopped had not a third Person intervened.

16. Brothers, you can perceive that great counsel
was called for were Heaven to keep its glorious peace
and unhappy earth were to attain, sometime, to peace.
With this purpose in view, "The Angel of Great
Counsel" and strong succour,* the Son, one of the
three Persons of the Blessed Trinity, was sent out on
his mission, but not dismissed. It was his saving birth
in time that left heaven undisturbed and called earth
to peace. A multitude of thousands of angels hymned
that birth in the words, "Glory to God in high heaven
and peace on earth."*

17. Great and marvellous the plan that does not
diminish the eternal Trinity in God and makes a new
trinity spring up in man, a trinity that enables man to
rise above the internecine strife of his fallen state to
peace never before experienced and never after to be

*Is 9:6 (LXX)

*Lk 2:14

disturbed. O great plan truly worthy of God which so arranged things that God's coming into man should bring about a needful trinity and man's going into God should not make for a needful quaternity! For God's coming to man, as we have said, means that the Son of God and Son of man unites in himself two natures and three substances. While the divine Trinity, one God, is one nature in three Persons, Father, Son and Holy Spirit.

18. Christ, the new man, is three substances, Word, soul, and body, in one Person. One substance and three Persons in God; one Person and three substances in Christ. Trinity of nature and diversity of Persons in God. All three divine Persons are "co-eternal and coequal;"[8] the three substances in Christ are diverse and not equal. In other words, there is neither more nor less in the Trinity, while in Christ there is, to some degree, a going up and coming down;* one substance is greater or less than another. This should teach you to go step by step ever higher, from what is less to what is more, from flesh to spirit, from spirit to God; from the second kind of marriage (to which you came through the first kind of marriage) to the third kind, that of the mediator, himself the ladder, to the fourth kind of marriage.

*See Jn 1:51, Eph 4:10

19. Carnal man, born of Adam through concupiscence, should be spiritually born again to Christ through grace; and, through Christ, should come to the Father, who makes regenerate man the fellow heir of the Son. In other words, man should come from the old self through the new self to the eternally real self; from vanity to virtue by way of truth; from waywardness by the straight way to true Life. 20. And do not forget, dear friends, that the marriage to which you have been invited with Jesus (I take it you are his disciples and so apply to you the words, "Jesus himself, and his disciples, had been invited to the wedding"),* this marriage can take place only if you are zealous for conversion.[9]

*Jn 2:2

However, this discourse has taken so long,[10] and the hour is so late that only with difficulty shall we be able to finish this morning's quota of work. Let us hasten now, so that later, when the evening's work is over, we may be able to enjoy the little that remains of my sermon, like a mouthful of fish with barley-bread,* which the Word, our Lord Jesus Christ will, in his generosity, give us. Amen.

*Jn 6:9

NOTES

1. Story = *historia;* secret moral meaning = *tropologia.* See Jerome *Comml Joel;* PL 25:971; and Cassian, *Conf* 14:8; PL 49:963-64.

2. For the theme of the six books of instruction Isaac uses here, see the note by G. Salet in the Hoste edition, p. 342.

3. "The likeness of all things" (*similitudo omnium*) is found in reverse (*omnium similitudo*) in our author's *Ep an;* PL 194:1886, where it is credited to "the philosopher." See the quotation ascribed to Varro (*mens rerum omnium similitudine insignita*) in Hugh of St Victor's *Eruditionis Didascalia* 1:2; PL 176:742.

4. St Augustine deals with "evening and morning vision" in *Gen litt* 4, 26, 41; and *Civ Dei* 11:29.

5. Intelligence and intellect are used here, though in descending order, as in Sermon 4, sections 7, 8 and 9; and in *Ep an;* PL 194:1886. For the fall of man seen as fall from contemplation, see Gregory, *Mor* 11, 43, 59; PL 75; 979, and Eriugena, *Super I C* 2:1; PL 122:146.

6. The idea of the Incarnation as a marriage between God and our nature and/or the Church is based on Jn 3:29, which itself looks back to Ho 2:19, etc. With regard to the wedding at Cana, see Augustine, *In Joan* 8:4.

7. On the doctrine of the four senses of Scripture in Isaac, see the note on pp. 343–44 of the Hoste edition.

8. A phrase from the so-called Athanasian Creed; see Isaac's *Ep an;* PL 194:1888.

9. Literally, "comes about only in desire of transmigration." "Transmigration" in this context is best explained by Gregory, *In Evang* 21:5, where "Galilee" is taken to mean "transmigration achieved" (*transmigratio perpetrata*).

10. *Detinuimus.* See Ovid, *Metamorphoses,* 1:683.

SERMON TEN
A Second Sermon for the First Sunday after the Octave of the Epiphany

*Jn 2:2

"JESUS had been invited with his disciples to the marriage."* As I said before, this marriage is achieved only if one's life is a conversion–process. I have now to explain what you heard from me earlier, that is, from where, how and to where this process takes us. And this not only that we may return to where we have fallen from, but that we may get a foothold in the very place of our fall and so rise up from it.

The two feet we are to use in the business of our conversion are our understanding and our love.[1] We must change from letter to spirit in the case of the understanding; our love must shift from vice to virtue. And not merely change, brothers, but change-over to ever greater understanding, ever greater virtue, until with fullest knowledge you see him who is your true love, yes, even until with the full embrace of love you grasp him whom at last you have been granted to see. To your abounding joy and amazement, so intimate your knowledge, you will be able to use the words: "Such is my beloved."

2. And your love will find expression in, "He is my intimate friend,"* and, "All mine, my true love, and I all his; he shall lodge on my bosom."* This is the purpose that conversion should have. It is not for the tepid, not for the half-hearted and lazy; you must be generous,[2] must go at it with zest and fervor, and yet with an ease past all describing, as you are caught away where the impulse of the Spirit would have you go.*

Take note of the zest with which the Son of God crossed over to what, since he could not surpass himself, was beneath him. He crossed over to you, the lowest he might go. He gave all for you so that he could come to this marriage mentioned in our text. Since, brothers, "yours is to be the mind which Christ Jesus showed,"* you must seek to understand from what, why and for what reason he "dispossessed himself of the prerogatives of God"* and took on "the likeness of sinful flesh."*

3. Now, why did he do so? Not, surely, because he feared to lose or in order to gain anything; no, he did so solely because he loved us.* We, in our turn have to emerge gradually and escape from the pit of sinful flesh (in which he neither could nor ought descend), not like slaves who dread punishment, nor like hirelings with an eye on the kingdom to be gained, but only from love of God, as becomes his children. It is in this spirit that we should go to meet Christ "in the likeness of sinful flesh,"* that in him "mercy and truth may meet, justice and peace may be united in one embrace."*

4. Our itinerary, then, is from the pit of sin, through the likeness of sinful flesh to the form of God; in other words, we must pass from sin through repentance to God. Thus shall we really grow in understanding and virtue, and come, as I have said, to that maturity of mind called wisdom and that clarity that is perfect love, to fellowship, so to say, with the highest angels, with cherubim and seraphim thanks to Christ who in contrast "emptied himself"* even to folly and weakness. He tries, as it were, to make the guests at the marriage drunk when he uses foolish

Sg 5:16
Sg 2:16

Ezk 1:12

Ph 2:5

Ph 2:6-7
Rm 8:3

Ga 2:20

Rm 8:3

Ps 84:11

Ph 2:6-7

things such as preaching and the weakness of the Passion to save those who believe.*

5. The water mentioned could symbolize the folly and weakness which Christ changes into the wine of wisdom and virtue, "so much wiser than men is God's foolishness" found; "so much stronger than men does God's weakness" prove.* The world with all its wisdom could not find its way to God;* it lacked the wine. Christ would remind the world of its lack and so when he gave the guests wine to drink it was wine that he had changed from water, wisdom that came through folly.

6. We are assured that the wine is truly the best.* The wisdom Christ gives is such that the wine that preceded it, the wisdom of the pagan philosophers is unsatisfactory and stands condemned; the wisdom of "God has turned worldly wisdom to folly."* No doubt about it: "Truth has grown rare amid the sons of men, none but exchanges empty forms of speech with his neighbor,"* the teacher with his disciple. The pagan philosophers have been absorbed and joined to the rock which is Christ.* What has become of the wise men, the scribe, the philosopher of this age we live in?* "The so-called wise have been tricked by their own cleverness."* "They reel and stagger to and fro as a drunkard does, all their cunning forgotten;"* the wine they drank has failed them.

7. This should remind you, brothers, what a good and useful thing it is that your wine has failed and that you are not able to follow your own understanding. Let Jesus fill your mind and heart, let him fill them first with water that he will later change into wine. Do what the Doctor of the Gentiles recommends; he is one of the servants who know from where and how the good wine has come. His words are, "If any of you thinks he is wise, he must turn himself into a fool, so as to be truly wise."* In terms of Cana, this means that one must get rid of the illusion of having a sufficiency of wine if one is to have one's fill of the best wine, Out with self-complacency, for "If anybody claims to have superior knowledge, it means he had not yet attained the knowledge which is true

*Sg 5:1,
1 Co 1:21

*1 Co 1:25
*1 Co 1:21

*Sg 7:7

*1 Co 1:20

*Ps 11:2-3

*Ps 140:6

*1 Co 1:20
*Jb 5:13
*Ps 106:27

*1 Co 3:18

*1 Co 8:2
*Is 5:21
*Rm 1:22
knowledge."* "Woe to those who are wise in their own eyes."* As St Paul says, "They, who claimed to be so wise, turned fools."*

8. Let a man be filled with water, that is, let him acknowledge his folly and weakness. The sooner he sees himself as he really is, the sooner he will come to be what he should be: "He must turn himself into a

*1 Co 3:18
fool, so as to be truly wise."* If he would drink the wine he must not refuse the water. He must renounce his pet notions and himself if he is to advance in wisdom and charity on the way to the virtue of obedience. You remember, brothers, those words of the Psalm, "You take their life from them, and they breathe no more, go back to the dust they came from. Then you

*Ps 103:29
send forth your spirit and there is fresh creation."* Take it that "life," "dust" and "spirit" are equivalent to the wine that failed, to the water and to the wine that Christ prescribed and provided respectively.

9. It follows that the words, "You send forth

*Ibid.
your spirit, and there is fresh creation"* tells us that if Christ supplies the wine, men experience the inebriation of being part of the new creation.

*Jn 2:1
"And Jesus' Mother was there."* This means that her suggestion to her Son was more than a hint, it was an instance of her intercession. If he granted her a miracle it was precisely because she grasped the mystery. When her Son replied, "Nay, woman, what

*Jn 2:4
is that to me and you?,"* as if to say, "I have power in common with my Father, weakness with my mother," she understood perfectly and advised the servants to do all that Jesus should tell them.

10. Many of the world's sages have treated at length of the soul's relation to God, of its creation by him, of its purification through him, and its beatitude in him. "All their inquiry," nonetheless, "has played

*Ps 63:7
them false."* They took it on themselves, without thought of Jesus, to be the bridegroom's friend. It was as if they had not invited Jesus to the wedding, with the result that they strayed far from the truth. Not so the Apostle; he would have "Christ find a

*Eph 3:17
dwelling place, through faith, in your hearts."* And if we ask how we have deserved that this Jesus, this

faith I mean, should come to us, what mother has brought forth this faith in us, what merits have preceded it, we have but to turn to the Apostle, but to listen to the disciple who penetrated so deeply into the mysterious marriage of our salvation when he tells us, "It was grace that saved you with faith for its instrument."*

Eph 2:8

11. Grace, then, is the mother that brings Jesus to birth in our hearts; grace that forestalls the unworthy; grace that is the unseen depth that gives birth and growth to the length, breadth and height that is seen.* Justice may seem to answer this mother roughly with "Nay, woman" (loving kind and full of charity), "why do you trouble me with that?" Nonetheless, Mercy has its way. The Apostle sums it all up in the words "It was not thanks to anything we had done for our own justification; in accordance with his own merciful design he saved us."* "Mother" grace was there through whom faith, the first of the virtues, is created. Faith is made operative through the love that is Jesus, lest he be inactive and his disciples not believe in him.*

Eph 3:18

Tt 3:5

Jn 2:11

12. And what do these disciples, these followers of Jesus stand for, unless it be the virtues that follow and obey faith, that but for it are useless? Without faith they may resemble true virtues, yet they in fact are not. It is impossible they should please God without faith.* Why whatever does not proceed from faith is sin!*

Hb 11:6
Rm 14:23

What do the six hard and cold waterpots signify? Perhaps they are to remind us of the insufficiency of men's efforts. Six we know is a symbol of work-time, just as seven refers to rest from work and eight is about the resurrection that follows once all labor is over. 13. The worship the Gentiles paid to demons and the traditional purifications practised by the Jews have all been so dissolved by the water of christian faith that while they have been rendered null and void, the saving tang of reality has been found to be in the same faith. This, incidentally, is just what a teacher should do: first show up the folly of error, and then teach wisdom to the converted. St Paul sums it up briefly: "There is no virtue," he says, "either in circumcision or in the lack of it."* In terms of the Cana scene, they are mere water.[14] Under circumcision and the lack of it Paul includes all gentile worship and the external rites and observances of the Jews. He pours cold water on all that futile folly and puts saving wine in its place with the words, "It is keeping the commandment of God that has meaning."* In line with this, Jesus annuls the old Sabbath observance and his disciples eat with unwashed hands,* hence, the old dispensation must be understood spiritually, and water must be changed into wine. Peter's query at another time of the meaning of Jesus' parable provoked the reply: "What, are you still without wits?"*

The water pots, you recall, held two or three measures apiece.* This reminds us that while the pagans interpreted their sacred functions either in the cosmological or moral sense, we, for our part, find in the Old Testament not only the literal and moral sense, but the allegorical and often even the anagogical meaning. That wise man Solomon concentrates his wide discussion of so many things in a single small barrel of wine when he tells us (much as St. Paul has done), "Fear God and keep his commandments: this is the whole meaning of man."* 15. This kind of fear might well be taken as represented by the water in our text. Once a man sheds his smugness he has no difficulty in admitting his folly and weakness, he begins to fear and advances towards wisdom, for "the fear of the Lord is the beginning of wisdom."* Wisdom puts the finishing touches on the love that "drives out fear,"* turns the water into wine. This fear is doubled or tripled when because of our own fault we dread falling from glory into punishment. The water in question, may also stand for the change of heart which turns away from lifeless deeds;* six (a multiple of two and three) represents the time given us to work out our salvation, while the wine is the Kingdom of God.

16. Jesus' first miracle, like his first preaching, warns us: "Repent, the Kingdom of heaven is at

*1 Co 7:19

*Ibid.

*Mt 15:20,
Mk 7:2

*Mt 15:16

*Jn 2:6

*Qo 12:13

*Ps 110:10

*1 Jn 4:18

*Hb 6:1

Mt 4:17 hand." Repentance itself may be seen as doubled or tripled if it embraces heartfelt sorrow, oral confession, and if possible deeds of reparation. The servants who imbue a sinner with self-knowledge or the fear of God, or, at least with sorrow for sin, are the angels or the Apostles or preachers. Aware of the mystery, they draw the mysterious liquid whence and when Jesus orders and bring it to whom he orders.

Jn 2:9   17. "The master of the feast tasted ... " What a rebuke this to those who occupy the first place and yet are the last to drink of the Saviour's wine! The first draught was meant for them, for them first to taste and experience. They have become drunk, however, on another kind of wine, they cannot keep their heads up; in the sense that they have become worldly businessmen though their election was supposed to set them up as teachers of the spiritual life. They take care not to go too far into the desert, and, instead of leading, they drive their flocks. Enemies to themselves, they try to be friends to others. Since they talk of others' souls but their own bodies, they are worthy to hear: "Do what they say; do not imitate
Mt 23:3 their actions."

    18. So, my brothers, the community whose Superior spends his time travelling about dealing with secular affairs and what is foreign to his vocation and yet manages to force his subjects to keep to the regular life seems to me to resemble a handsome man who goes around with his head where his feet ought to be. I say this, although it would be no harm if we kept ourselves sometimes from passing judgment on the servant of another, or, better still, perhaps, if we shut up altogether. When it comes to each of us individually, I take it that the master of the feast symbolizes man's free choice: free choice to which first is offered the gift of faith; free choice which alone has to answer to God for either the contempt or its obedience, free choice that is arbiter of man's soul and its three-fold power of reason, desire and anger.[3]

NOTES

1. Cf. Sermon 3:19; Sermon 4:2 and 16; and Bernard, *Asc* 3; *SC* 8:6; 85:3.

2. These clauses contain verbal reminiscences of RB, Prologue and chap. 6.

3. *Rationabilitas, concupiscibilitas, irascibilitas.* For a fuller treatment, see Isaac's *Ep an* (CF 24:155-77).

SERMON ELEVEN
The First Sermon for the Third Sunday
after the Epiphany.

Mt 8:1

"WHEN JESUS had come down from the mountain, etc."* Heaven is mountain, the earth valley; God is mountain, man valley; the divine nature is mountain, the slave-nature valley. When God "possessing the divine nature" came down to earth, dispossessed himself and took on "the nature of a slave, fashioned in the likeness of man"* the crowds that waited for Him were able to follow him, crowds which separated from him could not go where he goes.* In what direction does he lead them? He leads them, first of all, to the healing of the leper—perhaps they were such and did not know it. While it is wretched to be ill, it is still more so to be unaware of the fact and not to seek a remedy. Worst of all is it to refuse the offer of what will really put matters right.

Ph 2:6-7

*Lk 8:40, Jn 13:
33, 36-37; 15:5*

2. So God, wise and loving-kind physician that he is,[1] leads them to learn their lesson, leads them to a man aware of his infirmity and consequently seeking a cure, confessing his disorder and appealing to Christ's goodwill. The crowd was meant to learn the

inner meaning of what it witnessed, to learn that the sick man who sees he is will will be followed by someone even sicker who does not.[2] The Apostle tells us: "The promises were made to Abraham and his offspring;" this is further explained by the fact that "Christ came to relieve the needs of the circumcised for the sake of God's truth; he must make good his promises to the Father. The Gentiles, in their turn, must praise God for his mercy."*

*Ga 3:16,
Rm 15:8-9

3. These words of St. Paul, as I see it, refer to two peoples—the crowd that awaits Christ and follows him represents the Jews; the leper who comes to him and is made clean stands for the Gentiles. The followers of circumcision were first when it came to awaiting and perceiving Christ's bodily presence, yet the uncircumcised, though they came to Christ later, so willingly believed the preaching of the Apostles, so sincerely confessed their leprous state, so humbly besought their Physician, that they were the first to receive the marvellous effects of his grace. He had not yet healed anyone in the crowd that followed.

4. This following of the crowd, what does it mean? You recall how the Pharisees were watching Christ in order to find fault with him; how they put questions to him not that they might learn from him, but to make him betray himself in his talk.* Far from following his teaching, they sought for some means to make away with him.* Such was the following these followers of circumcision gave him—not to go his way but to get him out of the way, not to catch his teaching but to catch him out. Those Jews, however, who on meeting Christ admitted their sinfulness, worshipped his glory and implored his goodness are to be counted as mystically one with this leper of our text.

*Mt 22:15

*Mk 11:18

5. Time was when the followers of circumcision got first preference; their worshipping one God was meant to rouse the Gentiles to emulation.* But later the Gentiles became the favorites so that the Jews might be moved to faith in the divine Trinity. Such is the state of things this very day, "the last have become first and the first last";* the teachers need to be taught and those willing to learn have become

*Ps 17:58,
Rm 10:19

*Mt 20:16

teachers; those who were once blind now see and those who once had sight have become blind.

6. Israel not only missed its mark, it persecuted its Saviour; but the chosen servant has attained to him. Israel's fields are ravaged daily before his eyes,* and the desolation of the letter that has been changed into the fertile field of spiritual understanding is being enjoyed by strangers. The kingdom of God has been taken away from them and given to a people which yields the fruit that belongs to it.* In the presence of the self-styled healthy the honest sick man is healed; his confession of sin wins him justification. "A just man is first to accuse himself,"* meaning that the beginning of his justification is his self-accusation; he begins to be just once he becomes his own accuser.

7. Justice comes to a sinner in three states: sin's confession, sin's correction and sin's avoidance, in the spirit of "I shall be ever stainless in his presence, ever watchful to keep myself from guilt."* Note these three stages in the approach of the leper. "Lord, if it be your will, you have power to make me clean."* He confesses his uncleanness and the power of the Lord; he implores the Lord to be good to him. He praises and invokes the Lord and is sent away cured of leprosy. The appeal for grace follows immediately on the giving of praise: petition cannot be separated from the two aspects of confession, namely of guilt and of praise.[3] "For everyone who so calls upon the name of the Lord will be saved,"* will hear the words, "It is my will; be made clean."* As the holy Prophet puts it, "Praising I will invoke the Lord and will be secure from my enemies."*

8. He is made clean by Jesus' touch and yet is forbidden by him who made him clean to declare himself clean until such time as he had shown himself to the priest and offered the gift ordained by the Law. What is the meaning of all this, brothers? How could a man made clean by Christ refrain from giving Christ the credit? Was the man who had praised Christ's power even before he experienced it to tell no one of the grace he had experienced? Does one

*Is 1:7

*Mt 21:43

*Pr 18:17

*Ps 17:24

*Mt 8:2

*Jl 2:32, Rm 10:13
*Mt 8:3

*Ps 17:4

made clean by Christ have need for a priest, a priest who is perhaps unclean? Far be it from us to think Christ's order pointless; he must have been speaking of mysteries.

God alone has the right to receive our confession and the power to release us from our sins; our duty lies in confessing our sin to him and expecting pardon from him. 9. Or rather, since God alone is able to really forgive sins we have no business in confessing to anyone else. True, but do not forget that the Almighty, the most High, has wedded what was weak and lowly. He has made the slave-girl his queen; she who took her place behind at his feet he has enthrowed at his side—after all, she came forth from his side, from the very side whence he pledged her to himself.† All that the Father has belongs to the Son and all that the Son has belongs to the Father* because they are one in nature. And so the Bridegroom has made the Bride one with himself and the Father because he has given her all that belongs to him and taken his share of all that belongs to her.* This is the very purpose of the prayer the Son makes to the Father on behalf of his bride in the words: "Father it is my will that as you and I are one so may these disciples be one in us."*

10. We see then, that the Bridegroom is one in nature with the Father and one in spirit with the Bride. Whatever he found improper in his Bride the Bridegroom has swept it away, nailing it to the cross,* the wood on which he bore the weight of her sins and took them away.* He took upon himself, he clothed himself in whatever really belonged to his Bride's nature and bestowed on her his very own divine nature. In becoming man the Son took away the devil's nature, assumed human nature, and conferred the divine nature so that Bridegroom and Bride could hold everything in common. Yes, and to such an extent that he who did no wrong, on whose lips no treachery was found, can make his own the words, "Lord have pity on me, I have no strength left, bring healing to a soul that has sinned against you."* He who is her partner in weakness is her

*†Jn 19:34,
Gen 2:21-22*

*Jn 16:15; 17:10

**Mt 13:46,
Ph 4:15*

*Jn 17:21

*Col 2:14

*1 P 2:24

**Ps 6:3,
40:5*

partner too in tears. Bridegroom and Bride are as one, be it in receiving confession or in bestowing absolution. All this makes clear why Christ had to tell each of us, "Go, show yourself to the priest."*

Mt 8:4

11. That the Church has this right does not make it belong any the less to Christ alone. Indeed, if this right does not belong to the Church, it does not belong to the whole Christ. You might as well say that because Christ has this right, it therefore does not pertain to God alone. Did this right not pertain to Christ, it would not pertain, so to say, to the whole of God.

A sinner who has sorrowed interiorly so that Christ alone and not the whole Christ has pardoned him must not tell anyone he has been healed.* I

Ibid.

mean, of course, if he scorns showing himself to a priest who has received the commission of pronouncing absolution and, consequently, has the right to receive confession. Were such a sinner to say he was clean his leperosy would return and his uncleanness would be all the greater for his disdaining the ministry of Christ, who cleansed on condition that he tell no one of it, but show himself to the priest and offer the appropriate gift.

12. Just as forgiven transgressions are incurred all over again by the unforgiving,* it profits a man nothing that his sins have been forgiven interiorly should he refuse to confess them exteriorly. Just as

Mt 6:15

to deny reverence to the Son is to deny reverence to the Father who sent him,* to despise the Bride is to cast a slur on the Bridegroom who has made her his own. So to treat the Bridegroom, that is the Son, means despising the Father and resisting the Holy Spirit, the Spirit apart from whom neither the Father nor the Son nor the Church ever grants pardon.[4]

1 Jn 5:23

13. God's mercy is irresistible, yet he wills to give and forgive under certain conditions only. "Give", says our Lord, "and gifts will be yours,"* otherwise one is likely to lose whatever gift one has. "Forgive," we are told, "and you will be forgiven;"* refusal to do so is to expose oneself to an angry Lord demanding repayment of a forgiven debt to the last farthing. It is only right to see the same conditions at work in

Lk 6:38

Lk 6:37

such passages as "Look, you have recovered your strength, do not sin any more, for fear that worse should befall you."* And, "I will not condemn you either. Go, and do not sin again henceforward."* We may take it that even when such an oft-repeated warning is not expressed it is implied; the text we are discussing, "It is my will; be you made clean. Go and show yourself,"* is no exception.

*Jn 5:15
*Jn 8:11

*Mt 8:3-4

14. It follows that apart from Christ the Church cannot grant forgiveness and that Christ has no will to forgive apart from the Church. The Church's authority to forgive extends only to the repentant, to those, that is, whom Christ has already touched; Christ, on his part, has no intention of regarding as forgiven one who despises the Church. Doubtless, Christ need accept no restraints to his power of baptizing, consecrating the Eucharist, ordaining ministers, forgiving sins and the like, but the humble and faithful Bridegroom prefers to confer such blessings with the cooperation of his Bride. "What God," then, "has joined, let no man put asunder."* "I say this is a great mystery and refers to Christ and the Church."* The sacrificial turtle-dove's neck might not be completely severed from its body;* no man may separate Christ, the Head, from his Body.

*Mt 19:6
*Eph 5:32

*Lv 5:8

15. Christ in fact, did not allow himself to be decapitated. He was extended and stretched out and hung on a cross to join in one the depths, the heights and what lay between. To remove the Head from the Body were to ruin the whole Christ irreparably. Christ apart from the Church is no more the whole Christ than the Church is complete if separated from Christ. Head and Body go to make the whole and entire Christ. That is the meaning of the words: "No man has ever gone up into heaven; but there is one that has come down from heaven, the Son of Man who dwells in heaven."* This man alone forgives sins. He first touches the sinner interiorly and heartfelt repentance comes about; then, he sends him to the priest, sends him on an external errand to make confession orally. The priest, in turn, sends him to offer to God the gifts that make amends.

*Jn 3:13

16. So these three achieve full cleanness: heart-felt contrition, vocal confession and deeds of amendment. No one who has failed in any of them can say he is cleansed. However, brothers, I clearly perceive that I have not quite fulfilled your desires. You very much prefer that the moral sense of Scripture be explained, so that you may be built-up on the foundation on which you rest.* Be sure, that I shall, as far as may be granted me, try to comply with your wishes, although my own preference is for the delight I find in the allegorical sense. Meanwhile, since "mere words do not build up the kingdom of God,"* let us get back to work since much remains to be done of today's quota.

*1 Co 3:10-11

*1 Co 4:20

17. Attending to discourses should not get in the way of our work; yet from time to time we should ease off on our work and find leisure for the Word of God. Man is neither flesh alone nor spirit alone, nor has he been made fully spiritual as yet by the life-giving Spirit. The whole man cannot live by the bread alone for which we work,* nor by the word alone to which we consecrate ourselves. No, he is part animal, part angel until, through Christ our Lord, he sheds all mere animal likeness and becomes as the angels of God through Christ our Lord, Amen.

*Mt 4:4

NOTES

1. On God as the wise physician, see RB 27.
2. The leper of Mt 8:2, symbolising the penitent who confesses, can be found in Abelard, *Ethica* 26: PL 178:674, and Hugh of St Victor, *Sacram* 2, 14, 8; PL 176:584.
3. For these two senses of confession, see Augustine, *In Ps* 29:19; *Sermo* 29; and Bernard, SC 56:7.
4. The argument is that despising confession means despising the Holy Spirit, hence despising the forgiving Spirit (Jn 20:22-23); cf. Hugh of St Victor, *Sacram* 2, 14, 9; PL 176:564.

SERMON TWELVE
For the same Third Sunday after Epiphany.

"WHEN JESUS had come down from the mountain."* This passage, brothers, should remind you of
that other passage according to which Jesus "when
he saw how great the crowds were, went up to the
mountain-side."* Thus, matching what is spiritual
with what is spiritual,* you will go ever higher in the
spirit and exemplify that counsel the Apostle gives:
"Since you live by the Spirit, let the spirit be your
rule of life.* This is what right order requires, what
reason demands; this is what I keep telling you with
scarce a respite: if a person wishes to be really
spiritual in meditation, understanding, and teaching,
then life, habits, virtues must first be spiritual. What
one desires is far more important than what one
comprehends: hence the words: "Since you live by
the Spirit, let the Spirit be your rule of life.

2.   "Aglow with the Spirit,"* the disciples cheerfully
and readily followed their master up the mountain,
while the crowd, slow and sluggish, could only await
his descent.*

My Lord Jesus, the Saviour of all, has to such an

Mt 8:1

Mt 5:1
1 Co 2:13

Ga 5:25

Rm 12:1

Mt 5:1; 3:26

*1 Co 9:22

extent become everything to everyone,* that, search
as you may, you will never find anyone to surpass
him in either lowliness or loftiness. When he bent
down to set free from the accusations of the devil that
soul caught in adultery, he wrote on the ground with

*Jn 8:6-10

his finger;* and this was but a sequel to the fact of his
having himself been formed by the finger of God,
earth of the earth, for the sake of those on earth. But
lifting himself up, he mounted above the very Cheru-

*Ps 17:11

bim and so soared upon the wings of the wind,* surpassing the virtues of all the just and the contempla-
tions of the angels.

3. For who is there above the clouds to rival the
Lord; where is the Lord's like among all the sons of

*Ps 88:7

God?* He is, as I see it, the valley into which he
descends, and the level place in which he walks with

*Lk 6:17
*Mt 5:1
*Mt 17:1
*Mt 14:23

the crowd,* and the mountain, up which he goes, at
one time with all his disciples,* at another with only
a few,* and yet again sometimes by himself to pray
to the Father.* Being fully divine he cannot go
higher than himself, cannot be greater than God.
Unchangeably and perfectly human, he ought not
descend below himself, ought not become a brute

*Ps 72:26

beast.*

4. He is then the high and holy ladder which that
traveller saw in sleep (meaning, perhaps that he would
have had no sight of it had he been at home and
awake), the ladder that reached from the earth up to
God and stretched down from God to the earth.[1] At
his own discretion Christ ascends through himself to
himself, now with a few, now with many, and now

*cf. Serm. 1,6-8

with no one being able to follow.* When it so pleases
him, he condescends to speak to an ordinary crowd
in a fashion suited to its capacity. At times he attends
to lepers and even gets the name of glutton and lover

*Mt 11:19, 9:11

of wine by eating with tax-collectors and sinners.*
He sometimes is not content with merely saying, "It

*Mt 8:3

is my will, be you made clean;"* but heals and
strengthens the sick by his touch.

5. Happy the soul, dear brothers, that is able to
follow the Lord Jesus in every way; that hastens "by
the very fragrance of his perfumes allured wherever

*Sg 1:3

he goes,"* soaring upwards unemcumbered in contemplation and seeing how truly Christ is God, or sharing on a lower level the ministry of his charity in the way of obedient service, willing poverty, endurance of hunger and thirst of weariness, of labor, of tears, of constant prayer, of sympathy and suffering. He came and accepted an obedience which

*Ph 2:8

brought him to death.* He came not to have service done him, but to serve others, and to give not silver, not gold, but good counsel and assistance to many,

*Mk 10:45

even his life as a ransom for the lives of many.* How blest the soul of Paul, how steadfastly he walked in Jesus' steps, when he could truly say: "If we are out of our senses, it is for God; if we are in our right

*2 Co 5:13
*Ph 1:23
†Mt 17:4

mind, it is for you."* He knew that to "be with Christ is much more than a better thing"* (obviously, it is good to be there).† Yet he did not refuse to stay on in the prison of the flesh for the sake of the brothers

*Ph 1:24

he loved.*

6. Let this be the model to which your lives conform, brothers. This you see is the true norm of monastic life[2]—to be in thought and desire at home in the everlasting fatherland with Christ, and yet shirk no kind service that can be done for Christ's sake during the toilsome journey through his life; to be willing to follow Christ the Lord on his upward journey to the Father and thus become clear-sighted, purified and revived in mediation, not to refuse to follow Christ's going down to one's brothers, and though such activity being everywhere

*1 Co 9:22

by turns to everyone,* and being full of distractions and interruptions. Nothing that may be done for Christ's sake must be despised and nothing must be desired that is not for Christ's sake; Christ is ever the one and only source of that longing for him that finds expression both in the leisure that concerns itself with Christ as one, and in the willing service of many where Christ is manifold.

7. Note how rightly the Psalmist divides his right-ordered offering of his whole self: "For you my

*Ps 62:2

soul has thirsted and in so many ways my flesh."* He would tell us with what simplicity his soul and with what diversity his body tends each to Christ; his soul as one; his body as at once a unity and a plurality, as doing many things for the sake of the one Christ. The soul ascends, the body descends, so that the whole man may go the way of the whole Christ, may be fully at the service of the whole Christ. The whole Christ is God and man; the whole of man is rational soul and flesh. It is for the soul as it contemplates truth to welcome the company of those of its kind in the realms above; the body in dutiful charity should care for those at its side; thus neither will fail in its duty to itself. As Job has it, "You will care for your own kind and not sin."*

Jb 5:24

8. Should the body notice one of its own kind happen through weakness to fall below itself, it must not show repugnance, must not shirk doing a service, must not refuse the touch that true pity inspires. Never does the soul better deserve to have true sight of its kind in the realms above as when the body stoops in charity to such of its own kind as have fallen below its level.[3] It was for your instruction that divine Wisdom, our Medicine and our Doctrine, chose to heal the leper by touching him, though a word would have sufficed. You should show kindness not in the easiest, but in the most loving way possible. There must be no shrinking back; keeping Christ ever-present in intention you must prove yourself fully compassionate. 9. After all, Christ, no matter what the person, place or work, is ever beautiful, pure, noble and worthy.

His words, you remember, were: "It is my will; be you made clean."* What business have we, brothers, discussing those who are more able than willing to do good when every day I must listen to your complaints and groans and sighs? I mean your groans that you are unable to achieve, no matter how much you will it, all that you desire, in either rising to the Father and the one thing necessary, or in descending to the manifold business of helping a brother.

Mt 8:3

"If it be your will," said the leper, "you have power to make me clean."* 10. Such is the power at his free disposal, dear friends, that everything is

Mt 8:2

possible to the Almighty; this does not mean that
he always wills all that he is able to do. He is able to
do much that he has no intention of doing and will
never be able to do in spite of himself. When confessing one's sins one need have no doubt whatever
of God's power; and yet, since he who can do all
whatsoever he wills does not will to do all that he
can, one rightly implores his favor and adores his
power. In God we must consider both will and
power. His willingness to heal the leper because he

*Mt 8:3

is able to—"it is my will; be you made clean,"*
understood as implying "because you say I am able
to"—teaches us not to shy away from whatever good
deeds are in our power. Rather, we should as the
Apostle says: "Practice generosity to all, while the
opportunity is ours without discouragement; we shall

*Ga 6:9-10

reap when the time comes."*

*Qo 3:1-8

11. There is a time for sowing and a time for
reaping.* Work then, brothers, while you can do good,
what good you can to whom you can. The night will
come when even if you would like to you may no
longer do good either to yourself or anyone else, if
while daylight lasted you were unwilling to do what

*Jn 9:4

you are able to.* While it is pitiful indeed to be unable to do the good you would, it is diabolical to
refuse to confer the benefit that is well within your
power. Rightly did this latter kind of man lose, as a
result of his refusal, the power to do good, and make
himself liable to one day lose both the desire and the
doing of any good, or to lose all possibility of achiev-
ing any good he might desire. It will be given to another so that he may have both will and power.
Then God will give us fullness of power in perfection
for the sake of his own good will. At present he
enables us to will according to his will so that what
at first is a pure gift of his grace will become at the

*Cf. Bernard,
Gra 14:51

last a sure claim to his reward.* 12. We conclude
then, that Christ, the Power and the Wisdom of

*1 Co 1:24

God,* cured the leper by touching him, though he
could easily have done it by merely speaking to him,
to teach us that his will is to rid us by his deed and
word of our leprosy and ignorance. Such is the will

of Jesus Christ, living and ruling with God the Father.
Amen.

NOTES

1. Gn 28:12. On Christ as the ladder of Jacob, see Ambrose, *De Jacob et vita beata* 2, 4, 16; PL 14:620-21. Isaac also uses Jacob's ladder in his *Ep an.*

2. *Haec sanctae conversationis vera est disciplina,* terms found in Gregory, *Dial* 2:1; PL 66:128, on Benedict's reception of the monastic habit.

3. The way to the contemplation of truth is the way of compassion; see Bernard, *Hum* 6-7.

SERMON THIRTEEN
The First Sermon for the Fourth Sunday after the Epiphany

*Mt 8:23

"JESUS went up into a boat and his disciples followed him."* We read that the Lord Jesus at various times went up at other times went down. And yet, brothers, if we consider the whole reality of Christ it amazes us how either could be true. Could God most high go higher? How could the most humble of men go lower? While he could not go higher than God, he ought not go lower than men; the latter is unbecoming, the former is simply impossible. If this going up and down be understood only and exclusively of local motion, it is a marvel that this man should come and go at all: is he not ever-present everywhere and are not all things present to him? Should he go towards any place, he is already there; he is never absent from the place he leaves. Such is the greatness of his divine nature. Let us for the present look rather at the gracious courtesy of his manhood.

2. The boat entered stands for the Church[1] that as yet is cruising the vast ocean stretching wide on every side of this present world.* But if this be true,

*Ps 103:25

should we not rather say that he went down into
the boat and not that he went up? For he dis-
Ph 2:7 possessed himself, and took the nature of a slave,*
and in and through this nature he entered into the
Church, coming to and down upon it as the Head on
Eph 5:23 the Body.* Every society and community and private
family for its due ordering must have some in charge
and others who obey.

3. However, that one unversed in cooperation
and obedience should become a superior and give
orders is most unbecoming.[2] To prove it sovereign
Greatness, whose very nature is to be second to none,
whose inalienable right is to rule all things, to whom
all arrangements and authority in the universe owe
their origin, "made amends for what he had not
Ps 68:5 stolen,"* bent down to take our nature, did our duty,
paid the debt he did not owe. So well did he accom-
modate himself to his surroundings that amid all his
marvellous deeds none was a greater wonder, none a
brighter lesson than the holy life he lived as a man
among men. Thus to the amazed, overawed Baptist
who cried, "It is I that ought to be baptized by you,
and do you come to me instead?"* he responded, "Let
Mt 3:14 it be so for the present." That is, wait awhile and
don't spoil God's plan. By following the plan and
beginning with humility, we will fulfill all due
Mt 3:15 observance.*

4. This due observance expected of us is obtained,
practised and finds its full accomplishment in the
two already-mentioned levels of those responsible for
authority and those responsible to authority. In due
observance one is in charge according to order and one
obeys according to subordination; far from presuming
to a position of authority, one consents to govern
only where legitimately called by another. This agrees
with what the holy Apostle says: "Nobody can take
on himself such a privilege as this, his vocation must
Hb 5:4 come from God, as Aaron's did."* The Lord Jesus
behaved the same; at the beginning of his mission he
was subject to the people, he came as one of them to
Lk 3:21 John's baptism,* he did not take it on himself to rise
to the level of one in authority (we have the emphatic

assertion of the Blessed Apostle writing to the
Hebrews to this effect),* but was elected and
appointed by God the Father who definitively
declared him in authority with the words, "This is
my beloved Son, in whom I am well pleased,"*
pleased, that is, with the way he did his duty during
his time of subjection.

5. We must listen to him who learned to obey.
He who up to then had been silent had a right to
preach. Preaching is not for one who had not learnt
to be silent. The Teacher who has really learned what
he teaches deserves disciples. He is a worthy leader
who did not disdain being under others. Thirty years
in the lowest place had well earned the words: "My
friend, go higher."* So much, then, on the text that
told us that Jesus went up into the boat.

6. Then comes: "His disciples followed him."*
You will not find a disciple of Christ who is not
patterned in this way in the likeness of his Master.
Not for such a man to take on himself such a privilege
as this, to make himself an apostle or evangelist. If he
preached it is because he has been sent to do so;* not
for nothing did the apostle write: "Some he appointed
to be apostles, others to be evangelists".* When
Zebedee's sons were coveting positions to which
they had not been invited, they were told, "You do
not know what it is you ask."* Christ's disciples
today, brothers, follow their Master, willingly taking
a low place until they are called higher. Those who
push themselves forward, who take on themselves
such privileges as they may, are no disciples, no
followers of Christ; far from being sent by him, they
have allowed their ambition to forestall any call he
might give them. In Christ's view they rank as thieves
and robbers.*

7. What more absurd petition or presumption or
pretension could there be than that of one who would
have himself alone placed above all and sundry? Was
not this what that reckless angel told himself in the
words: "I will soar above the level of the clouds, I will
set my throne higher than God's stars,"* higher, that
is, than his fellow angels? Such ambition comes of a

*Hb 5:5-6

*Mt 3:17

*Lk 14:10

*Mt 8:23

*Rm 10:15

*Eph 4:11

*Mt 20:22

*Jn 10:18

*Is 14:13

mind either conceited or crazy. To regard oneself as more wise and more worthy than anyone else is not only self-satisfaction but self-delusion. 8. Is he not blind who in his own eyes is so important and enflated?

Once pride is born it blinds the mind as surely as disease does the eye. This explains why the proud cannot believe that they are proud; unable to see themselves as they are, they cannot admit that they are proud. As for one who is ambitious for what he knows he is unfit for, such a person is obviously crazy!

9. The Gospel continues: "A great storm arose on the sea."* The wind that was against them is the hot north wind from which comes all evil. Well knowing its fury, the soul banishes it by saying, "North wind, be off; wind of the south, blow through this garden of mine, and set its fragrance astir."* There can be no doubt that the contrary wind is the devil, is Satan who stirs up the depths of the sea, namely, the children of this world, and attempts by instigating frequent storms of opposition to shipwreck the Church. In his power he disturbs even the mountains because of the bitter trials that overtake them.* Where now, I ask, is the Power of him whom they have followed on to the boat, the power that made them boast in their confidence: "Not for us to be afraid, though earth should tremble about us, and the hills be carried away into the depth of the sea?"*

10. By now the waters, the mountainous waves of the deep, rage and roar, and those mountains of his Church or mountains of the little ship, are in a proper panic over the force and fury of the elements.[3] Why have they lost their bearings? Why are they afraid? Their strong Saviour is asleep. Where Christ their Strength sleeps their fear holds sway, for then the sea's fury rises and a man forgets his faith in Christ.

11. While Christ's power is inoperative it is a good thing that fear should dominate; it will in due time force the frightened and their slight and sleepy faith to seek safety with him with whom they should have kept their strength, and far from being afraid could have claimed: "God is our refuge and strong-

Mt 8:24

Sg 4:16

Ps 45:4

Ps 45:3

*Ps 45:2

*Mt 8:25

hold amid the bitter trials that overtake us."*
Instead, they have to beg Christ to wake up and save
them because if he sleeps on they will drown.* The
best thing the disciples could have done would have
been to keep their Master from sleeping; they did the
next best thing and woke him from sleep. In place of
courage and glowing faith they had but fear and a
confession of need. Love keeps Christ awake;
necessity wakes him from sleep. What a good thing
it is, nonetheless, to have to make a virtue of necessity!
12.   For seeking counsel and help is indeed virtuous,
though not as virtuous as having the courage that
prevents fear.

So, brothers, whenever persecution rages against us,
let us, after the holy Apostle's example, have recourse
to Christ. Let us enliven our faith in Christ and awake
the memory of his Passion, that sleeping of his that
this sleeping in the boat fittingly refers to.[4] By ourselves we become either weak and fearful or indulge
in foolhardy fortitude; in Christ we find the very
pattern of patience and he endows us with really
virtuous endurance teaching us true constancy.
Separated from him we are forever failures; joined to
him we are fit for anything; as the blessed Apostle
says, "Nothing is beyond my powers, thanks to the

*Ph 4:13

*Ps 10:5

strength he gives me."* How true it is that the Lord's
eyelids appraise us!* When he closes his eyes the sea
rages, everything becomes savagely difficult. May we
not be broken! He opens his eyes, all is calm, it is all
smooth sailing. May we not become proud! For when
all is quiet, all is safe, may we not become lazy. In
foul weather we must hope for fair and in fair
weather we must beware of foul. Changes are always
going on and one thing follows another. The truly
wise man will be more anxious in prosperity than in
adversity, and in neither will such a person grow lazy
and surrender to slumber; not for such to either
despair or become complacent. So, brothers, with fear
and hope for escort, let us keep ever alive in us faith
in our Lord Jesus Christ. Amen.

NOTES

1. On the boat as the Church, see Hilary of Poitiers, *In Matt* 7:9;
8:4; 13:1; 15:10.
2. See Bernard, *Mor* 8:31-32.
3. On the Apostles as mountains, see Hilary, *In Psalmis* 146:9;
PL 9:873; and Gregory, *Mor* 33, 1, 2; PL 76:668.
4. On this theme, see Jerome, *In Matt* 1:8; PL 26:53.

SERMON FOURTEEN
A Second Sermon for the Fourth Sunday after Epiphany

"SUDDENLY a great storm arose on the sea, but he lay asleep."* What, dear friends, did our Lord achieve while his body slept? What, if not wake-up the disciples, whose hearts were asleep? It was while Christ slept that Power was at work bringing "the winds out of his storehouse."* Silent and fast asleep the Word spoke, teaching the disciples how perilous it were for them should they allow their Master to stay silent, to be idle, to sleep. Wisdom is learnt when at leisure, but not by the lazy. No leisure is more busy, no free time more full of toil than when wisdom is being learnt, when the Word of God is being consulted.

2. Martha toiled, Mary kept quiet, but not inactive.* It was Lazarus who was sick, passing from inactivity to death, and from death to corruption.* How many today are like him! They are remiss and idle internally, though without the excuse of useful external work. Well provided with the necessities of life, they busy themselves with tall tales and silly scheming. No doubt, they have escaped Martha's

*Mt 8:24

*Ps 134:7

*Lk 10:39-40
*Jn 11:1-39

solicitude, but have not experienced Mary's devotion! No wonder that in Bethany, the very House of Obedience,[1] they are afflicted with the languor of sloth![2]

3. What wretchedness! Weak in the presence of Power, fools in Wisdom's company; blind to the Light, dumb to the Word, they are wasted with hunger at the table piled high with the bread of long life and good discernment. It is of such the Scripture says, "With no stomach for food, they are close to death's door."* And just as our Lord allowed sick Lazarus to die that he might raise him to life,* so is it here in the text we are discussing; he allowed himself to fall asleep for the benefit of the sickly apostles or whom they signify, so that at least in their peril they might wake him. Outwardly then he slept, he to whom the men we are discussing had, as it were, fallen asleep inwardly. Their inner state was shown by his outward state. But when gentle and subtle instruction could find no place in them, he warned them externally all the more roughly.

4. Hence "the magnificent rage of the sea" that enables "the Lord to appear magnificent in the deeps"* Asleep, he instructs those falsely secure by means of the tempest; awake he teaches by the ensuing calm those rightly terrified. Take my word for it, brothers, the storm and the calm, the sleeping and the awaking are, each of them, a word of that holy Word. Sleeping, he condemns by the word of the tempest that spiritual sloth which is followed by such confusion of mind as makes it a sort of interior and intolerable storm. Once roused and awake, Jesus, by the calm his word wrought, shows the need for vigilance and spiritual eagerness.

5. So, brothers, we must spare no effort to keep awake. The very remoteness of the monastery[3] we have chosen should be a further reason for our making sure that in the boat of our innermost being, surrounded as it is by our outer nature as by a sea, the Word of God should never fall asleep; in himself, of course, he neither sleeps nor slumbers. If Christ has nothing to do for us he cannot keep awake to us; he is, to put it briefly, interested only in being asked

*Ps 105:18
*Jn 11:11

*Ps 92:4

favors or being asked questions. At very least, he
desires attentive listeners should he himself speak.
Just you start sleeping to him, brothers, while he is
speaking to you, and at that very instant he sleeps
to you. Woe betide you should he sleep to you!

6. Let him but sleep to you and the wind, sea,
storm wake up; the tidal-waves of fancy and the
surgings of a thousand temptations will break upon
you. Good cause have you to pray to him as the
Psalmist does: "Give light, o Lord, to these eyes of
of mine lest they close in death."* If you keep from
sleeping, he will keep unwearied watch over you.
Peter proved well able to deny Christ three times
simply because he proved unable to stay awake with
Christ for a single hour. He slept although our Lord
had told him, "Watch and pray, that you may not
enter into temptation,"* that is, into a spiritual
storm. What excuse, now, have those who nod over
their books in the cloister or snore during readings in
church or sleep during sermons in the chapter-room?
In all these instances God's very Word speaks and
goes unheeded.

7. Our Lord and Teacher speaks and man, the
disciple, sleeps.

We must consider three practices: reading, meditation and prayer.[4] By means of reading or preaching
(this latter is a kind of reading) God speaks to you.
That is why we are told, "Listen, you that have ears
to hear with."* In meditation you put him queries
and in prayer you put requests to him. That is why he
says: "Ask, and the gift will come; seek and you shall
find; knock and the door shall be opened to you".*
That prayer does, indeed, obtain, that meditation
does discover, they know better than I can tell you
who in their zeal for things spiritual have trained
their faculties by due exercise.* Mere man by his
natural gifts cannot take in such things, even if his
form of life be spiritual. 8. I am but repeating
(and I do wish you would remember the fact) that just
as you will find people unspiritual in mind but spiritual in form of life, so you will find some unspiritual
in form of life but spiritual in mind.[5]

*Ps 12:4

*Mt 26:41

*Mt 11:15

*Mt 7:7

*Hb 5:14

A third kind are those whose lives and values are just natural; a fourth, those whose lives and values both are spiritual. There can be no doubt that reading, meditation and prayer are the whole formation of the spiritual mind; why, they are a dwelling of the mind in heavenly realms, like Moses, on the mountain, one who makes use of them speaks and listens to, holds conversation with God as with his neighbour,* though it be only in his mind. 9. But a person's life itself can be a going aside and coming near to the Lord. It is in this sense that our Lord says, "Come close to me, and I will come close to you."* To repeat: some are near God in their understanding, but far from him in their manner of life; others live close to him in manner of life, though not in understanding; still others are far from God in both their conduct and their mind; while others are close to God in both ways. Understanding brings one close to God; manner of life brings closer; lastly, understanding and life bring one as close as possible.

*Ex 33:11

*Jm 4:8

10. Let us keep awake, then, brothers, and be on our guard most specially against the plague of spiritual laziness that comes usually of immature self-assurance and infects even such as really have made some progress. They tell themselves that, having overcome all evil tendencies, they may lie down to rest in all safety, with nothing to terrify them. In the case of the less advanced, the fact that their bodily needs are taken care of by others leaves them, they think, nothing further to do.

This explains, dearest friends, why the holy Fathers whose sublime and severe way of life we have the nerve to attempt to follow (we who are so laden and lax, not to say pampered and sleek*) made poverty the corner-stone that holds together the two walls of the spiritual building. By making poverty twofold it is applicable to both our exterior and our interior, that is to being poor in pocket and in spirit. The idea being that once a person becomes aware of how lacking he is on both counts, he should take good care to prove himself lacking in neither.

*Dt 32:15

11. Here you have the reason, dearest friends,

why we have led you into this remote, waste and for-
bidding wilderness, and did it so craftily! Here you
can be as humble as you like, you cannot become
wealthy. This indeed is solitude worthy of the name,
far out, at sea, cut off almost completely from all the
rest of the world. Here then destitute of all worldly
comfort and very nearly all human solace, it should
not be difficult to give worldliness a rest. What can
the world offer to us on this tiny last island at the
end of the world?

Yes, Lord, I have gone afar off and made good my
escape: fled so far away* that I have no idea whether
there be a place still more remote to which I might
further withdraw; you know. 12. There was a time
when my thirst for solitude made me long to escape;
at last I reached this desert-isle, so desolate and
remote. Some of my, so to say, fellow-conspirators
lost heart and only a handful have come with me.
Even these dread this howling wilderness, and there
are times, I must admit, when I dread it. It is true,
Lord, solitude has been added to solitude, silence has
been piled on silence. We are more and more forced
to silence among ourselves, but only that we may
converse all the more freely and familiarly with you
alone.

As for ourselves, dearest friends, is it not in our
own best interest to focus our attention with thanksgiving and praise on the mercy that God has shown
us, mercy beyond our hopes? 13. His favor has so
arranged this exile of ours that on the one hand we
have leisure for prayer, meditation and reading, on
the other we have no option but to work if we are
to have the means of sharing with those in need,*
that is with our own animal bodies. Rather than with
the sweat of hired-help or of oxen, we must be ready
to earn our bread with the sweat of our own brow.

14. So, brothers, my dear fellow-prisoners* and
fellow-refugees, take the advice offered by the
Prophet in the words, "You that keep the Lord in
remembrance take no rest nor let him rest either."*
Keep awake to him, unless you would have him
sleep to you. For my part, "to you, Lord, shall I

*Ps 54:8

*Eph 4:28

*Rm 16:7

*Is 62:6

118

cry" at all times, and "do you, my God, not leave my cry unanswered. Listen to me"* or I shall become like those at sea shipping water perilously. Open to one who knocks in meditation, and answers his queries; do but listen to his prayers! Your great and generous love is more than ready, we know, to do this, provided that when you speak we listen. If you are listened to, you listen; you listen carefully to those who listen carefully to you. To turn a deaf ear to your law is to make prayer a sacriledge.*

15. "Speak, then, Lord, your servant is listening."* In your turn make answer to him who speaks to you. While we are both of us at sea neither of us should sleep! Were you to sleep to me, the world and all the memories it brings would rise up against me; what towering waves, what turbulent thoughts would assail me, were you to fall asleep! Were I to sleep to you, my flesh would not sleep to me. Lord, though you could have so strengthened me that I should not have to seek safety with you, nonetheless be my refuge and pay heed to my sobs and the groanings of my heart, and not least, to the unceasing clamor of my cares. Wake and rise up! 16. Bestir yourself, check the winds, and the sea,* rescue me from the fears that daunt me, from the storm around me* so that within me and without there be deep calm. Let men and angels alike, to whom we present such a spectacle,* see your power and in their amazement exclaim: What kind of man is this, who is obeyed even by the winds and the sea? * This, brothers, is to be the experience of both you and me on condition that we obey him who so truly lives and rules. Amen.

*Ps 27:1

*Pr 28:9
*1 S 3:10

*Mt 8:26
*Ps 54:9

*1 Co 4:9

*Mt 8:27

NOTES

1. An etymology taken from Jerome, *Nom hebr;* PL 23:839-40.

2. "Spiritual sloth", *acedia,* has its classic description in John Cassian, *Coen Inst* 10; PL 49:359 ff.

3. Literally *eremum* (desert), a common term for monastery in the Cistercian tradition, one with biblical roots in such texts as Dt 1:19, Ps 77:15, Ws 18:20.

4. Compare with Sermon 5:7, and see the rules laid down in RB 8, 20, 48, 49, 58.

5. The "spiritual form of life" is, of course, the monastic life. Cf. Bernard *Apo* 2:4, 5:11; 12:29; and *Ded* 1:2.

SERMON FIFTEEN
A Third Sermon for the Fourth Sunday after the Epiphany

*Mt 8:23

"JESUS took ship".* There is no limit to the things man will try, no contraption too fragile for him to take a chance on! Wherever did poor mortals get the idea of risking their lives crossing the sea on wood so perishable? Was it that they found the land-mass too confined?

There is the sea before our eyes; the boat, you notice, brothers, is battling with the waves. What, I ask you, makes the difference between life and death for those poor fellows sailing there unless it be, as we have said, a fragile and flimsy piece of wood? Let us sit down for a while, brothers, and ponder this matter more deeply, and, as usual, let us make these outer sights a lesson for our inner life. We are tired and time permits. 2. Take my word for it, brothers, those whom you see at sea there are not, in my opinion, living more dangerously than any other men who are in this present world and in these mortal bodies. Surely, we may compare this world and these bodies of ours to the sea? If so, those fellows there have

something at least to put between the lively, life-
giving wind and the heavy, deadly brine, although
it is something flimsy, fragile and untrustworthy.
But in our case, nothing at all comes between soul
and body, nor does anything separate the body from
the world about it.

This explains why coming into the perishable
body means coming to our death. Conception in such
flesh is but reception in such depths; shown into life
yet sunk in death; a man and a sinner simultaneously;
shipwrecked on entering this world. 3. It could not
be otherwise, since we came into this world soiled
then and there by this world. Yes, as long as we live
the life of nature we cannot be acceptable to God;* a
choice must be made between belonging to the world
and belonging to the kingdom of Christ. The blessed
Psalmist, foreseeing this shipwreck of ours, cries out
loudly: "Save me, o God; the waters close about
me . . . I have ventured out into mid-ocean, to be
drowned by the storm."*

Were you to ask: "Has everyone been so sunk in
the life of nature as to be in danger? Do all who come
into this world suffer of this shipwreck?" 4. Yes,
most certainly. What else are we to make of that universal and well-known Flood? Why did the deep cover
the earth like a cloak when the waters stood high above
the mountains* and there was no sign whatever of
dry land? That thanks to a piece of wood a few souls
found refuge,* like our friends in the boat there, is a
type of the living wood, the life-giving Cross of
Christ by the presence and protection of which the
chosen few were saved, while many who are merely
called (and those still more numerous who are not
called) are lost.[1]

5. The sound wood of faith for us is the only
thing between life and death. I gladly welcome the
idea that the boat our Savior went up into is none
other than the Cross whereby he created the difference between death and us, between what we are
and death.[2] He led us away, separated us and won us
freedom from world, flesh and devil.* "He went up
into"* says the text, and with every good reason, for

*Rm 8:8

*Ps 68:2-3

*Ps 103:6

*1 P 3:20

*Ac 10:38
*Mt 15:39

he went up of his own choice, there could be no question of being either unwilling or forced. He willingly offered sacrifice to the Father: both offering and offerer, "he was offered because it was his own will."* He laid down his life when, as, and for as long as he willed, he who ran with joy the race for which he was entered.*

Is 53:7

Hb 12:1

6. Where are they, those who go about whispering and complaining, those so half-hearted, timid and slow that they must be pulled and pushed towards the cross and passion of our way of life and the penitence they have dedicated themselves to under oath? What can they make of the text that says, "His disciples followed him"?* It is surely right that disciples go the way of their teacher, servants of their master, sons of their father. All those who are resolved to live a holy life in Christ Jesus will meet with persecution!* Should persecution from others be lacking, the outer self of Jesus' disciples is to be "crucified with all its passions, all its impulses,"* while the inner self must hang with Jesus on the gibbet of obedience. A humble disciple should be able in all circumstances whatever to address his spiritual father with the words, "Abba, father, ask me not what I want, but what you will."*

Mt 8:23

2 Tm 3:12

Ga 5:24

Mk 14:36
Mk 14:38

7. And if "the flesh is weak,"* if it becomes heavy, if the soul be distressed, grow dismayed and daunted, let the spirit nonetheless, be always willing* to restrain and win the obedience of what is subject to it, and be obedient to its superior, since it alone God judges. Well may I call the Rule you have made profession of and your living in this remote monastery your cross. Not only does solitude separate you from other men, the duty of obedience cuts you off from your very selves. You may not do as you like; you own neither the things you use nor your bodies; neither your work nor your leisure is at your free disposal. What is this dependence on the will of another but for Christ's love to be nailed to the Cross, to be crucified with Christ by means of the nails of obedience?*

*Ibid.

*Rm 6:8,
Col 2:20; 3:3

8. At this point the meaning of Christ's sleeping in the boat becomes abundantly clear from what has

been said earlier. To sleep in the boat is to die on the cross, as the Psalm says: "I have slept and have taken my rest."* No one else finds it so easy, so much within his power, either to sleep while staying awake or keep awake while sleeping; our Lord laid down his life when he chose to and when he willed took it up again.*

*Ps 3:6

*Jn 10:17; Is 53:17

While he sleeps the sea rises, whipped-up by the wind, and the frightened disciples fear shipwreck. It recalls the exulting and insulting the Jews were driven to by the devil while he was dying, a time the disciples were so overcome with fear that they were close to despair. 9. There is, I am sure, brothers, no need to discuss such well-known gospel-scenes in detail. Christ's awakening, his rising from the dead, brought calm first to the hearts of the Apostles and later to the whole Church once the world had been overcome and its prince put in bonds. If all this does not make for wondering joy, it can only be because a person is in such stupor and sorrow that he is a marvel to be wondered at.

10. Let us, for our part, brothers, consider how great Christ is and how safe it is to sail in his company and for his sake, yes, "to share his sufferings"* and die with him, that in ourselves, that is, in his members, we may make good the debt which his afflictions still leave to be paid.* It needs must be that all the members should suffer with their Head when he suffers; yes, that the whole Christ should suffer, be made perfect through suffering and so enter into his glory.* Sharing his kingdom is simply out of the question if his suffering is not shared.

*Rm 8:17

*Col 1:24

*Lk 24:26

"Even the winds and the sea obey him."* Unless he permit it by sleeping, no temptation, internal or external, from above or from below, can do a thing; still less, should he rise and rebuke it!* 11. You remember the sacred Psalm: "At his word the stormy winds rose, churning up its waves; high up towards heaven they were carried, then sank into the trough . . . And he stilled the storm into a whisper, till all the waves were quiet."* He is faithful and will not allow those who belong to him to be tempted

*Mt 8:27

*Lk 8:24

*Ps 106:25-26, 29

*1 Co 10:13
*Ibid.

*Ibid.

*Nb 21:6-9

*1 P 2:21

*Sg 2:14

+Ps 83:4

*Ps 50:19

*Sg 4:6

*Ps 41:7,12

*Jn 17:5
*Ps 41:7-8
*Ibid.

beyond what they are able to bear;* why, he makes "profit from temptation"* possible; virtuous patience grows should the trial grow making the victory all the greater, the crown that perseverance alone achieves.

12. Consequently, brothers, whenever temptation comes upon you,* be it sickness, poverty, severe observance, long continuance in the same old place, be it the frustration that results from the remoteness of the monastery and its strict silence, plus other possibilities past counting, let us, through reading, meditation or prayer, rouse Christ from sleeping in our regard. Let us give our full attention to the lesson his Cross and Passion has for us; bitten suddenly by the serpent below let us look to the Serpent lifted on high.* 13. As the blessed Apostle Peter tells us, "Christ suffered for our sakes, and left you his own example, you were to follow in his footsteps."* Let us take him, dear friends, not only as an example to follow, but as our medicine, lest when bitten we die. He must not only inspire endurance, he must bestow the gift of perseverance. He is not merely the pattern in the fight, he is the power that carries to victory. Here the wary and innocent dove makes her nest in the cleft Rock and crannied Wall.* 14. "Where else should the swallow find a nest for her brood, but at your altars, Lord of hosts?"* From these altars does the sweet scent, all myrrh and incense, go up, as it is written: "Here, o God, is sacrifice, a broken spirit; a heart that is contrite and humbled you, o God, will never disdain."* Ignorance of this had no place in that soul that knowing both the destination and the direction said, "I will betake myself to the mountain of myrrh and to the hill of frankincense."* Weary of itself and sad of mood, the soul calls to him* the Lord Jesus, its Saviour, not in the highest heaven to which he ascended to "the glory which he had with the Father before the world began," but "in this land of Jordan,"* that is, of descent,[3] the land of "Hermon's foot-hills where one depth makes answer to another."* This means that our self-denial, our suffering, our endurance looks to the death, passion and endurance

*Col 3:3

of Christ our Lord for effective inspiration. 15. It is those on this mountain of myrrh that Saint Paul addresses in the words: "You have undergone death, and your life is hidden away now with Christ in God."*

Ever mindful then, of our Saviour, most particularly of his love, suffering and endurance, that greatest evidence of his undeserved love "for" us and best pattern of what he expects of us, let us never grow weary, but stand firm against all trials whatever, partners of his sufferings for his sake so that we may share glory with him. Such the gift Christ himself gladly makes us. Apart from him we have no such power. Nothing is beyond our powers thanks to him who lives and rules with the Father and the Holy Spirit. Amen.

NOTES

1. For linking Noah's Ark and the Cross, see Augustine, *Catech rud* 19:32; and *In Joan* 9:11.

2. The boat of Mt 15:39 and parallels symbolizes the Cross according to Bede, *In Marc* 2; PL 92:173.

3. Jordan as descent is from Jerome, *Nom hebr;* PL 23:781. Migne and Hoste have *ascensionis* here. It seems better to follow Tissier's *decensionis.*

SERMON SIXTEEN
The First Sermon for Septuagesima

"HERE IS an image of the kingdom of heaven; a
Mt 20:1   rich man . . . "* God's wisdom, dear friends, is indeed
subtle and, nonetheless, absolutely straightforward;
it is found to be both really one and truly manifold.[1]
As the prophet says, "Great numbers will understand,
Dn 12:4   and knowledge shall be manifold."* Wisdom is aptly
described as "a fountain bordered with gardens, a
Sg 4:15   well of running water."* It is a fountain because it
never ceases to flow; its unfathomable depth makes
it a well, a well of running water of ever-fresh bub-
bling up insights.[2]

    2. Take this parable of our text. It seems a
straightforward piece of Scripture if ever there was
one, and yet it is rightly explained and commented on
by many different authors in many different ways,
but no one can so get to the bottom of it that all possible interpretations are exhausted, that posterity
cannot add a word to what has already been said. In any
case, whatever may be said of anything with wisdom
and truth, no matter what form it takes, exists from
eternity, totally contained at once and forever in

every possible way in eternal wisdom and truth.

3. There is a Spirit that penetrates to the depths of God by enclosing not by enquiring,* the Spirit that, as the Scripture tells us, is "the bond that holds all things in being, that knows every sound we utter."* When he speaks through someone, be the truth or worth of the message what it may,[3] the Spirit knows it, understands it, intends it. Sometimes the person through whom he speaks finds no meaning, sometimes, a single meaning, sometimes he is illumined by many meanings at the same time, no one is ever granted the fulness of interpretation. This explains why it has often been possible to attribute to the Holy Spirit and to find in agreement with him differing and even discordant interpretations of the same Scripture text; provided such meanings are proved consonant with the true faith and with both what builds up love and banishes selfishness, over all of which Holy Scripture keeps an ever-vigilant eye.

4. Take any exegete you like who takes the same text in different ways at various times; as long as he agrees with truth and love he can claim the approval of the one Holy Spirit. What goes against love must not be passed off as truth; what is contrary to truth cannot be called love. These few remarks, brothers, are a sort of short preface so that should you hear something unusual or something that differs from what you have elsewhere read (I may be somewhat bold) you will not think that I am altogether unaware of the Fathers or despise their opinions or that I am foolishly rejoicing in my own pet ideas. 5. No, a careful listener seeks ever the meaning of what is said in the motive for saying it. My purpose is not so much to explain the readings from the holy Gospel as it is to take the opportunity they offer to say something towards the building-up of the brethren and of ourselves, making all due allowance for time, place and persons. I must say something, since you refuse to let me share your silence. Moreover, the Apostle entreats us not to offer any portion of God's grace an ineffectual welcome,* and David goes further and warns us against giving such treatment to our rational intellect

*1 Co 2:10;
Ws 1:7

*Ws 1:7

*2 Co 6:1

when he praises one who has not been false to his
own soul.* The Gospel expects every talent to be
doubled.* The child of the promise not only kept
the wells his father had, but opened fresh ones.*

*Ps 23:4
*Mt 25:20
*Gn 26:15 ff.

6. Have all due respect for the opinion that
faithfully and fittingly interprets this vineyard of our
text as the whole Church, Christ being the vine,
Christians the branches, the Father the gardener and
the rich man, the daylight the whole of time or the
life of man, the hours the ages of the world or of
individuals, the market-place this world's grasping
and insatiable business.[4] 7. For my part, I view my
whole self, soul and body both and not just my soul,
as the one vine that I may not neglect, but must dig
about it and cultivate it to prevent it being overrun
by unwelcome weeds and by the roots of other plants
or be smothered by its own offshoots. Pruned it must
be or it will grow wild: trimmed so that it may yield
more fruit.* It must be altogether fenced-in or every
passer-by will freely plunder it;* the greatest danger
of all being that the wild boar from the thickets
that solitary beast, may ravage it.* To sum all this
up briefly: it must be cultivated with the greatest
care, otherwise the noble shoots of this choice vine
will go to seed, will turn into a worthless vine and,
far from delighting both God and man, may only
succeed in saddening both of them. It must also
be guarded with the utmost watchfulness that all the
exertion spent on it and hopes placed in it may not
be wiped-out, either by stealthy stealing of those who
devour the poor in secret* or by sudden and unlooked-
for disaster. 8. It was in this sense, as though referring to a vine in his keeping, that the First Man was
given Paradise that, as Scripture says, "he should cultivate it and keep it".[5]

*Jn 15:2
*Is 5:2,5

*Ps 79:13-14

*Hab 3:14

Truly, dear friends, just as time itself is punctuated by
light and darkness, day and night, so too is man's life, this
transient one, passed sometimes in darkness at the midday-
sun,* at other times in light though it be midnight. God did
not bid night come from day, but "bade light shine out
from darkness."* Children of this world, children of night
and darkness, are born in darkness; yes, and children of the

*Dt 28:29

*2 Co 4:6

light and of the day have no other birthplace!* The Apostle not only wrote to the latter, "You are all born to the
light, born to the day; you do not belong to the night and
its darkness,"* but also, "Once you were all darkness;
now, in the Lord, you are all daylight."* 9. So true
is this parentage that the children of light are called
light, the children of darkness darkness; it is ever a
case of, "Like father, like son." It follows that
unbelief is night and faith is day; sin is night, virtue
is day; ignorance is darkness, while wisdom is light;
hatred and love are as darkness and light; the devil
is darkness, God is light,* which explains why Adam
is darkness and Christ is light. To draw this list to a
close: a guilty conscience and delight in sin are night
and deep darkness; a good conscience and love of
virtue are dazzling daylight. Worldly wisdom and life
are darkness; spiritual wisdom and life are daylight.

10. Night then, obtains in such cases as have been
cited, the sort of night in which, as our Saviour says,
"no one can work."* Whoever does evil does not so
much work at as suffer from the night: all bad
actions are passions[6] to beings made good. To
misuse the good that by nature one is or has not
only corrupts oneself, it means being corrupted,
means oneself reaping the corruption one causes.
The things that pertain to the night and the darkness
are passions, not real actions; real actions belong to
the day and the daylight alone. Because of this the
passions the holy martyrs suffered for Christ's sake
are rather called acts and achievements, the day of
their deaths their birthdays. No work could be more
laborious than what achieves the immortality that is
far beyond all suffering. 11. No deed takes more
doing than the unflinching constancy that at one
single stroke vanquishes the flesh, the present world
and the devil, rage and tempt as they may.

It is abundantly clear, I take it, how subtle and
valid that message of Truth always is that tells us
there is no working at night only during daylight can
it be done. Truth's words are, "While daylight lasts I
must work; the night is coming when there is no working any more."* Yet this may be applied, fittingly

*1 Th 5:5

*Ibid.
*Eph 5:8

*1 Jn 1:5

*Jn 9:4

*Ibd.

enough, to that other night in which no one can work, but always and eternally all that is is to suffer. In the nether-world night and suffering are ever-present and everlasting; in heaven, on the other hand, the only business of eternal day is eternal praise and thanksgiving.* 12. Good reason had the Prophet to sing "How blest, Lord, are those who dwell in your house! They will be ever praising you."* The first kind of night, then, is that from which daylight may shine out and doing good may follow it, though it cannot take place in it. The second night consists of such lasting darkness that not only is there no working in it, it is so dark, there never will be any after it, it is everlasting. There is no doing, no scheming, no wisdom in the lower regions that soon shall be the home* of the children of this world's light and of that darkness.

Is 51:3

Ps 83:5

Qo 9:10

Therefore, dearest friends, while the opportunity is ours, while we have this day, not, of course, the day of man, of which the Prophet says, "It was no wish of mine that that day should befall mankind"* (no need to remind you how holy Job put that "day" under a solemn curse).* Let us, I say, practise generosity to all beginning without any hesitation with our very selves. 13. Whose friends is he that is his own enemy?* "Befriend yourself, doing God's will."† counsels Ben Sirach. One who neglects his own vine has no business cultivating some one else's. When it was night we were incapable of any good, so the Light freely came into the world and took the world by surprise. We were born when it was night, we were brought up in the night, but though composed of clay from beneath, we are also of spittle from above—spittle from the Head, clay from beneath the foot. When mud made of this clay and spittle was smeared on the eyes of the man born blind his eyes were opened.* That universal night is past in which all have sinned;* it has gone, the Sun is shining, the darkness has so vanished that those who could not work previously have not the least excuse now if they refuse to work in the daylight. As he who is the Day says: "If I had not come and given them my message," meaning,

Jr 17:16

Jb 3:1 ff

*Si 14:5
†Si 30:24*

Jn 9:6
Rm 5:12

"if I had not shone on them they would not have been at fault; as it is their fault can find no excuse."*

*Jn 15:22

14. Whoever does not make use of grace given is neglecting the duties of the daylight and is rightly rebuked for idleness. There is a time, to be sure, when there is no working, when, as the Psalmist puts it, "You decree darkness, and the night falls. In the night all the forest is astir with prowling beasts."* Against these the vineyard is to be fenced-in and guarded. He gives the reason why man could not go out to his work in the words, "The young lions go roaring after their prey."* The case if different now, dearest friends, the sun rises, and shining on the earth makes it day* so that man, man who is no longer a brute beast, may go out to his work in the morning. Forestalled by the grace that hastened to his help, man goes out to sweat at his toil till the evening. Whatever the hour at which he began to work, labor till evening is demanded of him; no wages are paid to him earlier than at evening. Perseverance in doing good comes last and is rewarded first.

*Ps 103:20
*Ps 103:23
*Ps 103:21-22

15. So—to tidy-up a little as it grows late—the night when there is no working any more stands for turning-away from God, be it of thought from truth or of life from love. The day in which man goes out to his own proper work symbolizes turning towards God in investigation and imitation, to knowing and loving God, and, not least, to delighting in such knowledge and love. Man has been made in the image and likeness of God* for the sake of this knowledge and love; and by means of this knowledge and love man is made new and formed again to God's image and likeness: through understanding to the image, through form of life to the likeness. 16. Yet notice, man made to the image and likeness is made new to the likeness and to the image; in order to be formed again and come to share God's nature man must first shape his life according to Christ's. Eternal life is knowing the true God;* the true way to it is to love with one's whole heart.† Love, then, is the way, the truth, and the life;* truth is the image, love the likeness; love is the price, truth is the prize, by love we

*Gn 1:26
*Jn 17:3
†Jn 15:1
*Jn 14:6

make our journey, in truth, we stand fast. No wonder that Lucifer, though he heralded the dawn,* was cut off before evening. He did not reach fulfillment in the truth because he turned aside from the way of love. Moreover, since love will never come to an end,* when truth is attained love is not at an end, but the life with the truth that comes of love and the love that comes of truth will be supremely satisfying and will never stop.

*Is 14:12

*1 Co 13:8

17. Therefore, dearest friends, at the very first enlightenment of grace at the decisive day-break of one's turning to God when a person emerges from the night of sin and of carnal behavior and begins to attend to man's proper work, one comes up against one's conscience and sees how evil one's evil life was. One perceives in the light what one was like in the darkness. Conscience, you see, is sent into the vineyard first of all in the sense that when self-accusation calls everything possible to mind, brings all to memory, such humble self-abasement certainly means digging deep, means cutting-out the roots of injustice and turning to self-cultivation unto justice. 18. So true is it that the just man is ever his own accuser.* But turning to God and earnestly accusing oneself of past sins is not all; one must also carefully judge and severely examine the seriousness, number and motive of one's misdeeds. In this way, reason will shrewdly evaluate the disapproving conscience and the way it works in the vineyard; and so reason's careful judgment of what is presented to it may be followed by sorrow and grievous contrition of heart.

*Pr 18:17

In the chapter of faults of our inner selves then, brothers, it is for conscience to accuse, for reason to judge the case, and sorrow must act as torturer, so that while we accuse, judge and condemn ourselves, the Lord may pardon us and we may not incur condemnation as this world incurs it. 19. Contrition of heart is followed by confession of the lips, and this, in its turn, finally by amendment of life. Amendment comes last, but is first to win a reward. Without amendment of life, confession is no better than make-believe mouthing and contrition is merely a wishful

*Rm 2:15

warmth. In such a case, the judgment of reason, with conscience witnessing for the prosecution, is in favor of condemnation.* He is a mocker and no penitent who weeps for what he has done and keeps doing what he must weep for. 20. It can be said then that, provided there is amendment of life, contrition and confession are worthwhile and earn their reward; should it be lacking, far from being helpful, they justly pronounce our condemnation.

Much else, brothers, could be said, perhaps, with more depth, about the various times and the different workers in the vineyard; but, as was said already, time did not permit me. What you have heard, I have merely touched on and have not really treated in detail. Such being the case, I prefer to keep for another sermon to be delivered to you, my brothers, whatever, thanks to your prayers, he may deign give to me, he who is the very Wisdom of God, the Father's Word, Christ our Lord living and ruling with the Father and the Holy Spirit. Amen.

NOTES

1. Ws 7:27, 22. On wisdom as one and manifold, see Eriugena, *Comm Joan* 3; PL 122:314.

2. For Bernard Scripture is also an unfailing source of water. See *SC* 10:1; 51:2,4.

3. For the idea of spiritual utility, see Augustine, *Trin* 1,10,20; and Gregory, *In Evang.* 2:40. The idea is common in Bernard, e.g., *SC* 51:2,4.

4. This "historical" interpretation is common in the Fathers, e.g., Jerome, *In Matt* 3; PL 26:141; Augustine, *Sermo* 87:7; Gregory, *In Evang* 1,19,1-3.

5. Gn 2:15. See Sermon 6:14 on this theme taken from Ambrose and Eriugena.

6. "Passions" in the technical philosophical sense of "states of being acted upon".

SERMON SEVENTEEN
A Second Sermon for Septuagesima Sunday.

WHAT I SAID yesterday dearest friends, about
the day in the Gospel parable and labor and labor's
reward, with division into morning, third, sixth,
ninth, eleventh hour and evening,* I have no intention of changing today. Turning to God in mind and
heart will still be represented by daylight; turning
away from God will continue to be seen as the night
when there is no working any more. Endowed with
sense-knowledge and sense-appetite,[1] and to this
extent indistinguishable from the brutes, men are
said to be animals. 2. However, once reason is added
to such knowledge and appetite in order to rule
them, animal sense and appetite coexist with rational
mind and with the death-penalty that comes of sin.
Men must die since and because of Adam's sin;*
apart from that sin they need not die did they but
keep themselves from sin. When sense-knowledge and
appetite, far from following reason, fight against it
(as alas happens in some cases), reason is misused
against itself. 3. Such people, no matter how
clever, how crafty, how sensible, charming and gentle

*Mt 20:1-6

*Rm 8:10

they may be, do not yet really belong to mankind. If they are, in a manner of speaking referred to as men, in reality they are to be judged not as men, but as monstrosities born of mankind, since they live with their heads where their feet ought to be. Even the pagan poet tells us God gave men an uplifted gaze.[2] But, dear friends, when it comes to the people just mentioned, though they may on occasion offer some resistance they are soon overcome: poor lonely reason is promptly vanquished and made captive. "With the lonely it goes hard; when the lonely fall there is none to raise them."* 4. It sometimes happens that reason is so ennervated, daunted, unmanned, that of its own accord it follows, submits to, and gladly gives itself over completely to every kind of abomination. Those who put up some resistance are evil. Those who freely give in are worse; both are children of the night and of the darkness. The latter love the night they have made their own; the former long for the day. Those have nothing human about them; these have kept a bit of humanity. These last feel their chains; the others fancy themselves free. Both groups are in darkness and walk in darkness;* they have become in the night the prey of both the beasts of the forest,* (that is, not only carnal appetites and worldly desires), and of the young lions,* (meaning, malign influences in an order higher than ours*). It is all summed-up in the words of the Psalm: "You decree darkness and night falls; in the night all the forest is astir with prowling beasts, the young lions."*

5. And yet even when a man comes to himself, be it because he turns to sense-knowledge, to desires or to reason, yes, even though he should make such progress that he strips off all likeness to brute beasts and clothes himself in man's true nature, he neither escapes the night nor enters completely into the daylight. "My soul is a trouble to me," sings the Seer, and therefore he began to be mindful of God, as of the daylight.* For God is all light, and in him alone no darkness can find any place.* Though the holy angels find their morning in him, yet they stumble in the evening they find in themselves; this evening of theirs

*Qo 4:10

*Ps 81:5

*Ps 103:20
*Ps 103:21
*Eph 6:12

*Ps 103:20-21

*Ps 41:7
*1 Jn 1:5

and the morning of God go to make that one, first

Gn 1:5 day. God alone finds the light of day in himself, and once he begins thanks to his purely gratuitous grace to shine in rational minds, he creates morning and

Gn 1:4 separates light from darkness.

6. Grace, then, is the dawn of the spiritual day; it not only anticipates reason, it turns it from itself to God and leads it from the darkness of ignorance or, as previously mentioned, of weakness and even of ill-will, into the daylight of wisdom, virtue and justice, the day, in other words, of Christ our Lord. Not that I consider that the term "the day of Christ" refers only to one single day; Christ himself mentions several when he says: "Your father Abraham was overjoyed to see my days, he saw them and was

Jn 8:56 glad." 7. There is a day of fear, a day of love, a day of joy, or, in other words, a day of toil, a day of rest, a day of exulting. As the Psalmist puts it: "Let us rejoice and be glad in this day of the Lord's choos-

Ps 117:24 ing." Still more plainly, there is the day of the Cross, the day of the Tomb, the day of the Resurrection. "He will give us life after two days, on the third day

Ho 6:3 he will raise us up," Hosea tells us. He refers to that sixth day in which all work is completed. He also refers to the Sabbath-rest from all divine doing. Third is the Lord's day on which there is the resurgence into newness of joy; the great day when amid the thick dark-

Ps 117:27 ness joy reached to the very horns of the altar, namely, to the glory that came of the Passion, the reward of Christ's toil, to the exaltation of the Cross.

8. How blessed the soul still weighted down by

Ws 9:15 mortal dwelling-place, that was nonetheless caught up on the Lord's day and heard that voice behind

Rv 1:10 him, that voice that I long to listen to, though it be only from far ahead of me. For the present, dearest friends, let us control this impulse of our spirit, and,

2 Co 10:12 measuring ourselves by our own standard, let us go back to the day of Fear, the day of dismay and distress, so that we may have some share in Christ's dismay and distress. We must, also, take part in the day of his toil and of his sweat so that we may suffer and be crucified with him. In his day of battle our

*1 P 2:21; et al.
Lord Jesus truly endured it all for our sake,* prefiguring in mystery what we must endure.

9.   One who emerges from darkness and the
*Ps 106:14
shadow of death,* in other words from turning-away from God and from perverted turning to the world or to self in order to turn back to God, moves, as it were, from the back to the front of the head. In so doing, the very first thing one meets is the memory of past evil deeds and the fear of things to come, anguish over what one has done and dread of what one has still to suffer. The process begins with recalling one's evil life and fearing being still more evil when one comes to die; here you have the first to labor in the vineyard, conscience accusing itself.

10.   This self-accusation is the first grace given to
*Mt 20:4-6
the penitent, the first hour of conversion.* The next stage is that what memory recalls it presents to the heart, that is, the power of desire. This power is said to reside in the heart, just as power of understanding is supposed to have its place in the head. Rational understanding is usually spoken of as including the threefold faculty of discernment, reason and memory;[3] it is considered that in the heads of animals these three faculties occupy each a particular section, in the order of front, middle and back of the head, where each exercises its particular function.[4]

11.   When, then, one comes to his senses, passing from the back to the front of the head, forgetting, as the Apostle says, what has been left behind, pressing
*Ph 3:13
on to what lies ahead,* the first thing met, as already mentioned, is the memory of past deeds. One begins to see how ill things were with one when one was evil. As to power of desire or affection, it is to be understood in two ways, corresponding to the heart's two reactions of either love or hatred to what discernment, reason and memory put before it. These two reactions, according to the different points of view that differences of time bring to the changeable, time-affected heart, give rise to those four well-known and noted emotions that are the very substance and stuff of all virtues and vices; as one might say, the first principles of whatever virtue and vice there may

be. 12. It was of these that Lady Philosophy sang as she consoled her foster-son:

Drive out both joy and fear!
And from all hope keep clear!
Let sadness not come near!
Rule any of their kind
They ever cloud the mind
And with a bridle bind.[5]

13. Conditioned then by present, past and future, joy and hope come of love, fear and sorrow arise from hatred. Love and hatred each proceed from our capacity for coveting and for rejecting respectively.[6] So, if the head is described as having three compartments, the heart may be said to have two. Man's soul itself, fully constituted by the powers of understanding and of desire that belong to its nature, is in its complete actuality a coveting, rational and irascible thing. This explains why the first of this trio to meet the transgressor who returns to himself is what he had taken leave of last on his departure, the capacity for rejecting that third aspect of the whole soul.

14. Becomingly enough, at the third hour the second grace is sent into the vineyard,* so that, when conscience working through memory brings forward its well-reasoned accusations compunction or interior sorrow, in the measure and degree of the guilt involved, may inflict its penalty through the power of rejection. In this way, the sweet self-indulgence of one's past life becomes the unforgetable self-reproach of compunction; as Scripture expresses it, "With bitter heart I pass all my years in review".* Reconsideration comes first, later comes bitterness, the latter is the third hour, the former is daybreak. 15. It is misery and madness to forget one's sins; still more wretched is it to remember them with unrepentant heart; the most hateful thing of all is delighting in the recalling of one's sins.

At the sixth hour* good-will comes into operation—six and work have been long associated.[7] The power of desire, as you remember, gives each deed its name;[8] it is by the fruit of the labor invested that the quality of the intention is ascertained. As the poet says: you

*Mt 20:2-3

*Is 38:15

*Lk 23:44

144

will easily perceive the inner disposition from the outer deportment.[9] 16. Conversely, a change of heart leads, inevitably, to change of behavior. The disposition of the heart, lording it as it does over the deportment of the body, uses it as its subject and slave. Consequently, in so far as the movement of the body depends on the free choice of the will, it is not to be held answerable for its actions. Only the movement of the heart, be it obedience or disobedience, virtuous or vicious, is liable to judgment, because to it alone has freedom of choice come from God. Consequently, turning from God and delighting with the evil one means making over one's natural powers as slaves to what the devil himself was slave to, "to impurity and wickedness, till all was wickedness".* Conversion to God, on the other hand, consists of making over one's natural powers as slaves to right-doing, till all is sanctified.* 17. At the sixth hour the third grace, training of the body, is sent into the vineyard,* so that as sorrow furrows one's inner being, labor should furrow one's outer self, with fasting chastening, toil tiring and vigils wearying one. When man comes out from the darkness of the flesh into the light of the world, though born to labor,* he starts out from sorrow. In like manner, one who comes out from carnal darkness to spiritual light not only starts out from sorrow, but grows up to toil, as Scripture has it: "Man is born to toil."* 18. Yes, and the words that follow, "and the bird to fly,"* fit in perfectly with the sequence I have been developing. The word "bird" is rightly understood as referring to the faculty of reason by which man transcends the brute beasts and their earth-bound ways and shares the same nature as the angels. At the ninth hour the fourth grace is sent into the vineyard,* and man is raised far above the active life with its use of the less excellent faculties of the soul, and, in his search for God, soars on the wings of reading, meditation and prayer with the love of God for his objective.

19. As at the ninth hour reason, so at the eleventh delight is sent into the vineyard.* Once the active life has achieved its purpose, what is left for

*Rm 6:19

*Ibid.

*Mt 20:3,5

*Jb 5:7

*Ibid.
*Ibid.

*Mt 20:2

*Mt 20:5-6

the soul except the contemplative life, the consumma-
tion of which is the sight of and delight in God. During
this pitiable pilgrimage of ours, however, everything
is imperfect, nothing is found perfect. As the Parable
shows the active life does not attain to the ten of the
denarius, nor does the contemplative life reach the
twelfth hour of the day.[10] So delight comes last,
labour is least and is rewarded first. As the Psalm
says, "The way of your commandments has brought
Ps 118:14 me delight greater than all riches."

20. It follows that whatever comfort, delight
and enjoyment we find in our observances and toil is
an undoubted foretaste of the reward of our labors, if
only because until we learn to delight in the correc-
Hb 12:5,7 tion which the Lord sends and come to live it, we
scarcely support, barely stand-up to the day's burden
Mt 20:12 and the heat. In grief and constraint, subject to fear
and grumbling everything makes us sad and spiritless.
But at the eleventh hour when the fifth grace joins
love with observance and good-will is linked with our
efforts, so that we are able to delight in and to enjoy
whatever comes, as every burden is light, every yoke is
Mt 11:30 easy, there begins a death of fear and of labor, of
grief and of sadness. 21. The evening of the first and
morning of the second day, on the other hand, are
the beginning of love and of enjoyment, of zeal and of
merriment; in other words, of pure pleasure and
encouragement, and genuine gaiety and mirth of
mind. Such joy as this is known only to the one who
Rv 2:17 receives it. This is indeed the beginning of the perfection that puts an end to our first lessons; the beginning of the fulfilment that sweeps away what is
imperfect; the beginning, lastly, of the perfect love
1 Jn 4:18 that drives out fear, that takes away labor and wipes
away sorrow.

22. So, once remembrance of one's sins has done
a thorough job, once the capacity for rejection and
training of the body have borne the day's burden and
Mt 20:12 the heat, once reason in its turn has toiled, love the
last to come is the first to snatch the prize and bring
labor to an end and receive the reward. Love not
only labors less than all, it lessens the labor for all;

first to receive the reward, it makes reception possible; at rest itself, it draws all to rest. Consequently, the spirit that delights in God, that sometime before had felt so distressed and dismayed, so sad, anxious, troubled, so spent with cares, can now comfort itself with the words: "Return, my soul, to where your peace lies; the Lord has dealt kindly with you; yes, he has saved my life from death," that is, from sin, "my eyes from the pit," that is, from the sorrow that comes from past sin, "my feet from falling," that is, from fear of future sin.* 23. Absolutely nothing can grieve, toil or burden one who finds delight in all that he does and suffers, one who, under the light yoke and easy burden, has really found the reward for his work, has indeed found rest for his soul, as our Saviour promises in the words, "You shall find rest for your souls."* And so a person rejoicing and singing on the Second Day mentioned, that of the love that drives out fear, runs glad of heart the way of God's commandments by holy living, runs with the unutterable ease that comes of virtuous habit.[11] 24. And this was the person who on the First Day, that of Fear, was oppressed by the burden and heat of the work in the vineyard into which he had found a narrow road and entered through a small gate, and where once inside he had dug its hard and stubborn soil.*

Yes, dearest friends, when we attain to the treasures of the loving-kindness of God which he has stored up for those who fear him* and made manifest to those who love him, we shall find that nothing is hard, harsh or heavy if it must be borne for Christ's sake. 25. Far from complaining of difficulties when we find ease and delight in all circumstances, our only complaint then will be that we do so little for it. Cheerfully, even impetuously, shall we gird ourselves for ever-stricter observance and this in turn will enable us to experience ever-greater joy and delight. The very remembrance of our sins, far from driving us to fear and compunction, will impel us to thanksgiving.

Those as yet in this mortal life and crucified with

Ps 114:7-8

Mt 11:29

Ps 30:20

Ibid.

Ga 2:19

Christ* are those on the sixth day, the day of weariness and labor, the day of divine doing, the day of suffering and of the Cross. Such, indeed, are grieved in their distress. 26. But on the day of peace and of rest, the day of calm and of withdrawal, the day of burial and of the Sabbath, dead to sin and to the world, in themselves they are buried with and rest

Rm 6:4

with Christ.* And all this that on the Third Day, the day of deliverance and of victory, the day of festival and of joy, the day of Resurrection and of glory, on what in all truth is the Lord's Day, on the eighth day, that is in fact, the first day of new light, on this Day that just as Christ was raised up by his Father's power from the dead, so these that have been raised up with him should live and move in a new kind of existence. As the blessed Apostle says, "Since we live by the

Ga 5:25

Spirit, let the Spirit be our rule of life."* May the Holy Spirit himself generously make this his gift to us, the gift of him who, with the Father and the Son, is the one God that lives and rules for evermore. Amen.

1. Cf. *Serm* 6:14; and *Ep an.*
2. Ovid, *Metamorphoses* 1:84. These words are cited in a number of patristic collections, e.g. Isidore, *Etymologiae* 11; PL 82:397; Bede, *Hex* 1; PL 91:29.
3. See *Ep an* for a fuller treatment of these powers of the soul.
4. The determination of three cells in the head is found in Augustine, *Gen litt* 7, 18, 24. It was very popular in the twelfth century among authors connected with the School of Chartres.
5. Boethius, *Consol Phil* 1, 1, metr. 7, 11. 25-31. The four fundamental emotions (*metus, gaudium, cupiditas, dolor*) were a commonplace of ancient philosophy widely known in the Middle Ages.
6. "Capacity for coveting" (*concupiscibilitas*) and "capacity for rejecting" (*irascibilitas*) along with the "capacity for reasoning" (*rationabilitas*) forms a Platonic Triad commonplace in medieval anthropology and central to Isaac's thought. For a study of these themes, see McGinn, *The Golden Chain*, 146 ff.
7. See Serm 10:12.
8. Serm 3:2. See Ambrose, *Off* 1, 30, 147; PL 16:66.
9. Perhaps a paraphrase of Juvenal, *Satires* 2:7. A similar idea is found in Ambrose, *Off* 1, 18, 71; PL 16:44.
10. The denarius stands for perfection in Gregory, *In Ezech* 2, 6, 5; PL 76:1000. Twelve hours, of course, make up the perfection of the working day.
11. See RB, Prol. and chap. 7.

SERMON EIGHTEEN
The First Sermon for Sexagesima

*Lk 8:5

"THE SOWER went out to sow . . . . "* Our poverty, so peaceful and so desireable, brings with it, as you can see, abundant want and generous dearth, particularly of books and of Scripture commentaries. Like the praiseworthy monk who could boast "I gave

*Historia Lausiaca 15-16; PL 73: 1198.

away my Gospel for the sake of the Gospel"*, we have been led by books to leave books. 2. Holy books gave us lessons on the value of monastic solitude—its fruits of quiet, the gifts its poverty brings— to such effect that we have not only forsaken, as we

*Gn 12:1

once did, our home and relatives,* but have in a sense forgotten a host of saintly brothers and the house of our spiritual father, with much else,* including a well-

*Ps 44:10-15

stocked library. We are no better than a few survivors of shipwreck with scarcely the clothes on our backs; the world and almost all contact with our fellowmen are lost to us who, clinging nakedly to the bare cross of the naked Christ,[1] have been cast up on this ocean-encompassed island.

3. You do not permit me to be silent. You are foolish in compelling me to make up for your reading by frequent discourse. The result is that I do not

always keep to the usual interpretations of gospel passages, preferring to discuss what I consider best suits the season, the place and the purpose of my listeners. An instruction that aims at destroying the rule of selfishness and at developing that of charity in its hearers by unravelling Scripture difficulties is not *Ps 44:2* at variance with the mind of the sovereign scribe,* the Finger of God. Such unfettered liberty is, however, excluded in this gospel reading, since he who put the parable showed it application.

Lk 8:9   4. The seed is the Word of God;* the Sower is the Son of Man, himself God's Word. Seed and Sower being the same, the Word himself sows himself and is sown. Sure enough, he alone is able worthily to sow, that is, to preach himself. "We proclaim not our-*2 Co 4:5* selves," said that great preacher, "but Jesus."*

5. In our days, I fear that people preach themselves, seek to make a name for themselves when preaching of Jesus. They recount the great deeds of another while looking for glory or gain for themselves. Their seed-ground, ever outside themselves, is the empty *Jb 6:26, Qo 5: 15, Jr 5:13, etc.* air.* Fruitless themselves, what harvest could they claim in others? They herald truth and hoard complacency; prescribing remedies, they drink poison. The better they treat of humility, the worse grows their pride. Lovers of riches exhort to love of poverty. The covetous to contempt for worldliness, misers to almsgiving, the ambitious to subjection, and other similar inconsistencies.

6. Not so the Father's holy Word. He preaches what he is, he does what he teaches. "Jesus set out to *Ac 1:1* do and to teach,"* Scripture tells us. When he says, "Learn from me, from what you observe in me, I am *Mt 11:29* gentle and humble of heart",* this Sower sows himself both by the example of his deeds and by his words of doctrine.

From where, I ask, has he come to do his sowing? *Lk 8:5* "He came out to sow,"* Scripture says, without departing, that is, from where he was. The Word alone came out from the Father's bosom into the Virgin's womb; from there, made man, the Son of Man came into the world of men, came as a sower

into a field. When people set about sowing, they fill
baskets with seed from some shady storehouse and go
out into a field to sow it. The Seed and the Sower of
whom I speak came out from the secret unfathomable storehouse where the fulness of Deity dwells and
his virgin birth put him into the basket of man's
nature. From this he, Seed, Sower, Basket, sows himself and sows of himself.

8. "And as he sowed, etc."* This wise husbandman knows well that all parts of his land are not
equally fertile, yet he sows in it as if such were not
the case, as though he were unaware, owing to pressure
of work, of the waste of precious seed. What does this
mean? Is it that the sowing, not the Seed, varies? Yes,
there are in fact various sowings of the Word: interior,
to ear of heart; exterior, to ear of body. One kind,
teaching by word, affects the ear. Another, by example, strikes the eye. A third, by inspiration of grace,
enters the heart. 9. These three kinds found their
perfection in Christ's heaven-sent teaching; only one
who has his chair in heaven teaches interiorly. Moses'
disciples, Scribe and Pharisee, teach one thing and do
another,* affect ears but not eyes. Christ's disciples,
who join doing to doctrine, thereby sowing to ear
and eye, give fuller measure of justice. Christ, the one
true Master, alone sows externally by example and
word, helps internally by gift of grace. Consequently,
though his words are addressed to all without distinction, his sowing does vary. He himself tells us: "The
Spirit breathes where he will and you can hear his
voice, but know nothing of the way it came or the
way it goes"*—meaning that, while all men can hear
his message, no man can tell the particular purpose,
condition, abundance, measure of grace that goes
with it as, in fulfilment of God's high and hidden
design, it finds its way to the individual benefit of
this or that person.

10. There are four classes of hearers in the
audience. There are those with hearts trodden down
and unyielding. The Word reaches their outer ears but
their hearts give it no welcome. The seed has fallen by
the wayside, since the way of faith and obedience is

*Ibid.

*Mt 23:3

*Jn 3:8

*2 Th 3:2,
Rm 10:16

not theirs. Faith, we are told, does not reach all hearts; some do not obey the call of the Gospel.* Poised between their ears and hearts, the devil bars the way to the heart, as the saying goes, by taking out through one ear what has entered by the other. As a preacher rises to proclaim the Word exteriorly, the devil prompts counter-utterance within, denies the truth of what is said, changing its meaning, criticizing the preacher, distracting the hearer with drowsiness or daydreams.

*Ps 77:9

*1 Co 13:7

11.   There are others who find no difficulty in obeying, but lack the virtue of endurance; like the bow-bending sons of Ephraim, they are routed in the day of battle.* Ever prepared to mend their ways, they are still more prone to relapse. To all appearances they are live-wood, but in fact they are deadwood, time-servers and shallow-minded. Lacking the taproot of love, they cannot believe and endure to the last.* In time of peace they keep faith, but in time of temptation, internal or external, they fall away. They are chaste while passion slumbers, courageous when no one opposes them, meek if let alone. Their devotion depends on how well things go. They are the sort who praise God as long as he blesses them.* Adam's true descendants, they are worthy sons of the father who held his ground so courageously while no incitement was offered, kept his feet until a very slight push sent him headlong. The first kind of hearer was too obdurate, too obstinate to give the Word a welcome; this sort is too soft and yielding. He all too soon surrenders.

*Ps 48:19

12.   Those of the third class keep the Word, but fruitlessly, or rather, as witnesses against themselves. They resemble ground under the primal curse, unclean and uncultivated, overgrown with thorns and and thistles. They well deserve the prophet's rebuke: "You must use your fallow land, sow no longer among the briars."* 13.   Evil obstinacy renders the first sort callous, lack of courage is fatal to the second; this third class shows all the ill-effects of avarice, distracting cares, oppressive worry, of stifling wealth, ennervating pleasures, dissipation and drunkenness.

*Jr 4:3

Small wonder that the thorns which instead of wheat
are found in the hand of the drunkard should pierce
and wound it.*

*Pr 26:9

14. Thorns—so God's word describes them. Truth
itself declares them so. The Wisdom that unerringly
assesses each thing and its worth, its number measure,
weight, its nature, form, and purpose reckons them so.
Yet who in our day accounts riches as thorns and
refuses to cling to them when he has embraced them?
For our part we must put our faith in the Word of
God, must be convinced that riches are no better
than thorns, that whoever clings to them is as one
who the more he clutches a bundle of thorns, the
greater hurt he does himself. Let us leave it to such
fools to make a bramble thicket their welcome
refuge,* to discover from their own undoubted
experience of grief what comes to those led astray by
delights so false and fleeting. 15. I remember, dear
friends, that when we preach and turn men away from
these thorns, the food of hell, they all cry out that
riches truly are thorns. They disparage, they loathe,
they curse the world more than we have ever done.
They detest the weary treadmill of this present world
and its prickly pursuits, but they do not desert them.
While lamenting and condemning their own condition,
they so praise and congratulate us that you would
think we were already safe among the blessed. They
curse worldliness and go on loving it. They both loathe
it and labor for it. They complain of the worthless
burden, yet keep carrying it. Worldliness is not their
toy but it has them in its toils. Like the legendary
fire-spouting giant bent beyond escape under the
weight of the mountain,[2] they cannot rid themselves
of the load that oppresses them. In those in thrall to
worldliness, the love of the Father cannot find (to use
the country saying) the least ground for growth.
Lacking this love they are simply unable to welcome
the seed the Son is and to yield his harvest.

16. Let us give thanks to the Father, the heavenly
husbandman who through the Holy Spirit has made
us capable of receiving the seed, the Son. The fire
of love that he has poured out upon our hearts* has

*Jb 30:7

*Rm 5:5

burnt up the thorns, cleansed our field, has enabled us to endure and to yield a harvest thirty, sixty, even a hundredfold.* It is obedience that welcomes the seed of the Word, patience that makes it fruitful, perseverance that reaps it. What the Apostle said of athletes—"the race is for all, but the prize is for one"* holds good of the virtues: they all bring us on the way of God's kingdom, but only one enables us to attain the price. 17. Otherworldliness, poverty, vigils, almsgiving, fasting, obedience, patience all help us on our course, but perseverance alone wins us the victory. "That man will be saved who endures to the last."* The Lord sits in judgment† on the ends of the earth. It is not going half-way, much less is it making a beginning that decides one's lot. How one finishes, not one's first effort, is reckoned virtue. We conclude then that patience wins approval for obedience, perseverance crowns patience with all blessing. Patience tests and proves obedience. Perseverance brings glory to patience. May he who has granted us obedience and not denied us patience utterly, may he, the Father through the Son, in the Spirit, bestow on us the gift of perseverance. Amen.

*Mk 4:20

*1 Co 9:24

*Mt 10:22
†1 S 2:10

NOTES

1. Cf. Jerome, *Ep* 52, 4. For the theme of nakedly following the naked Christ, see the note in Hoste, Vol. II: 8-11.
2. For this giant, see Gregory, *Mor: Epist miss* 3; PL 75:513.

SERMON NINETEEN
A Second Sermon for Sexagesima[1]

*Lk 8:5

"THE SOWER went out to sow his seed."* Yes, the Son of Man went out from the Virgin's womb and sowed the Word of God, that is, himself in men's ears by his preaching, in their eyes by his example, in their hearts by his grace. Yet even as he sows, his hearers are ranging themselves into four different groups.

Firstly, there are those who listen but are kept from believing and right living by the Evil One whose thralls they have made themselves, so devoted are they in his service, so conquered and sold into the slavery of sin. Next are they who listen and entertain the Word with joy, that is, make no difficulty about receiving it, but under stress of trial with like facility reject it and make it useless. Jeremiah describes them in the words, "Loyalty is dead, the Word is on their

*Jr 7:28

lips no more."* Then there are those who profess it with their lips but suppress it in their lives. Lastly, the fourth group consists of those who believe in heart and are justified, whose lips make the confession that

*Rm 10:10

brings them salvation.*

2. Yet to one who looks deeper it is clear that

just as the four yields of the field are nothing new to the Sower, so neither the going out nor the sowing are the first he has ever done. "I came out from the Father," he tells us, "and I have entered the world."* Yes, he entered this world through his birth of the Virgin. Hence his first coming-out was not from mankind, his first sowing not in men. Men were not the first God spoke to, nor were angels. As Elihu says, "God speaks but once and does not repeat his Word".* Here indeed, brothers, is a question worth discussing, reverently not insolently, with devotion not presumption. To whom did God once utter what even he cannot repeat? What did almighty God say that it exceeds his power to replace it?

3. Ours, my brothers, must be the dispositions of that god-loving soul that with all the impatience of desire sought its beloved, sought him in secret, sought in city alley-way and street, and all to no purpose until beyond the watchmen, the sleepless angels, it found him. Only there, at the other side of the towering angel host, it found him and clung to him and would not let him go.* What joy it had that sought so earnestly, was so blessed to find, clasped so strongly, so wisely kept! 4. Have we, my brothers, any other business? Sought, found, held, not let go—is not this the whole spiritual life? What more remains to be done?

5. It was thus that John, the sharp-eyed, god-thirsting eagle, sought what we too seek, sought that first and only Word and, spurning all that ever came to be, found "in the beginning" what never began. In the beginning, he tells us, the Word already was.* Yet how was he in the beginning if he cannot be without beginning? Can a word be that never begins? No word but is someone's word and must, surely, come from a speaker in order to be a word.

6. The word therefore proceeded from him to whom it belongs. As to how he proceeded, when, in what manner, and from where; as to who spoke first, what he spoke, how he spoke, and to whom—if we are to go somewhat fully into all that we must conduct our discussion at a deeper level than is usual and customary.

*Jn 16:28

*Jb 33:14

*Sg 3:1-4

*Jn 1:1

Now, the first requirement, if anything whatever
is to be in any way whatever, is that it should simply
be. What has no being of any kind is mere nothing;
what has no being, what lacks every mode of being is
absolutely non-existent. Consequently, existence[2]
logically precedes the composition of every being and
is what last remains when it is analyzed. Nothing
subject to forms is prior to it. Suppose the forms
removed. Nothing remains if it does not. The mind
may posit division where actually there is none. It
may envisage some necessary constituent of something as either present or absent, but a thing's form,
which can unite with matter or be separated from it,
must exist for there to be anything at all.

8. Therefore, everything that exists has received
the form of being and exists and subsists so that it
can be this or that particular being, that is, can belong
to a particular species. Every single created thing
exists because it is numerically one; hence it can also
be measured and weighed. All created things fall
Ws 11:21 within the compass of number, measure and weight,
as only an ignoramus does not know.[3]

9. It follows that once the existence of something
is verified, the next points for investigation are its
nature, its properties, its uses: in other words, what it
may be; how it may be; and for what purpose it may
be. No wonder that those who study such matters
discovered (it was not of their own devising) that
there are, in fact, naturally three sciences that contain
pretty well the whole of philosophy: namely, physics,
logic, and ethics; natural, rational, and ethical science.[4]

10. Natural science, in the first place, provides us
with notions wide enough to include whatever being
ever comes to be. It teaches that things must exist
either in themselves or as a modification of something
else. What exists in itself is obviously of greater worth
than what, if it is to exist, needs the support of
another thing. Since our study is God, than whom
we believe there is nothing more worthy, we need
only follow what is best and most worthy, dearly
beloved, until we arrive at what is supremely worthy,
that than which nothing could be better. Arriving at

it at least by reason, let us hold to it by love and guard it with diligence.

11. Having left aside what does not exist in itself but needs the support of something else for its very being and hence is rightly called "something added" or an accident, let us deal with what exists in itself. To perceive clearly, however, how a thing can exist in itself, we need the second branch of philosophy mentioned above.

12. A thing subsists either as a nature or in act, in reason or in reality. For instance, *man* as a concept or nature is fully accounted for in the words: *rational, mortal, animal.* This is the whole being of man, and for *man* as such to subsist nothing need be added. No need to discuss whether *man* in the abstract be wise or not, one size or another, a father or a son, white or black, seated or not, here or there at a particular moment, doing or enduring, armed or defenceless. Such attributes do not affect abstract manhood, but do actually condition every individual man. 13. *Man*-in-general and *man*-in-particular each subsists in itself. Hence, each is a "substance", be it concept-*man* or an individual. Of course, a given, actual being subsisting in itself is properly, especially and most fittingly called "substance" and, therefore, First Substance. What exists only in the mind and ideally is in itself in only a secondary sense and, consequently, is named Second Substance.[5]

14. Every substance then has its own existence in one of these two senses: First Substance subsisting by itself in itself; Second, by itself, but not really in itself. The only way Second can exist is in First. Second exists only as a concept, a universal nature, an abstraction; while First Substance exists both in reason and reality as a universal nature and a particular, as an abstraction and as a kind of existence.[6]

15. It follows that the truer and better substance is that which partakes both of abstract and of objective existence as numerically one. It is far and away superior to what exists only as an idea, a concept, something vague and up in the air, never met with as such. No living man but is a definite individual. Yet to be

this or that man would be impossible were there not a generic thing called *man.* 16. So that if a Second Substance finds a footing only in First, there is no First Substance but it follows Second. Reason gives priority to Second Substance when it comes to regarding First as possible. Still, it is the actuality of First Substance that alone gives Second its existence. If the universal *man* is not, man is not. There is no universal called *man* unless individual man exists. The same holds for substance as such. If there be no substance-in-general, there can be no particular substance. Substance-in-general, on the other hand, exists only in this or that particular substance.

17. Substance-in-general, then, is the reason and cause, the stuff and quasi-matter of all that exists in itself, that is, of all particular substances. For it not only makes it possible for them to be, that is, to have existence, it makes it possible for them to be what they are, namely, substances. It itself, nonetheless, as common-to-all and generic, has no existence in itself. Though it has nothing prior to itself to use as material out of which to make itself, it does however contain within its ambit the necessary means of its own existence.

18. Our general conclusion then is that all substance is either First or Second. Second Substance exists through itself but not in itself. First Substance exists in itself but not of itself. It follows that both kinds of substance are incomplete, defective—Second not existing in itself and First not existing of itself. The latter needs something prior to itself if it is to be; the former needs something subsequent to itself in order to be at a particular place.

19. At this point, dear friends, I must confess— I know not with what impatience my mind exults before the fact—there already falls on us a ray of light that piercing through the imperfection of each and all these substances affords us a glimpse of what we may call "supersubstance",[7] which exists by itself, in itself, and of itself; is at once and absolutely ideal and real, and exists as essence and in act, both in the intellect and as a kind of existence. There is

nothing prior to make it possible, nothing subsequent to uphold it in being. It is not the effect of anything superior to it, nor does it need anything below it in order to subsist. No universal concept makes it possible, no kind of being perfects it, it is not specified by anything other than itself.

If anything be really such, if this be not some empty fancy that beguiles the mind, this being far surpasses any substance. First Substance and Second receive no worship from me so long as something better certainly can be conceived, even if perhaps it does not exist.[8]

20. As already said, accidents are posterior to substances and depend for their existence on substances, and this is why they have no existence save in substances. If then there be no substances, accidents are non-existent; if there be no accidents, covered by the nine categories,* there are no Second Substances, no specifying of lower by higher substances, no Second existing in First Substances. Moreover, if there are not forms, there are no actually existing First Substances. If there be no First there are no Second Substances, since these last only exist in the first. 21. From this it is clear that the non-existence of accidents spells the non-existence of substances. Accidents and substances stand or fall together.

*of Aristotle: Quantity, quality, relation, position, place, time, state, action, affection.

As for the abstraction called Second Substance, in itself it is in reality nothing. Our mind conceives it in a vague way and holds it ready for investing with some form or other, for insertion into this or that actual substance. First Substance, in its turn, is not more possible without a form than form without substance.

22. Therefore both subject and accident, or substance and form, are—each on its own—mere void and emptiness, which shows that the third, the composite, that comes of two nothings (matter by itself and form on its own) adds up to nothing. Of this the prophet has no doubt when he declares of men in general: "All the nations of the world are as though they did did not exist in his presence,* that is, the presence of

*Is 40:17

him who, by and in himself, truly is, owing nothing to anything prior or greater than himself. They shrink to nothing, emptiness, a very void beside him."* The man, brothers, who thinks himself something when in truth he is nothing is merely deluding himself.*

*Ibid.

*Ga 6:3

23. Let us then stop our querying, since we are nothing. Let us cease seeking what in all truth is, for we truly are not. He differs from all else, who said of himself "I am who am"*. All else can say of itself, "I am who am not" or "what I am is nothing".

*Ex 3:14

Is this, my brothers, what we have come to? Yes, to discover that our search for something has proved finding nothing: our seeking God has meant losing ourselves! The slightest hint of that which is not nothing has made it all too clear to us how much our nothingness is rooted in nothing. How true it is, Lord, that "in your light we shall see your light"* and our darkness!

*Ps 35:10

24. And now, dear friends, we must break off at this point for today. Work and words have made us weary. Such is the food we eat in the sweat of our brow while exiled from God's house, from its cries of joy and thanksgiving and all the bustle of feasting.* May he conduct us safely there, he for whose sake we live, exiles from almost all that is in the world, on this island and in this monastery.

*Ps 41:5

NOTES

1. Sermons 19–26 contain Isaac's doctrine of God as one and three and the metaphysical presuppositions of his theology. For a detailed study and commentary, see B. McGinn, "Isaac of Stella on the Divine Nature," *Analecta Cisterciensia* 29 (1973) 3–56.

2. "Existence" (*essentia*) is the "form of being" (*forma essendi*) of really existing things.

3. Isaac's doctrine in sections 7 and 8 is heavily influenced by Boethius, as are other sections of this sermon.

4. This Platonic–Stoic division of the sciences was well known to the Fathers, e.g., Augustine *Civ Dei* 11:25. For Isaac's understanding of the sciences, see B. McGinn "Theologia in Isaac of Stella," *Citeaux* 21 (1970) 219-35.

5. This doctrine of substance is Aristotelian in origin (see *Categories* 5:2a-b) as mediated through Boethius, *Cat Arist* i; PL 64:181.

6. "Kind of existence," literally *status*, a technical philosophical term much discussed in the twelfth-century Schools.

7. *Supersubstantia*, the term recalls the *ultra substantiam* of Boethius *De Trinitate* IV.

8. "*melius aliquid . . . certe cogitari possit.*" A reminiscence of Anselm's "ontological" argument for God's existence found in *Proslogion* 2-3, though the formulation *melius* rather than *maior cogitari* shows the influence of Bernard's *Csi* 5, 7, 15.

SERMON TWENTY
A Third Sermon for Sexagesima

YESTERDAY, dear friends, in our seeking God, as you know, we lost ourselves and thereby found ourselves. Nothing could be more just. Fallen below ourselves and outside ourselves, as it were, we had to come back to ourselves or our return to him could not come about. Struck by a slight and lattice-strained ray of the light that floods God's countenance, we fell face to earth,[1] that is, from the high opinion we had of ourselves to the admission of what we really are. After that, our seeking to know what God was led to our finding what he is not.

2. We went about, you recall, searching alley-way and street,* examining substances both universal and particular, and we found he could not be found in them, he who is not a particular being that comes under a general term, he whose essence is identical with his existence.[2] He is no part of whatever else is[3] or rather, all else is nothing and comes from nothing, while he alone neither is nor comes from nothing. Our search, you see, brothers, is for Being beyond all created beings, distinct from all and in no way

*Sg 3:2

described as a nothing.

3. But where, Lord our God, are we to seek, if no created thing suffices? Where are the wings to enable us men, weighed down by the flesh, heavy with sin, to make our way past all corporeal and incorporeal substance in our search for you, the uniquely sufficient one who alone can content us? Lord, here are we who have forsaken all for your sake.* Show us, supposing your favor is ours, your longed-for and loving self.* 4. Grief like ours there is no comforting,* the remembrance of you and the thoughts it gives rise to are our sole delight. To lack still the sight of you makes us fainthearted. If you are neither a corporeal nor an incorporeal substance, what are you? Let us make sure, brothers, that *God* is not an incorporeal substance such as those watchmen[4] who nonetheless were left behind by that soul whose earnest search found happy fulfilment.

5. Now, substance, taken in its most general sense, finds its first and sufficient classification in corporeal and incorporeal substance. Under pain of not being a substance, a substance is one of these two kinds. Yet what most emphatically constitutes and defines a substance is the capacity of being the subject of contrary accidents.[5] Whatever the substance, it has this capacity, fulfills this "Rule of Parity", the susceptibility to contraries. Both kinds of substance, consequently, have no choice but to be the subjects of contrary accidents; their changeableness results not merely from differing and varying elements, but from contrary ones. This leads to substance being referred to in another science as the basis of the elements of all their variations; a changeable, at once persevering and inconstant foundation.[6]

6. Our seeking, however, is not the fluctuating foundation of attributes but the unchangeable Father of all light, with whom there can be no variation, no shadow of change.* He, it is manifest, cannot properly be spoken of as substance, even incorporeal substance. It were a great wrong to believe him subject to contrary accidents. It is clear, for one thing,

*Mt 19:27

*Ex 33:13
*Ps 76:3

*Jm 1:17

that what is unchangeable is as such better than what is changeable. What is unchangeable, as what has been said earlier makes plain, is fittingly called *super-substance,* superior to all and every substance, neither substance nor in substance.

7.   Being already by definition the subject of contrary accidents, substance cannot as such accept the division into changeable and unchangeable. It can in no way be termed unchangeable. There is no division of upper and lower here, since changeable substance is not only not a kind of substance, but it adds nothing to substance, is merely the substance that in a general way contains all substances and sustains all forms.

8.   It follows that Unchangeable Substance, so far from meaning a kind of substance, can only refer to Being that surpasses all substance, whatever in excellence, is utterly other than it in nature, far exceeds it in sheer power. Created substance is ever supporting. Uncreated is ever surpassing. The latter is uniquely and sovereignly immutable; the former subject to constant modification. The latter is known only by the proper abstraction of the mind and exists in the subjects of its nature; no created mind is able fully to grasp the Infinite Substance that has no nature above it in which it might be conceived and no particular being below it in which it is fixed. It is one, simple, and unmoved; it can in no way be discovered among all that exists.

9.   Supreme above all, God is one; hence, above matter. Simple; consequently, beyond anything material. Immovable, hence superior to all created things. Every creature has inconstancy in being, a leaning towards non-existence built into it by the very fact of its transit from nothing to existence. "But you, Lord my God, are unchanging," being simple, "your years can never fail."* You are immutable, and therefore we recognize you as eternal.

*Ps 101:28

10.   Well, brothers, because this speculative flight has made us tired, back we go on our feet to what remains of today's work. This alternating of lowly work and soaring high on the wings of thought* has

*Jb 5:7

been taught to us and achieved in us by him who exemplified both during his mortal life, Jesus Christ our Lord, who lives with the Father and the Holy Spirit for ever and ever. Amen.

INDEX

1. The language and theme here recalls Augustine, *Conf* 7,10,16. For further background, see the note in Hoste II, pp. 40-41.

2. Literally, "he who through abstraction is not conceived of differently than he exists in reality".

3. *Nihil omnium est,* a formula that recalls the Pseudo-Dionysius, *DN* 1 and 5; PL 122:1116, 1148, 1150; and Eriugena, *Div nat* 1:66; PL 122:510.

4. Sg 3:3-4, referring to the angels, as mentioned in the previous sermon.

5. Aristotle, *Cat* 5:4a-6, and Boethius, *Cat Arist.;* PL 64:198-200.

6. Possibly derived from Chalcidius who says that one of the senses that *essentia* (N.B. not *substantia*) can be taken in is that of prime matter (*materia informis*) underlying all change. See *Comment in Tim* 222.

SERMON TWENTY-ONE
A Fourth Sermon for Sexagesima

*Ps 104:4
*Is 55:6

*Sg 3:2

*Sg 3:3-4

DEAR FRIENDS, in seeking that Lord of ours of whom it is written, "Seek his face always"* (he must be sought while he can be found),* we have gladly lost almost all contact with men and have lost ourselves into the bargain. Two days ago we went through alleyways and streets in our search* and yesterday we even went somewhat beyond the watchmen who go the city rounds.* Beyond matter and form, beyond even the incorporeal substance of a nature simple by reason of its opposition to matter, we found the One, the Simple, the Unchangeable.[1] If nothing better exists or could possibly exist, this is surely our God.[2] Today we must investigate no longer among all things, but now above all things; we must ask whether we have found the sovereign Good not only of all that is, but also, as we said, of all that could be.

2. Now, even at this stage we can see that the Unchangeable can neither improve nor fall away in any fashion. He cannot become greater or less, change his nature or his mode of being from what it is. Whatever he is now he will always necessarily remain.

Secondly, because he is simple, he is what he has.[3]
Being truly simple means that nature, form and properties are not other than the thing itself. Thirdly, the
One cannot have a cause prior to itself. The One
necessarily precedes all else. Many cannot be if there
be no one. The many cannot exist save as caused by
the One. The One precedes all that is, is the cause of
all that is, the absolutely unique principle of all
that is.[4]

3. Consequently, the One is prior to all else. The
Simple is the end of all that is. The Immutable transcends all. From the One come the many, from the
Simple the various, from the Unchangeable all change.
The numerable multitude is caused by the One, the
manifold composite by the Simple, motion of whatever kind by the Immovable. For just as all change
comes from the Unchangeable, so all that is composite is due to the Simple.[5]

4. My brothers, you whose eager hearts I clearly
perceive, what, I ask you, could excel this Being
already so clearly discovered to our grace-enlightened
search? It is prior to all, the source of all that is. There
is nothing beyond it or superior to it: the Beginning
from which comes whatever is; the End that keeps all
that is from ceasing to be; the Everlasting that moves
and guides all in being.

He is the Maker, Ruler, Upholder of all that is, the
Immutable Beginning for whose sake Jacob, God's
friend, worked seven years—such being the meaning
and significance of *Rachel.* * Yes, the Beginning where
that blessed theologian found what we too are seeking, God's holy Word,* the Beginning who is whatever
belongs to his nature, absolutely immutable not only
in disposition but in being.

5. Lord my God, whom I have sought amid all
that is and have found transcending all, are you really
such? Are you neither part of the universe nor nothing
at all, not half-way between all and nothing (Plato's
place for matter[6]), but rather the source whence
matter mysteriously flowed?*

6. O Lord, two lessons have you taught us, your
servants: that you are; and what you are not. We crave

*Gn 29:18-20

*Jn 8:25; 1:1

*Ps 84:8

a third: to know what you are. How true it is that in adding to our learning, you add to the load we bear. Precisely because that you are and what you are can neither be disguised nor prove deceptive, our longing to know what you are is all the greater. Would that we knew not what you are not and could beguile ourselves with some enticing fancy instead of you, or rather would that we knew what you are and could cling to you in truth and content. 7. Show your very self to us, Lord.* You know that our whole longing this day is for yourself, our love for you is for your own sake. Have we not forsaken worldliness completely, and this present world almost as fully, that nothing might hinder our seeking you? Since I may not yet slake my thirst with the clear sight of you, let me at least vent my indignation on the fool who blasphemed you. 8. You said in your heart, fool, being out of your mind, "there is no God",* as though such utterance would have been possible to you were he non-existent. Without him nothing could come to be. If you who so speak exist, surely he also does to whom you refer. All that exists is of necessity either cause or effect of existence. Consequently, if you are an effect, there is necessarily a cause of your existence. If you are a cause of existence, how can you deny your own existence?

*Ps 68:8

*Rm 4:17

9. Again, all that exists is either simple or composite, that is, coming necessarily from the Simple. You must choose between not being or being in one of these two ways. And likewise, what *is* is either immutable or its motion, of whatever sort, is an effect of the Immutable. All movement comes from the Motionless. We may then take it that all that exists is either one, simple, and immutable, or necessarily an effect of what is so. Should nothing at all exist, God nonetheless does, God to whom all that is not contradictory is possible. Present to him are not only actual things but all things possible. His call goes out to that which has no being, as if it already were.*

*Rm 4:17

10. Moreover, crazy fool, by your denial you corroborate what you deny. Should what you affirm be true, how well you have given yourself the lie.* If

*Dn 13:55

what you say be true, then something is true and if God *never* was, then this was *always* true. This everlasting truth means that something was always true; that truth, because this was true, was eternal. Consequently, before all else, with nothingness all about, this one thing, this one truth always was. But if it was composite, it was changeable. And if changeable, temporal. Time, then, was from eternity. What utterance could exceed such folly? 11. Yet such must be the consequence that follows the fool's assertion, if the one reality whose eternity is undeniable be composite and mutable. If, however, he is simple, he must be immutable. The conclusion, brothers, we so gladly came to earlier on, is affirmed by the fool if he denies it; his rejection is but reassertion.

12. Believe me, brothers, or rather believe what is certain and inseparably linked together: to deny God's existence is to demand it. And this is so from no mere logical necessity or verbal deduction. This is so from the nature of God. If aught exists, he exists. If nothing exists, as sure enough nothing did before it came to be what it is, he nonetheless does who has power to make what as yet is not. Nothing, you see, can by itself come to be. Nothing can precede and succeed itself.

13. Hence, of no truth am I more certain than of the existence of him whose existence the fool denied, of the existence of him without whom nothing can be, from whom all that is comes. The Unique, the Simple, Immutable, the Source of the number, measure, weight* found in every creature in its own way. Each creature is unique in the number it has from the One; it is confined to some class or other according to a measure defined by the Simple; it is ordered according to a "weight" by the Unchangeable. Every single thing is what it is because it is numerically one, because it is kept by its constitution to a measure lest it surpass its kind and because it is moved in proportion to its weight so that it finds rest.

14. Brothers, we have gone beyond all creatures and have found him and become *Iduthun,* that is "surpassing them".[8] For his sake we have spurned all

*Ws 11:21

else, the many for the One. And here he is, he whom we sought. Let us never leave him, never let him go. Let us earnestly, yes, shamelessly, ask him about himself. Not only does he allow us to insist, he longs to give in. You must get the better of him to win his blessing.* He asks to be released, saying, "Let me go, the dawn is up",* but his real desire is to be held.

*Gn 32:25,29
*Gn 32:26

15. Let us hold him, brothers, in our thoughts and desires, in our consciences and lives. Let us cling to him for his own sake, finding him our delight, making him our exemplar that, though many, we may be one in him, may be so united to the One, so simplified to the Simple that, as far as possible, we may have the constancy of the Immoveable. At rest in him, may we have that tranquility of which they know nothing who, neglecting God, have much to distract, engross, keep them all fuss and bother in their anxiety over the harvest of wheat, wine and oil.*

*Ps 4:8-9

16. He who would put a thick and many-stranded thread through the slit eye of a narrow needle must twist, tighten and sharpen it with his fingertips as much as he can. This work of ours, this keeping the mind constant in its search for wisdom, unless a man would fool himself and strive to no purpose, requires that the heart be free from anxious care, from curiosity, ambition and sensuality and that it be curbed by correction and that its intent be ever carefully guarded. 17. God's own Word himself assures us: "It is easier for a camel to pass through the eye of a needle than for a man to enter the kingdom of heaven when he is rich."* What is this kingdom but that of the sight and enjoyment of God? How could they attain it whose thoughts, delight and comfort are elsewhere? "Woe upon you who are rich," Christ says. "You have your comfort already."* Those poor in spirit by their own choice are told that theirs is the kingdom of heaven.*

*Mt 19:24

*Lk 6:24
*Mt 5:3

18. And yet, my brothers, you know what happens to the sick. They crave some particular morsel and for long their desire goes unsatisfied. Then it arrives and for all its goodness, its preparation, they simply cannot face it. Their appetite, their liking for it has gone. It finds them indisposed. Something

similar can happen to us who are yet ill from sin. The leisure once so longed for, the quiet so much desired, solitude, separation from the world, reflection, prayer, reading God's Word itself, each and all find us not quite keen. It is a different story when we have recovered. Then all such things find us eager. Far from having to make an effort, to overcome distaste, nothing so satisfies, contents, gives us joy.

19.   Not for us to avoid and loathe the life-giving food of our souls.* Generous fidelity will render its reception easy, give it relish and sweetness, make it the delight it becomes when it alone suffices. Thanks be, as always, to God's grace and love, that comes to the aid of our weakness through Jesus Christ our Lord, who lives and rules with the Father and the Holy Spirit. Amen.

*Ps 106:8

INDEX

1. Isaac's triad of *unum, simplex et immobile* as the fundamental attributes of the divine nature has affinities with Peter Abelard and his School, especially the *Sententiae Parisienses* where the same triad appears.

2. Again note the anselmian reminisences here and compare with *Mon* 27-28.

3. This formula was given classic expression by Augustine, e.g. *Civ Dei* 11, 10, 1.

4. This discussion of divine unity has deep roots in the Platonic tradition, especially in the Pseudo-Dionysius and in Eriugena among Christian authors. In Isaac's time it was characteristic of some authors associated with the "School of Chartres".

5. Anselm, *Mon* 17-18.

6. Plato, *Timaeus* 49a; 51a. For a listing of some Christian uses of this theme, see the note in Hoste II, 338-39.

7. This type of proof for God's existence finds its source in Augustine, e.g. *Lib arb* 2,3,7; *De vera religione* 30-32; *Conf* 10:24; etc.

8. Ps 38:1. The interpretation of the name is from Jerome, *Nom hebr;* PL 23:827.

SERMON TWENTY-TWO
A Fifth Sermon for Sexagesima

BECAUSE, owing to lack of books, my brothers, you demand I supply for your reading by my words, I must keep talking. Yet our frequent attempts to discover what he is whom we are seeking bring us many failures. Searching out such greatness, we are dazzled by its brightness.* Our enquiry is about what is far above us, yet our quest is well advised if it be done with reverence.

*Pr 25:27

2. Earlier discussions have taught us that all creatures are, of themselves, nothing; that only God is not nothing and yet that he is neither a thing nor half-way between something and nothing. Rather, he is really, truly, and not just ideally, supreme. He is the cause of all things; nothing can exist that is not from him. Should nothing else exist, he would still be the almighty source of all that could exist. It only remains for us to discuss the nature of him who has deigned to show himself to us as One, Simple, and Immutable.

3. What is really simple must of necessity be whatever it has.[1] Consequently, discovering God's attributes should put us on the way to knowing what

he is. Lest we get lost in so large a field, however, I shall only ask whether he has intellect and will. If these are not his, he seems to come short of the best form of being; if he does have them, he does not seem supreme. Intellect and will are in a subject, otherwise they cannot be. Yet if he has them and is identical with them, he needs a subject and is less than a substance.

4. What, brothers, are we to say? We must decide for his having them or for his lacking them, but whatever his attributes they are identical with his being. Unless of course we describe him as composite—which means he is neither one nor simple nor immutable. On the other hand, if he is intellect and will, power or wisdom (he must be if he has them), what becomes of our earlier, hard-won conclusion that he is other than all else, superior to and the source of it? If this is true, these realities, like the others, are caused by him. If he has them, how can he be supreme? If he does not have them, how can he be the best form of being?

5. Alas, our "search has played us false".* Just when I thought I had found all, I have lost all. Would that I had never studied! Not only is our light full of darkness, the darkness grows with the light.[2] "The Lord is light and no darkness can find any place in him"*, yet his unapproachable light itself produces our darkness. Two things, you see, cause darkness: insufficient light and over-abundant light.[3] Light's own source says, "Turn your eyes away, they compel me to depart."* "Lord, you have kept my lamp alight till now; dispel, I pray, this darkness of mine."*

6. Were we, brothers, to say that God is his wisdom, intellect, power, justice, it would be no more than facile repetition of what our reading and, still more, our unshaken faith have taught us. Its meaning is not so easy to grasp. What is God if he is justice? What justice, if it is God? Is he less than a substance, it more than a quality? The latter does not bear thinking, the former were to blaspheme. 7. It may be suggested that as God is One and neither number nor quantity, he is rather the source and beginning of number.[4] That is, as Simplicity he is neither a

*Ps 63:7

*1 Jn 1:5

*Sg 6:4
*Ps 17:29

quality nor a kind of thing, but cause and source
of wisdom, justice, power, and the like. He is not
wisdom as a kind of quality or a form of knowledge.
He ought not, therefore, to be described as wisdom
or anything of the sort; as well call him number,
measure, and weight. But he is the highest principle,
source, and efficient cause of all creatures whatsoever.

8. This, however, does not prevent his being
spoken of as infinite number, immense measure,
imponderable weight; and in the same strain, as substantial wisdom, as justice and virtue that do not
depend on will and habit of soul. Better still, I think,
is he named Superwisdom, Superjustice, and so on, in
the way we used Supersubstance—that is, not in the
manner of definition, but in order to give some account
of him.[5] Since he is in no sense a creature (he of whom
negations are more true), let him be understood by the
removal of all predicates. It is more proper to deny all
things in his case than to affirm anything of all
that exists.[6]

9. Hence, according to the proper character of his
own divine theology, he is not substance, he neither
has nor is wisdom. Within the narrow limits of our
reasoned theology he is said to be this or the other.
In symbolic and somewhat sensual theology[7] he is
called heaven and earth, the sun, first, a lion, an ox, a
bird, a tree, a stone, gold. One can use all these terms
the more freely of him because of a likeness of nature,
function, or use, but he has nothing of all of them in
the proper sense.

10. To call him heaven and the like is metaphor.
To speak of him as substance, wisdom, and so forth is
meiosis.[8] In the former case we exceed truth and go
beyond the faith. In the latter we come short of both
truth and exactitude. In every case we try to say something of the Ineffable, of him of whom nothing fitting
can be said. Our choice is between silence and make-
shift terms.

11. You see, brothers, what straits are ours,
under what lack of words our weakness labors once we
attempt to say something worthy of the Ineffable, to
give lessons on the Incomprehensible. It all goes to

*Is 43:10

teach you not only to believe others but to understand* yourselves that God is not for our explaining
and comprehending. This is so, dear friends, not
because of our weakness and slowness or obtuseness,
but on account of his power and subtlety.

12. No wonder the seraphim, for all their holiness and towering nature and those wings that
indicate the soaring of contemplation, are seen to

*Is 6:2

cover his face and feet.* It was to teach us that it was
not their own ignorance that kept the beginning and
the end from them, it was God's own fathomless
superwisdom.[9] Unseen darkness and inaudible silence
leave us blind and deaf; we cannot see and endure his
more than abundant, more than unbearable light,
because seeing the Unseen means being vanquished,
not just blinded, by light.

13. Yes, Lord, "I have exhausted myself in seek-

*Ps 76:4
*Ps 83:3
*Sg 5:6

ing you and my mind grows faint,"* not because of
you but beholding you.* The sight of him for whom
it longs make the mind faint, the soul faints and melts*
as it delights in the sight of him. Nonetheless this
delight spurs me on, ever makes me still more avid to
behold. Sight is but fresh fuel to delight. Seeing and
enjoying correspond to the middle wings[10] which are
the pinions that bear me towards you on whom the

*1 P 1:12
*Gn 18:27

angels are eager to gaze.* 14. Dust and ashes though
I be,* I have taken it upon myself to speak and speak
I will. And I will ask one question of you about your-
self: how are you the source and beginning of all the
aforesaid? This query, my brothers, is worth making,
I think, even if its meaning, I know, can vary greatly.

15. A river, to be sure, has its source and beginning in a spring, but the water in the course and in the
source is of like nature. A tree springs from its roots,
species starts from its genus.[11] Shoot comes from
seed, seed from seedground, seedground from elements, and elements from primordial matter called
hyle or *silva*.[12] In these and suchlike cases, consideration of the natural causes involved, say, of head
producing body, a species its like, non-free agents
their effects—in a word of nature taking its usual
course—we arrive at the fundamental truth that every

maker is the cause or principle of his work.

16. There is one kind of maker who exists beyond and before nature itself, there is another who only imitates her.[13] The latter kind of craftsman merely rearranges the material in which he works: golden objects he must make from gold, stone ones of stone, wooden from wood. He may copy, he cannot change, nature. All his work is inescapably hedged-in by three things: the material he uses, the form he intends to produce, the particular purpose of his endeavor. If we take into consideration the maker himself from which the work comes, there are necessarily four different causes: material, formal, final, and efficient.

17. Not so the maker who is able to draw something from nothing, and then annihilate it, who can transpose an existing thing into another species, increase or lessen without adding to or subtracting from a thing. He certainly is before and beyond Nature; he is the author of Nature and is necessarily different from whatever he creates. Cause, source, origin, in ways that come to mind at the moment and in a manner infinitely exceeding all else in sovereign supremacy: who can doubt that he must needs be confessed God most high and transcendent?

18. He is One, not numerically, but as the principle of number, the principle or cause of number neither in the final nor formal nor material nor natural senses (natural according to the seminal causes of things).[14] He is One, but not through relation of similar things or through the unity of a body. No, he is the One efficient and creator-cause of many that share neither his nature nor his existence. He is One, while all number is many. He is Simple, they composite. He is Unchangeable, they are divisible. Absolutely self-existing, he bestows existence of another order on other beings.

19. He cannot be two. Two is a number and has its being from the One, that being which is the One itself. Since two is twice one or twice unity, only one really exists in two. One does not go to make two as part of a whole but as the efficient principle of its being without which it cannot be. What becomes of two

should one disappear? 20. If one is accounted part of two or a simple element part of a compromise, or time part of age-long duration, such terms must be viewed in the light of the speaker's intention. If one is part of two, what is the other part? If it is one, then you have two unities; and if there are two, there are really none. The One who is prior to all else is the cause of all else. Two First Causes are not possible. Two such would be equal, neither could cause the other and therefore could not cause all things or be before all or be really and truly one. The One is, therefore, unique and is one by his own uniqueness.[15]

21. It follows, as already said, that a true two is twice one and not two ones or two unities, and that all number is a multiple of one; at least, to anyone who is able to rise from things and the attribute of quantity that numbers them to the unity of number of which I speak. There is nothing then in number that really has being and can be said to give it existence except the One who is not number or part of number nor shares its nature, but is its maker. He pre-exists number, is its only adequate cause and true home because its exemplar. The same must be said of the Simple and what is composite, of the Immutable and what is changeable. Two Simple Beings or two Immutables reason will not tolerate. The Simple, existing beyond all things, preserves them from nothing; the Immutable, existing above all, rules them and moves them towards a goal.

22. One, Simple, Immutable are three, and these three are altogether and equally simple and identically Immutable. These three or rather this One and Only bestows, without becoming part of, whatever existence there be. Were he to withdraw himself* nothing whatever could be or be of use or benefit to anything. Left to themselves all creatures are void and empty; "a shadow's shadow, a world of shadows"* a wise man says. In him they are alive and eternal; rather, in him they are eternity and life, as the blessed Apostle puts it, "What was made in him was life."* But there they are what he is.

23. All things then are in him. He is in all things,

the being of all things,[16] not in their changeable
nature, that is, insofar as they are shadows, not real
being but an image and kind of vestige of being;
rather, he is in them as what gives truth and life all at
once and forever to those empty and vain things that
are moved through space and time. He is the source
and efficient principle of what existence, wisdom,
justice and the like is theirs. This does not mean that
he has or is the attribute of any creature, but that he
is the indispensable cause and giver of the created
beauty and goodness that gives the seeker some clue
to the knowledge of their all-beautiful, sovereignly
excellent Maker, the living, all-ruling God. Amen.

NOTES

1. The augustinian motif noted in the last sermon becomes the starting point for this new stage in the argument.

2. See Sermon 4:5. Practically a verbatim quotation from the Pseudo-Dionysius, *Ep* 1; PL 122:1177; also found in Eriugena, *Div nat* 5:26; PL 122:920.

3. For the importance of negative theology in Isaac and its dionysian and eriugenean roots, so evident in this sermon, besides the two articles of B. McGinn, see also A. Fracheboud, "Le Pseudo-Denys l'Aréopagite parmi les sources du Cistercien Isaac de l'Étoile," *Collectanea* OCR 9 (1947), 328-41; 10 (1948) 19-34.

4. God as One and the source of number is a theme of ultimately Neopythagorean origin available to Isaac in such sources as Macrobius, *Comment* 1,6,7; and Eriugena, *Div nat* 3:11; PL 122:652 ff.

5. The superiority of the eminent theology is central to the thought of the Pseudo-Dionysius, e.g. *DN* 2; MT 1. This passage may owe something to Eriugena, *Div nat* 1:72; PL 122:518.

6. This axiom is taken from Pseudo-Dionysius, *CH* 2:3.

7. For a discussion of the dionysian–eriugenean source and significance of Isaac's three divisions of theology, see McGinn, "*Theologia* in Isaac of Stella."

8. Literally, "that figure of speech which is the opposite of hyperbole," that is, meiosis, or expressive understatement.

9. This interpretation referring the "face and feet" to God follows Jerome, *Ep* 18:7; PL 22:365-66.

10. That is, the middle wings of the Seraphim (Is 6:2) by which they are poised in flight.

11. Boethius, *In Porph D* 1; PL 64:48.

12. For Isaac's position on prime matter, see the complementary note in Hoste II, 338-39.

13. These two kinds seem to be a Christian transposition of the two causalities of *Timaeus* 28 ab. See, McGinn, "Isaac of Stella on the Divine Nature," 33-34.

14. Seminal causes or reasons shows the influence of Augustine, e.g., *Gen litt* 11, 17, 32-18, 33.

15. For the roots of this discussion of unity and binarity in Boethius and others, see the note in Hoste II, 76-77. Among Isaac's

contemporaries his discussion is closest to that of Thierry of Chartres in the treatise *De septem diebus.* See the passages cited in McGinn, "Isaac of Stella on the Divine Nature," 34-35.

16. "The being of all things," *omnium essentia,* is to be understood in terms of universal causality and divine omnipresence. For the history of this and related terms, see the material cited in McGinn, "Isaac of Stella on the Divine Nature," 17.

SERMON TWENTY-THREE
A Sixth Sermon for Sexagesima

*Mt 7:7

*1 Co 16:9

*Si 18:1

*Is 62:7

TRUTH promised, "Knock and the door shall be opened to you,"* and, dearest brothers, he has proved true to his promise. We knocked and, you can see for yourselves, a door, great and plain to view,* was opened, enabling us clearly to see that the One, to whom we give the name God, is before all else and able to exist without all else. Without him nothing can exist; everything that exists is from him. Creatures not only come from him but he is in all of them because they are in him not only before, but more truly than, they are in themselves. Whatever he brings about in time or with time has been in him from everlasting, as we are told by a philosopher when he says: "In the mind of the sovereignly Beautiful lay the lovely cosmos".[1] Another writes: "He made things that are yet to be."[2] The Son of Sirach declares: "He who lives forever created all things at once."*

    2. Now, then, dear friends, with boldness God's bounty has inspired, let us give him no rest.* Is not this the very purpose of our separation from the rest of the world, of our silence among ourselves? Let us

cry to him loudly that he speak to us, that he leave us not unanswered and we be like men sunk in the grave of ignorance and forgetfulness,* fallen from the high sight of the Lord on his towering throne,* not better than "the fool who saw as in a mirror his own face and forgot what sort of creature he was".* 3. God's purpose in showing or disclosing to us, in this present life, something about himself is not to satisfy us, but to intensify our seeking. We are not meant to settle down contented. He would have our thirst for him grow ever greater. "When your glory dawns I shall be well content," sings the Psalmist.* His song for the present is, "My whole soul thirsts for God, the fountain of life."* Complacency over one's past seeing means losing all that one should still seek out.

4. On with our search then, brothers, and let us consider that holy Mind of his that bore the cosmos before its creation, that already contained all that was to come, when he created everything at once.* If God has a mind, it cannot be other than himself; being and having are all one in him. Does not a philosopher tell us that even a man's mind is himself?[3] When Scripture says, "God made man in his own image and likeness",* we can be sure this treats of man's mind. God cannot lack a mind, if he would have wisdom and justice.

These two truths go together then: He is and he has Mind. He is being and has what, belonging to and proceeding from his being, is himself. 5. Hence, the strange—call it what you like—conclusion that what is really and truly one is just as truly two—what he is and what is his, what is from nothing and what is from himself—yet the two are truly one since what he has is what he is. But this one is two because a single being cannot proceed from itself, cannot owe itself to itself, cannot and ought not to be said to be its own possession.

6. Consequently, in the blessed, ineffable Unity discovered to us there is proved to be a more than marvellous duality, a duality, moreover, that does not cancel the unity since one reality exists or comes from the other. They are two but one; one yet two—that is, the principle and what comes from the principle. What

*Ps 27:1
*Is 6:1

*Jm 1:23-24

*Ps 16:15

*Ps 41:3

*Si 18:1; Is 45:11

*Gn 1:27

comes from the principle is the same principle or cause that is before all things, the Mind that contains all. There are not two principles, for he is what he has; Father and Offspring, Unbegotten and necessarily Begotten. The eternally begetting Unbegotten, what better name for him—to borrow a word—than *Father* of what from him proceeds? What name more unquestionably suitable than *Offspring* for what proceeds from him?[4]

7. So God, the One, Simple, and Immutable, has been shown to be two, since he both is and has what is his, and nonetheless, he is only one because his having is himself. Moreover, what he possesses in himself and with himself, all that immeasurable truth proceeds from the Unbegotten, from him whom we call the *Father*. To what alone proceeds from this unbegotten Father as his offspring we give the name *Son*. He differs in personal property from his Father, being of, in, and with him. He is the same in unity of being with him who is identical with whatever he has, since all of it is his being, so that what comes of his simple and indivisble nature cannot be other than that being itself.

8. We are not, then, dividing Simplicity and making two of the One. The Unmoved remains eternally unchanged; the Immutable does not cease to be what it always was. The One always keeps his primacy, his unbestowed being, and what proceeds from him is ever with him. Always he is the Father, sole begetter of his eternal Son. Never, on the other hand, is the Unbegotten begotten, the only Begotten unbegotten; the Father never becomes his Son, the Son is never his own Father. The Unbegotten and his Offspring in him both remain ever one and the same, simple, eternal, Father and Offspring of one nature, the same being and all that follows from this.

9. Consequently, the Father is eternity, the Son eternity that comes of eternity. The Father is the beginning, the Son the beginning that proceeds from the beginning. The Father is power; the Son the power from power. The same must be said of wisdom and justice and strength, and the like. In our rational

theology God's attributes are many, but in the
sovereign divine theology they are ineffably one,
their possession meaning that the only Father has
nonetheless only one unique Son in whom all is at
once, undividely and eternally, One. In themselves
they seem many, the reality is otherwise. Symbolic
theology for its part follows the same true teaching
when it uses such terms as *Word, image, radiance,*
express likeness, brightness, arm, hand, right hand, *
always giving us to understand it tells of a being
coming from a being, without any lessening of unity,
dividing of nature, confusing of persons.

*Jn 1:1; Col 1:15;
Hb 1:3; Ws 7:26;
Is 68:1; Ezk 1:3;
Jb 14:15.*

   10. Having come so far in our discussion, let us
now consider some reasons for calling the Son the
Word. Our rational minds, as you know, use three
different natural faculties: judgment, memory, and
discernment—depending on whether they deal with
present, past, or future.[5] Discernment explores the
unknown, judgment pronounces on its findings,
memory files away the decisions come to and produces them in the event of further enquiry. Both
discernment, then, and memory bring to the bar of
judgment, the one its findings, the other is contents.
And judgment deals with what is presented to it. Its
function in the mind's mouth, so to speak, is to chew
either what the teeth of discernment have grasped or
what the stomach of memory has sent back.

   11. What we have once learnt and has become our
knowledge is with us in two ways. It is in our mind's
mouth and we are able, as it were, to talk to ourselves
about it in its presence, to think on it or, to be more
precise, to make it our meditation, to examine it as it
lies before us, to deal with it immediately. Our present
discourse, word of mouth that gives expression to word
of mind, is a case in point. Secondly, our knowledge is
with us, but hidden even from ourselves in the depths
of our memory. No need to stress that everything we
know does not come back to us with equal ease. Nor
are we habitually conscious of the whole of our
knowledge. In time memory yields up its store bit by
bit and into the mouth of the mind comes a word
that finds external utterance in the mouth of the body.

12. It is clear from what we said earlier that for God, to whom all that exists or could exist in all its variety and possibility is present in one, single, all-including and unceasing glance, nothing is past or future. Not only has he no use for memory (because thought that never lets anything go or return has nothing to remember), he has no need for anything thought could discover. Discernment has nothing to bring forward for investigation, so neither power has a place there where nothing is lacking. The self-expressing of his Mind is so adequate, so irrevocable and eternal, that it can be categorically asserted that all things are supra-present to him, eternally unchanged in his Word.

13. Present, past, and future do not comprise the whole of his utterance; it includes everything in any way possible, whatever it proximate source, its particular nature and purpose, the explanation for its being or not being what it is. His asserting expresses no partial view, one aspect now and another later. With God there can be no change.* One only, eternally immutable vision; insight that is not merely adequate but, if the phrase be allowed, super-embracing in its totality; that not only excludes repetition because it is not finite, but includes the Infinite and is therefore, of necessity, itself infinite. To add to this Word or to change it is obviously impossible. It already expresses past all expressing whatever is in any manner possible.

14. Another Word or the same Word in another way or a second time can find no place where duration and innovation are excluded by ever-present eternity. No change, no play of passing shadow* are to be thought of when one inexhaustible utterance exhausts at once all that could ever be said. As object of knowledge, the Word is God's ceaseless, uniquely intimate knowledge in himself of all that is, Word eternal. 15. Not for him to gain knowledge of himself subsequent to his existence, to come by even a little more wisdom, to plan something in an idle moment. The Immutable can no more change his mind about something once decided upon and said within himself than the Infinite can put bounds to

*Jm 1:17

*Ibid.

what lacks beginning and end. The Word is that secret counsel that is begotten not begun, no part of which passes, all of which remains eternally. Fully formed, God's plans are perfect, exceeding not only beginning and ending, but beyond becoming generation after generation.* 16. Something that begins or ends can find no room in Mind where all is infinite and perfect. Things are neither past nor future nor even, strictly speaking, present to God. To say, "God has spoken" looks as if it were all over and he is now silent. "He will speak" suggests something yet to be, not yet begun. "God speaks" or "thinks" leaves us wondering whether what he has said or thought is final.

*Ps 32:11

17. You see what happens to a person forced to speak and not allowed to keep silent about God's super-being and Word? No effort of ours is able to give us a noun that expresses God's nature, no verb of ours can properly signify what is correctly said about him.[6]

18. Nevertheless, dear friends, our pursuit of the Word, himself become the lamp to guide our feet,* our holding on to him or going where he would go or turn his steps,* our not letting go of him, no matter where he enters or penetrates, has not been fruitless. Has he not led us at last into his Father's house, into the very chamber where he is begotten,* into the unbegotten being, wisdom, and power of the Father, the Father who begot a Son his equal in being? We, in our turn, have led the Word back to his Father, led him, as it were written, "to our mother's house".* While we have searched out the source of this holy sowing, that is, of God's Word, we have certainly found our own. It is from the same source but in a different way. One same Being is Father to his divine, eternal, beginningless, only Son and to all those other sons of his who come to be in time.

*Ps 118:105

*Rv 14:4

*Sg 3:4

*Ibid.

19. Thanks, then, to the bright lamp that, already mentioned, has guided my feet, I have caught at least a glimpse of what I set out to find, and I have expressed a part of this in word. Of this part only some of you perhaps have been able to catch glimpses, a glimpse of the Word's origin, the how and when of his

being and the manner of his existence. The Word's source—what it was, when and how that primordial utterance found expression—such was the course of my discourse. But this has merely shown the possibility of the Word being sown in other than the divine nature, not the actual fact of such a sowing. 20. We have yet, brothers, to deal in another sermon with the where, why, how and when of the Word's beginning in time. Meanwhile let us pray the Sower of this holy and mysterious Word graciously to implant insight of these wonders in me, and from you, brothers, to reap the fruit of that very insight from the stalk of this sermon of mine. For what is sown by means of this ministry yields an abundant harvest in good soil. May the Son of Man, God's Word, deign to grant us this, he the Seed and the Sower, our Lord Jesus Christ, to whom belongs glory and dominion through endless ages.* Amen.

*1 Tm 6:16

NOTES

1. Boethius, *Consol phil* 3, metr. 9, lines 7-8.
2. Is 45:11 in the LXX text hat served as the basis for the Old Latin translation. Isaac would have known this text through its use by patristic authors.
3. Cicero, *Somnium Scipionis* 8:2.
4. Compare this line of argumentation with Anselm, *Mon* 32; 39-42.
5. See Sermon 17:10 and *Ep an;.* PL 194:1876,1879.
6. See Pseudo-Dionysius, *DN* 1; PL 122:1116.

SERMON TWENTY-FOUR
A Seventh Sermon for Sexagesima

DEAR FRIENDS, we are a good example of how the whole man eats his food with the sweat of his brow.* *Gn 3:19* The sword pierces our flesh, of course, and does not spare our very soul.* *Jr 4:10* Clearing the ground of briers that would hinder sowing under a roasting almost mid-day sun has us bathed in sweat. Tired with our striving to win a harvest from the earth, let us rest a little in the generous shade of this nearby oak[1] and turn our minds to the not inconsiderable effort of threshing, grinding, mixing, baking and eating the seed of the Divine Word, lest we grow weary and discouraged.* *Mt 15:32*

2. The first loaf we must eat today will be seeking the reason for his going out who "went out to sow his seed".* *Lk 8:5* What had he to gain without, who could suffer no lack within? The One can no more decrease than the Infinite can multiply, the Simple decrease, the Immense grow, the Immutable be moved. This last remark, you notice, puts another loaf before us. We must discuss how the Immutable can go out.

3. Brothers, when this visible world had as yet no existence whatever, God was not a jot less great

than he is at this very instant; indeed he is infinitely more than what exists in this sensible realm. It is evident that everything which is in the copy has come from the model, but it does not follow that all that is in the model has passed into the copy.[2] Not, as I have already often said, that what exists exhausts the designs of him who knows every kind of possible being, knows it not as changeable and empty, but in beauty and truth proportionate to the truth and life that are his. The world we see is the last stage of a process at the opposite end of which stands that supreme Archetype whose activity in the universe is described as "bold in its sweep from world's end to world's end and everywhere manifesting his gracious ordering".*

*Ws 8:1

4. Take this oak tree. For all the blessing its cool shade affords us, it was fairer far and more marvellous as a little acorn than it is now in all its greatness. It finds its perfection in going full circle and producing acorns. Acorns are a sort of fixed point: from them in cycle come root, trunk, branch, leaf, flower, and acorns again. In their turn, the small seeds of such power are far less interesting and wonderful as acorns than they were in their previous stage in the generative power of mother-earth. The generative power, moreover, is less marvellous than the elements that compose it, and these are inferior to the matter from which they come. But never are matter and all else more glorious and true than they are in the mind of God.

5. This oak, we may conclude, while *actually* all that it is, as you can see, was *virtually* in an acorn, *radically* in the earth, *causally* in the elements, *possibly* in matter, and *potentially* in God. It is subject to change and destruction in its other causes; it lives eternally in God.

6. All creatures being in God, not only as possible but as foreknown, yes, as actually loved, what did that great pagan theologian[3] mean when he declared that God was filled "with great joy" on the completion of his work of creation?[4] Did he mean that God beheld in creation something new which he had not already foreseen? Was there some trace of beauty

in the copy that was not more fair in the Model?
Every work is more beautiful in design than in exe-
cution. Should he rejoice that there was far greater
reason within his own mind?

7. I do not mean to imply that this great philosopher—it was Plato, you recall—spoke childishly.
Moses, our theologian, has told us something similar:
"God saw all that he had made and found it very
good."*[5] Still, had God not seen things more glorious?
Did he not prize things of greater worth in his own
Mind? Or was it that both theologians, in mentioning
the work's completion, were subtly suggesting God's
ultimate purpose; Plato referring to the joy, Moses
to the goodness? 8. How great are the joy, gladness,
rejoicing, delight, and pleasure that he has within
once and for all and always from his great and glorious
power, that limitless world of beauty, that clear sight
of every possible purpose and arrangement, of every
cause and effect, that are his. How can he find
pleasure in seeing what is outside himself and therefore
incomparably less beautiful? The answer lies perhaps
in this very inexpressible, boundless joy and delight.

9. Be that as it may, mention of God's end—just
when we were meaning to end this sermon—enables
us to glimpse a third reality in his super-incomprehen-
sible, unique, simple, and immutable nature. This
third entity must proceed neither from nothing nor
from one Person only. God's internal joy and delight
in his light and with his light means that that joy and
delight clearly proceeds from both. Such delight and
joy belong with total equality both to him who
rejoices and to him because of and in whom he
rejoices. God's joy in his Son makes both of them the
principle of their unique joy.

10. Now, since both he who rejoices and he
because of whom and in whom he finds his joy are
one being—God being, as I have already shown, whatever he has—it follows that, since he is one with his
joy, his joy is himself, joy incapable of alloy, of fresh
growth, or failing decay, joy eternal, the joy that has
enabled us to glimpse the joy that is the Blessed
Trinity. Besides, because both he who rejoices and he

Gn 1:31

in whom he is delighted love one another, the love of each is not only in the other, it is love identical with both of them.

11. Father is the name we give to the one who comes from nothing in this Unity to be adored; we call him who proceeds from one alone the *Son*. But it would bring nothing but confusion to name him Son who, proceeding from both the other two Persons, belongs to both of them. So he is called *Holy Spirit*, a name that, distinguishing him from the other Persons, helps us regard him as the sweetness, love, peace, and delight of both Father and Son, while keeping us clear of any lessening of the Unity in our confession of the Trinity of God.

Jn 1:9

12. What need had God, the true Light,* already exulting and rejoicing in his light, what need had he of our darkness? Was it to see confusedly without what is so clear within his own Mind? If he was Light, he was certainly giving light. What else is it to be a light than to beget light? And the light that Light begets in emitting Light is nothing else than the Light itself. To be Light and to be Light-giving does not mean being two different lights. Yet the terms do not have exactly the same meaning. 13. The noun Light only refers to Light in itself. Light-giving signifies the light coming from light. The same Light is found in both cases, but different aspects are in question, another property of light, but not a different true light.

To be Light-giving is to be Light-bestowing, to make a gift of the same, not of some other, light. Yet Light, though it be light itself, cannot bestow light unless it itself be Light-giving. Light-giving without Light itself is impossible. We may conclude then that it is for Light to be Light-giving and that it takes both Light and Light-giving to be Light-bestowing.[6]

14. Moreover, it also follows that the idea of bestowing light includes, almost equivalently, the notion that light-giving light is bestowed. The idea of light-giving implies that light flashes out and by its brightness enlightens and bestows itself. The mere mention of light brings to mind something light-giving that

begets and bestows of itself light enlightening.

15. These subtleties are not just a little word game played in logical differences, they are found in the thing for which the words stand, in the nature of light which allows us to include these three properties in any one of them or one of them in all three of them. The one nature of light and its three properties are given expression in those three terms.

16. Rachel, as you remember, brothers, when she found herself still childless enlisted the help of her maid-servant.* The analogy suggested by ordinary light has enabled me, when I found it impossible to express the nature of the unapproachable Light, to give you some idea through likeness and enigma of what is both infinitely different and yet not unlike it.[7]

17. Light, we can say, exists and of itself begets Light, Light that reveals its Parent and, in so doing, both reveals Itself and makes a self-revealing Gift of Itself. And what makes Light more lovable, most especially to be sovereignly loved, than his being a Gift, Gift that we are enabled to welcome and enjoy? Great use to me were it that God is almighty, that all power, wisdom, justice, goodness are his, if some share and portion might not be mine!

18. The most compelling motive for loving God is surely that as Light he shines out, makes himself perceptible and a joy. Were there none to see or enjoy the gift, God, as Light, as far as he can, is ever open-handedly giving himself away. What is light-giving can no more avoid making a gift of light than light can refuse to be light-giving. Therefore every use of light comes from its own gift; from this comes its love, that by which it is held dear and beloved.

19. Summing up, then, we can say that love comes from use, use comes from the gift, and the gift from the form and natural image, that is, from the native radiance and brightness. Both Gift and Image, moreover, comes of Light's own eternity, from the very Being, own essence of Light himself. This essence, hidden away in unapproachable Light*—material light gives us some hint of it—is the utterly unbegun Beginning of the Radiance and Brightness.

*1 Tm 6:16

*Ps 26:1

20. This then, O Lord my God, my Light,* is the chief motive for my loving you, what enables me to love you, to know and to share your fellowship—your own natural gift by which you can be given, can be received and can be enjoyed. Be my prayer what it may, this is ever the Gift I look for, that is, your Holy Spirit, natural goodness and prodigal largess, your own, your eternal, ever-immutable self, no sudden, passing feeling stirred up in you by desire or device or deed of mine.

21. No wonder then, Holy Trinity, true Light, my God, this Gift of Light does not proceed from himself. We owe everything to him, including our fellowship with him, this Gift that himself owes himself to the Form and Brightness, to the Offspring of the Father's Light, and through him to the Father, himself the Light. The gift of Light comes from Light because it shines, and all use comes from the gift. No wonder we pay the same worship, give undivided love to the Holy Spirit, and in him to the Son through whom we love and reverence the Father, from whom come whatever gifts are worth having, whatever en-

*Jm 1:17

dowments are perfect of their kind.*

22. The Father bestows the Spirit in the name of the Son, that is, through the Son. The Son, who proceeds from the Father, makes us a gift of the Spirit. The Spirit of both Father and Son gives himself to us. Give to whom you are not in debt and you make a free gift. To forego a debt, to treat well him who has deserved ill can only be done by a great, a very great, indeed the greatest, gift. Such is the way God totally gives and forgives in the gift he makes of his Holy Spirit, the Spirit and all his uses that come to us through the Son, through whom, in the Spirit, the Father who is first and fontal goodness, the origin of

*Jn 6:37; 3:18

all that is, grants every gift and pardon.*

23. Let us, brothers, not only thank God the Trinity for light and enlightening given us, let us also pray the Father to disclose to us through the Son in the Holy Spirit why it pleased him to go out, he who within had no lack and nothing to gain without. And why he set about sowing what, if kept, could not

lessen, what when sown added nothing to, his store.
     Enough for today. We are tired. Tomorrow I shall
discuss this question to the extent granted me by the
gracious gift of the Holy Spirit, himself Giver and
Gift everlasting. To him belong glory and power
1 Tm 6:16   forever. Amen.

NOTES

1. Possibly a reminiscence of Vergil, *Bucolics* 1:1.

2. For model (*exemplar*) and copy (*exemplum*) in Plato, see *Timaeus* 28-30. Note also Chalcidius, *Comment* 304.

3. Plato is called *theologus* as early as Chalcidius, *Comment* 143, an appellation repeated by Cassiodorus and Eriugena among others.

4. *Tim* 37C in the Chalcidius version.

5. Isaac received the idea of linking these two texts from Augustine, *Civ Dei* 11:21 whose influence is very strong in this sermon. For a general study of the relation between Isaac and the bishop of Hippo, see A. Fracheboud, "L'Influence de Saint Augustin sur le Cistercien Isaac de l'Étoile," *Collectanea OCR* 11 (1949) 1-17; 264-27; 12 (1950), 5-16.

6. The trinitarian analogy based on Light (*lux*), Light-giving (*lucere*), and Light-bestowing (*lucem praebere*) is based on Augustine, *Sol* 1, 8, 15; PL 32:877.

7. Literally, *quod longe dissimiliter simile est,* a dionysian theme, see *Cl* 2.

8. Another threefold analogy adopted from Augustine, *Trin* 6, 10, 11, who in turn took it from Hilary of Poitiers. Cf. *Ep an;* PL 194:1887.

SERMON TWENTY-FIVE
An Eighth Sermon for Sexagesima

IN OUR SEEKING for the final cause of the universe, it is immediately obvious, dear friends, that it was not necessity that forced the Almighty nor covetousness the Lord of all, nor was Wisdom beguiled by curiosity, nor Truth by vainglory. No, it was free choice and the gift of his own generosity. It was no sudden whim, moreover, but a design eternally present to his Mind and Will, brought in due time to completion in deed. Besides, since his nature may in some sense give and share itself, and since his joy in and because of himself knows neither pause nor variation, he owed it not only to his native goodness but also to this Joy of his to look for fellowship in such great and glorious happiness.

2. Selfishness or self-complacency often drives us to share some personal joy of ours; the greater our gladness, the more pressing our urge. With God it is not so. His desire to pour himself out upon and into his creatures, to make them share his nature, is due exclusively to his lavish liberality and loving kindness, to the free gift of divine Joy. God's generosity is as

incompatible with miserliness as his goodness is with envy, his love with mere good wishes. His joy does not wish to be hidden and solitary.[1]

3. When the indivisible Trinity willed eternally and undividedly the existence of beings able to receive God, to have part in his delight, gladness, peace, joy, then the Trinity created from nothing the rational mind made in God's image. The very fact of creation from nothing, the truth of—as I've already mentioned—God's perfectly gratuitous generosity makes nonsense of the notion some have had of a certain compulsion inherent in his nature that could not be put to rest. Creation certainly is an effect of his natural goodness, but only because he wills it. Blessed, no less, the Being that demands doing good. Does not he who is compelled to do the good deeds demanded by the goodness of his own nature do them gratuitously and freely?

4. Native goodness and internal delight of mind were the cause of the work of creation. I mean of the rational spirit that is the cause for the material universe. The whole world of matter is at the service of the spirit's instruction; nowhere silent,* it ever keeps telling him of its Maker.   5.   Rational spirit has no other purpose than to enjoy and share God's delight in God and in all else. Rationality is his that he may be able to seek God himself in himself and in everything. The power of desire is his that he should love and long for God alone, the power of rejection is his that he should reject all that would hinder the contemplation and love of God.[2] To adapt Isaiah: man's mind should enable him to direct his desires toward good, his anger to reject evil.*

6. Consequently, the unique and highest good of a rational created spirit, the ultimate objective that alone befits its study of nature, that alone is logical and moral for its mind and will, the very meaning of its existence, is the contemplation and enjoyment of God. The way to this dwelling place* is the way of study and learning, of seeking and longing, loving quest and searching love. The only sin and evil for such a creature is that it should turn aside from such

*1 Co 14:10

*Is 7:15

*Jn 14:6

conversion, such seeking, such longing for God, and instead bend mind and heart on some other objective.

7.   Why, dearest brothers, do we keep on the weary search that laboriously leads to finding? What is sufficient is brief enough. What is perfect is near enough. Joy, love, delight, sight, sweetness, light, and glory—these are what God asks of us, the purpose for which he made us. To do what we were created *Jm 1:27   to do, this is right order and true religion.* Let us make sovereign Beauty our contemplation, set our hearts on highest Delight, be ruthless against whatever hinders such sight and enjoyment.

All our observances, our work and leisure, our speech and silence, all must be directed to such contemplation. To intend otherwise, to strive for what was not God's purpose in creating us, for what does not make his doing and ours one in motive and direction is not virtue at all and merits no reward.   8.   The reward of our good deeds lies with God who was the source of the gift of our being. He is beginning and *Rv 1:8   end to us:* the beginning to whom we come at last, the end that holds the primacy of importance; perfect beginning because of the end, infinite end because ever beginning. How could he ever lack or lose anything who always ends where he begins, always begins where he ends?

9.   In every case and place he who would offer service pure and unblemished in the sight of God, who is our Father, must do only this and for its sake *Jm 1:27   keep himself untainted by the world.* Yet the difficulty of actually living in this world and at the same time not being tainted by it is by itself reason enough for living away from it. As for the Apostle's mentioning, in the middle of the words just quoted, the "case of *Ibid.   widows and orphans in their need"*, it is, we may take it, a reminder that only well-ordered love[3] and concern for our neighbor offer any excuse, at all praiseworthy for allowing ourselves any slackening in the constant effort of mind, the unceasing longing of our hearts for the sweet and lovable rest of contemplation.

10.   That our observances be worthwhile then,

brothers, let us see to it that their purpose is to bring us both the delight of contemplation and true love of our neighbor, to gracious ease with God and well-ordered relations with our fellows. Well-ordered must our love of our neighbors be. It alone justifies, it alone makes useful our attending to our fellows and easing off somewhat the unceasing business of contemplation. As for exercising the body in work that enables us to "earn alms for those in need",* that is for the still-animal body, we have good reason for holding it not altogether outside the scope of charity to our neighbor. 11. What is closer to a man's soul than the body that not only must he cherish but cannot hate? While soul is merely living soul, not yet life-giving spirit,* and so cannot by itself impart life, it is consonant with right reason to supply from without what from within is lacking, a case of the spirit being a debtor to flesh by giving it life, not of its being led by it.*

*Eph 4:28

*1 Co 15:45

*Rm 8:12

12. All concern then, all taking pleasure in anything but God alone (with the aforesaid exception of doing kindness to our neighbor for God's sake) is simply wantonness, a form of adultery. It means going aside from the purpose of our creation as men and is contrary both to God's will for us and to our duty towards him.

13. Clearly, my brothers, great spiritual devotion and untiring effort are called for if we are to rid ourselves of "every thought that is unworthy of the spirit of instruction,"* the Holy Spirit who shrinks away from the touch of falsehood and, if we are to gaze upon the God-given light that both shows the way to truth and sets on fire with love. That such virtue might be all the more freely and surely yours, you have cast the care of your very bodies upon another. By means of this, work is enjoined on us, trouble is removed from us, involvement in cares is forbidden us.

*Wi 1:5

14. That worldly cares are troublesome is patent from the words of Scripture: "How many cares and troubles you have."* This life's affairs are fatal to our best interests; hence our Lord's warning: "Do not let

*Lk 10:41

*Lk 21:34

your hearts grow dull with revelry and drunkenness and the affairs of this life."* Busy cares are a deceptive escape. The burden of affairs is worse, utter thraldom. Neglect of one's spiritual life is the greatest danger of all. It ruins everything. Misuse of leisure spells loss of whatever one's efforts have gained; it means never attaining to the light of contemplation. A mind bent under a burden of affairs can rise to higher things about as much as a troubled mind can be at one and the same time calm. An unquiet heart is far from being tranquil and is equally far from being resplendent with light. 15. A heart that would contemplate must be bright as a mirror, shimmer like some still stretch of water crystal-clear, so that in it and through it the mind may see itself, as in and through a mirror,* an image in the image of God.

*1 Co 13:12

The heart, dear friends, that covets the sight of God as in a mirror must keep itself free from worldly cares, from harmful, unnecessary and even necessary ones. It must keep itself ever alert through reading, meditation and prayer. Blessed are the pure of heart; they shall see God.* May he grant that we do so. Amen.

*Mt 5:8

NOTES

1. This argument is based upon the famous text of the *Timaeus* (29e) denying envy as a characteristic of the framer of the universe. The fundamental premise of such a line of thought is well expressed in the famous axiom, "good diffuses itself" (*bonium est diffusivium sui*).

2. For this triad, see *Ep an;* PL 194:1877; and Sermons 10:17; 17:13-14; and 51.

3. Well-ordered love (*ordinata caritas*) is a central theme for the Cistercians, e.g., Bernard *SC* 49:6; *SC* 50.

SERMON TWENTY–SIX
A Ninth Sermon for Sexagesima

RATIONAL MINDS are the first and only beings made in God's image, thanks to the gift God wills to make of his Joy. They are for that reason the only creatures capable of sharing his knowledge and love. Their intellects and wills, faculties that enable them to understand and to love, fit them to share God's communicable nature. These faculties are, as it were, receptacles and tools belonging to their nature that the first gift of grace puts in being and the further gift of grace fills against both emptiness and the wrong kind of content.[1] 2. Wrong notions and misdirected love may occupy them with evil; God alone, their author and purpose, can satisfy them. Not that they will ever be able to contain him fully. "God," says the Apostle, "is greater than our heart and nothing is hidden from him."*

*1 Jn 3:20

Below God, no earlier, no greater beings exist than rational created spirit.[2] This is seen in the fact that no creature, occupy them as it may, can fully content them. For them to seek anything save God alone is to drink what intensifies their thirst. It is thankless for them to crave satiety from what is not God; money, power and the like leave them still dissatisfied. Such things are beneath them. 3. Created minds are the receptacles into which God's Wisdom and Power* pours himself, filling them with knowledge and love of him. Each of them is a field in which the Wisdom and Power of God sows himself, the Seed, from which comes the light of knowledge and the fervor of love.

*1 Co 1:24

4. God's first grace not only created these previously non-existent fields, but made them capable of receiving and multiplying the seed he would plant in them. These fields, as already said, are no other than the faculties of intellect and will that furnish created minds with free choice. In this field of free choice the Seed of the Word is sown by the second grace.[3] Thus to this lamp made ready for lighting the necessary kindling is brought.

5. In this field is sown, within and without, the Seed of the Word, as befits man's nature. All external creation speaks to the rational mind and teaches him from without about the Creator. From within the same is done by the deep nature of the rational spirit itself. Above and beyond these ways, God's gracious inspiration has at times a word for him. 6. But always, as an eye capable of seeing yet ever needing the light that enables it actually to see, and as an ear fit for hearing and hearing only what sound comes from outside itself —neither of these is sufficient of itself—so man's mind—though the initial gift of creating grace makes it capable of seeing God-given light always—needs a ray of light from above in order to really attain vision. The eye does not see the sun save in the light of the sun; created minds cannot have sight of the true divine sun and Light except in the light he bestows. "In your light," says the prophet, "shall we see light."* 7. The Word that lights up our minds is just like a ray of sunlight that enables us to see the sun, which otherwise we could not see, a ray that without cutting itself off from the sun comes from the sun and gives us sight of it. While still dwelling in God, he comes forth from him and

*Ps 35:10

enables us first to see the splendor that makes it possible for us to see anything at all and then shows us
the Father who neither forsakes nor is forsaken by
his Son.

8. Our bodily eyes perceive the light that streams
from the sun and in that light see everything else.
Following the sun's rays back to their source, we can
catch sight of the sun itself, fount and cause of the
brightness through which it shows itself by means of
its own gift and native benefit. Our minds first glimpse
1 Tm 6:16   the Radiance of unapproachable Light,* indispensable
condition of their seeing at all, and that Light lifts them
up, shows them where it came from, and unveils the
course of its origin, something it could by no means do
unless it came forth from there.

9. The son comes out to bestow light and does so
precisely because he comes from the Father. The privilege he has of his nature is one thing, his natural
source another. He owes both the brightness through
which he enlightens and the enlightenment that comes
of his splendor to the unique Source of all light. This
is not to say that he is first Light, then Radiance,
thirdly Enlightening, but that is because he is Light, his
brightness is ever, as far as his being is concerned, a
source of enlightenment, though it is not sufficient to
enlighten any particular object immediately. 10. If an
eye fit for seeing springs into existence in this sunlight, it would immediately, without any change in the
sun, be lit up by its rays. It could also, through no
fault or change in the sun, be darkened by chance or
totally blinded immediately, so that creation, illumination, and darkening would all take place in a
nearly indivisible instant.[4] Created minds that owe
their existence to the Light have their being in the
eternal and all-present Light, when at creation they
are filled with the light of God's presence that causes
no change in him. Should they of a sudden turn themselves into light-fleeing spirits, not the least shadow
can they cast on their Maker. He is like a permanent
and immobile sun in the sky, unaffected whether we
face towards it and are illumined, or turn from it
and are darkened.

11. Out he came, as has been said, the Sower of Light and the Word, himself the Light and the Word, and first of all he sowed the seed he brought from the Father's bosom.* He sowed it freely, that is, by the gift of the Holy Spirit, in the field of the angelic nature. He enlightened their minds from within, instructing them with nature's command. And as he sowed, grains fell—in the case of some, beside the path.* The Creator's bounty comes to his creatures by no other way than that of freely bestowed charity and love. Charity and love are in turn the only fitting way in which the service of created minds finds acceptance with their Creator.

*Mt 13:14;
Ps 73:11

*Lk 8:5

12. He sowed then, as has been said, first of all in the world of the angels and with two results. Some turned to God in thanksgiving and unselfishness, striking root deep in humility, bearing the high fruit of obedience; as Scripture says: "The saved remnant of Judah will strike deep root, bear high fruit."* Others turned to selfishness and "became fantastic in their notions, turned fools and claimed to be so wise". They turned their backs on the Light and their sense-less hearts grew benighted.* They refused due glory to the Source of their enlightenment, the Sower who had chosen them for the field of his sowing.* Instead they made much of themselves, all pride, vanity, self-impor-tance; thieves who made off with what light they had because they knew nothing of humility. They stifled every good thought, cast away the seed of blessedness sown in their hearts, made impossible the harvest, the fruit of love that springs from humble obedience. These were they who did not take their stand upon truth even for an hour; their creation, illumination, and blinding was, as I've already said, the work of an instant. Their wickedness blinded them to the free gift of enlightenment given by creating grace. Wisdom, the Sower, knew well what the loss of seed had been in the world of the angels, but his longing for a harvest would not allow him to stop his sowing.

*Is 37:31

*Rm 1:21-2

*Rm 1:28

14. "And as he sowed some grains fell on the rocks."* This rock-riddled ground is human nature in Adam, the nature that becomes aware of itself in

*Lk 8:6

the person of David, and in true self-knowledge says to the Lord, "For you my soul thirsts like a land parched with drought".* The Word of God did this by the second sowing interiorly through the gift of mind-endowed soul that enlightens every person born into the world.* He also did it exteriorly by the illumination implicit in the prohibition, "You shall not eat of the tree which brings knowledge of good and evil."* 15. This sowing took place in Eden, the former in heaven. Adam entertained the Word with joy and kept true to it for a while, but the heat of temptation from the woman who had been led astray proved too much for him. He criminally seconded the suggestion of her who wanted him to share her foolish credulity. Eve's word he preferred to God's Word; he withheld the inner moisture of charity from the root of humility and lost thereby the freshness of outer obedience.

*Ps 142:6

*Jn 1:9

*Gn 2:17

16. God, the stubborn Sower, sowed a third time; he sowed in the desert with Moses for spokesman, but "as he sowed some grains fell among briers".* The Jews, even when they kept the commandments and looked to the promised rewards, had eyes only for the things of time and earth. Their longing for the merely natural smothered the fruit, every bit of it, that comes of the spiritual understanding of the Law.

*Lk 8:5,7

17. And still, as though to prove the saying true that everything yields to persistent effort",[5] the Son of God became the Son of Man, and first he and later his Apostles sowed him, Sower and Seed, yet again, and won a welcome for the Word in the world of men. He won a welcome from both the remnant of Israel and the fullness of the Gentiles,* the good soil of those who not only welcomed the Word with joy but endured amid heat and cold and yielded a harvest.

*Rm 9:27, 11:25

18. There are then four sowings: one in heaven, another in Eden, the third in the desert, the fourth in the whole world. Of this last our Lord said: "Go out all over the world and preach the Gospel to the whole of creation."* The angels were first, then came our first parents; the Jews are next, and the Gentiles after

*Mk 16:15

them. First came a precept of nature befitting angels, then to men the precept of discipline; the Law was next, and finally the Gospel of grace. First was the Word impressed on minds; second was the Word expressed in words; third was the written Word; fourth was the Word made flesh. "The Word," John tells us,

Jn 1:14 "was made flesh and came to dwell among us." The Word came to the angels' minds from within, to Adam's ears from without; even to the eyes of the Hebrews at Sinai, and fourthly to man's very touch in Christ. "He it was to whom we listened, whom we

1 Jn 1:1 saw, whom we touched with our hands, the Word who is life."

19. So true is it that the story of these sowings and of the different reactions they occasioned is found through the whole of history, dear friends, that not only did the Incarnate Word himself, as he preached himself in person, encounter such differences, but every sower of the Word's seed meets them as a daily commonplace. Every sermon audience holds some who turn a deaf ear, others who accept the Word for a time. Those who smother the Word and those who endure and yield a harvest are there too—which reminds us that instead of endurance, what the angels needed was constancy, what Adam lacked was obedience.

It is not for us to be found with those who do not conceive the Word or with such as abort it or those who kill it as it begins to grow. We would be among those who cherish the Word with the tender care a mother shows. May this be the gift Jesus Christ our Lord bestows on us as he sows himself in our hearts. Amen.

NOTES

1. See Sermon 7:4, 7.

2. A favorite theme of Isaac (see Sermons 4:17; 5:16; 15:7; and *Ep an*) taken over from Augustine, e.g., *In Ioan* 23:5-6; *Quan an* 34:77.

3. The distinction between first (creating) and second (redeeming) grace is frequent in Isaac, e.g., *Ep an;* PL 194:1887-88. The connection between the faculties of intellect and will (i.e., the image of God) and free choice recalls Bernard, *Gra* 6:19.

4. For the instantaneous fall of the angels, see Augustine, *Civ Dei* 11:11-13.

5. Vergil, *Georgics* 1:145-46.

APPENDIX

Observations by the Translator

THE ORIGINAL intention of Cistercian Publications was an ecumenical version of the Sermons of Isaac of Stella: the selected-passages translated by Sister Penelope CSMV were to be supplemented by Sister Paul OCSO; this was to me very grateful news indeed. Some years earlier I had attempted a rendering into some sort of English of Isaac's remarkable Sermons for Sexagesima. There had been some idea of publishing them in some way, but the thing had only reached the stage of typescript. It was a pleasure to hand over the nine Sermons to Father Basil Pennington OCSO, Managing Editor of Cistercian Publications.

That, alas, was not the end of my troubles. Sister Paul asked me to become a kind of theological adviser to the venture; no great compliment to Isaac. Then she began, in her desire to get things moving, requesting that I translate this and the other Sermon; she found them too technical. By this time she had decided it would speedup the business if she left Sister Penelope's version to one side and translated straight from Dom Anselm Hoste's critical edition of the Latin original; ecumenism is, no doubt, a slow affair if you are in a hurry.

Time passed and Sister forged ahead, and then (why make a short story long?) she went off to help the Cistercian convent in Uganda. It was left to me to carry on.

All this goes to explain and, it is hoped, excuse the three-stage version of the Sermons of Isaac of Stella presented in this volume.

Sermons 1–4 were translated by Sister Paul; it is easy to see what a good job she would have made of the lot.

Sermons 5–17 represent my attempt to render, with ever increasing attention to scriptural sources and suggestions, the Latin text provided by Dom Hoste OSB, Sources Chrétiennes, No. 130, (Paris: Les Editions du Cerf, 1967).

Sermons 18–26 is the version of Sexagesima Sermons already mentioned, brought into line with the Latin of Dom Hoste's edition Sources Chrétiennes, No. 207 (Paris: Les Editions du Cerf, 1974).

A word of sincere thanks to the following: Father Basil Pennington OCSO, for encouraging me to continue where Sister Paul left off; Dr. E. Rozanne Elder, Father Basil's successor as Editor of Cistercian Publications, for her patient expertise; Dr Bernard McGinn for his expert editing and fine introduction; my Superiors for permitting the venture.

THE MAN AND THE MONK

It does seem a little strange that the learned should think it strange that it is difficult to discover much about an abbot of a small and unimportant monastery in middle and latter-half twelfth century Aquitaine.[1] After all, there is not much in the biographical line about the first three abbots of Cîteaux, even when the *Vita* of St Robert of Molesme is thrown in for good measure;[2] a delightful mosaic of "Noble by birth, nobler still in virtue" type of clichés is not all that informative, be the reader ever so learned.

Early Cistercian history and biography, especially if emanating from the Valley of Glory that Clairvaux then was, depends very much on the glory that was St Bernard. While Isaac, abbot of Stella, did not altogether escape that glory, he does not, at first glance, much reflect it, and could give the impression of rejecting it. Small wonder, then, he does not shine very extensively in the story of early Cistercian chronicle.

However, there is one compensatory factor, and, although it does not turn disappointment into dancing, it does suggest a special vote of thanks; apart from some slight use of Isaac's name in some letters and charters, all we know of him has been provided by his own writings. At the very end of these writings, in the Tissier and Migne editions, Isaac mentions that he is an Englishman. So final a location for mention of his place of origin would have amused one so emphatic that God is the Beginning and the End.[3] And, in fact, the incident that gave rise to this disclosure is itself entertaining, with just that spot of irony that Isaac heartily appreciated. The event, moreover, reveals the abbot of Stella so successfully that it occasions the kind of autobiography that, in a way, is biography enough.

At the request of his bishop, Isaac writes his Letter on the Service of the Mass.[4] In the last paragraph, after all the tremendous ascent from contrition to consecration to communion, there is a sudden stalling and decisive descent. To make sure, he tells his bishop, that the limits of a letter were not exceeded, a friend of the bishop's or, at least, one of his flock (though hardly a *laissez-faire* lamb), had just broken into the property of the abbey of Stella, given (and not by proxy) a good hiding to some of the brothers and made off with eight head of cattle. To crown all, to round off the rough-handling and robbery, Hugh of Chauvigny was boasting from the housetops that he had avenged himself on all the English; Henry II of England had, obviously, not consulted the said Hugo either when annexing Eleanor of Aquitaine or the

Aquitaine of Eleanor. The absurdity of Chauvigny's assertion provokes Isaac to a pious exaggeration that more fussy and fuzzy periods would regard as somewhat impious. He informs bishop John that Hugh's hand "is stretched-out still;"[5] high-handed Hugh is behaving like the Most High.

Amused irony was not our abbot's only reaction; he was, understandably, very angry. The fire that flamed-out in his meditation took the form: "Would that I were not an Englishman or, at least, never saw Englishmen in my place of exile!" This was not the most diplomatic language possible to include in and conclude with a letter to a bishop who was an Englishman. Such is Isaac of Stella in 1162; learned and devout, a man of amused irony and, very rarely, of intense anger.[6]

If length of tenure is anything to go by, Isaac seems to have performed efficiently; twenty years of rule (1147–1167) looks rather good, even for an age of for-life abbots. But he was something more than a superior who succeeded in administration of the earthly; he was a true church father to the assembly of God at Stella. So much so that the brethren came to resemble the Athenians of Acts; interested only in the newest notions, they were intolerant of anything less recent than their abbot's latest lecture.[7]

The irony of this was not only that it contradicted the very purpose of Isaac's discourses, but that his "new theology" was itself already dated; he was discussing the burning questions of the eleven-forties in the eleven-sixties.[8] Not that knowing this need have hindered their attending. Isaac's School of Chartres' style of an exciting blend of old things and new can be quite stimulating to the reader of today. Stella's most famous abbot does share his fun. Even if he represents a type of monastic theology that never really caught on among Cistercians,[9] he was neither failure nor freak; he was quite simply unique.

True, it was quite common, at that time, for young Englishmen to make a continental tour of intellectual watering-places.[10] Englishmen became and remained monks and abbots on the continent; one such contemporary of Isaac became abbot of Cîteaux itself.[11] Yet, apart from Isaac, it is difficult to find among twelfth-century continental Cistercians an Englishman who became monk, abbot and writer of note.

The case of Geoffrey of Auxerre (an Englishman for all the "Auxerre") only helps to bring out the solitary greatness of Isaac. For Geoffrey was, to put it rudely, no solitary sparrow on the housetop. He spent most of his life at the top, with the Best People. His switching from A to B, from disciple of Abelard to disciple of St Bernard, becoming the holy man's secretary and both his third biographer and third successor as abbot of Clairvaux, was not the record of an abject in the house of the Lord. An admirer of St Bernard and a zealous promoter of his canonisation, he was not able to imitate his independence. A friend of Henry II of England, he sided with him against Archbishop Becket; as they would say in certain places, he preferred the devil he knew to the saint he did not know. This earned him deposition, albeit illegal. There was no keeping him down though; he became abbot of Fossanova in Italy, and later abbot of Hautecombe, Savoy, where he died. In addition to his directly bernardine writings, he left a few letters and sermons; a complete commentary on the Song of Songs, and a commentary on the Apocalypse in twenty sermons. Still, the fact that Hautecombe and, its daughter-house, Fossanova were in the Clairvaux line is a reminder, were it needed, that St Bernard put Geoffrey into orbit.

Not so Isaac, not so. Second to none in his admiration for St Bernard, he made no secret of his enthusiasm for a brand of theological speculation that the abbot of Clairvaux, whether Bernard or Geoffrey, regarded as not quite diffident enough. Time was to justify both attitudes, and leave Isaac still standing on his own two feet.

But he was no mere theologian pushing his head as far as he might. He valued learning; but, as became a real disciple of St Bernard, he put life, living Cistercian life, first.[12] And then he did something that, although typically Isaac, was, in Bernard's view, rather bad form:[13] he opted-out from his responsibilities at Stella. There were, however, factors that Bernard would have appreciated; chiefly, the "folly" of making a once-for-all bid for a monastic ultimate.

Isaac left Stella for an even smaller set-up, the monastery of Châteliers on the little isle of Ré, near La Rochelle. He was not alone, but not all who approved the design had the courage to carry it through.[14] If the decision had been difficult, it was less so than the actual acceptance of the consequences, as Isaac himself admits, and in his own case.[15]

However, the living led to the learning. Isaac became more Isaac than ever. He had dreamed dreams; now, in the eagle-like renewal of his youth, he saw visions; he reached the peak of his theology; but only to go forward with the insatiability that the Infinite alone can satisfy to the world beyond the end of the world.[16]

Born in or close to 1100, dead by 1169 or later, Isaac, for quite some time abbot of Stella, gives the impression of a sturdy, energetic, intense man. Full of good sense, yet full also of enthusiasm for what in many another would be quite incompatible: scholasticism and monasticism. He keeps pushing ahead, but is ever mindful of the wisdom that is never past.

He understands the "impossibilities" of monastic living, but never tries to avoid them. He is, no doubt, severe (at least, on paper or, rather, parchment), yet never discouraging. He is not at all sure, at the very end of Sermon Twenty-six, that most are going to benefit by God's gift in Christ; he is absolutely convinced that man was made for the greatest possible intimacy with God.[17]

He loved discussing God's great cosmic, Christian and Cistercian dream; he was but speaking from what filled his unsentimental heart. But he did not just discuss; he decided to do and did the Cistercian thing. This included hard manual labor, and the still more laborious labor of monastic leisure: solitude, silence, reading, reflection, prayer.[18] Precisely because he was a good community man, there is an unmistakeable self-sufficiency about him, a certain distance between

him and the brethren; an undoubted ability to keep
to himself. He was, unquestionably, not afraid to be
alone with the Alone.[19] He would have relished the
irony of being thought strange and mysterious, when,
after all, he had succeeded in becoming a monk.

THE MEDIUM

Isaac's remark that a sermon is a kind of reading[20]
seems a trifle odd until the meaning of reading for
people of those days is recalled. They did not
differentiate, as we would, between reading and
reading aloud. For them reading was audible, unless
it was otherwise stated; they differentiated between
reading aloud and reading.[21] Reading for us usually
means eye-reading: for them it meant mouth-reading—
"the mouth of the just shall meditate Wisdom"—[22]
and ear-listening and the whole person tense with
attention, while, more often than not, literally labor-
ing to decipher some none too legible script on some
poor yet precious parchment.[23] Such being the case, it
is immaterial whether Isaac's sermons were ever
preached or not. Written to be read carefully, they
must be listened to, they expect an audience of, at
least, one.[24]

Our author leaves his reader in no doubt as to the
approach he intends to adopt. He does not purpose an
exegesis of the Gospel text, but uses it as a launching-
pad for a message that he hopes will help his listener
in his particular circumstances.[25] He would have his
disciples live ever-better lives, but he is far from content with merely tooling around some ethical and
ascetical Indianapolis. Life must be increasingly
grounded in the ever-living Christ.[26]

While accepting the historicity of the Gospel
accounts with a literalness that seems excessive to us,
and in the manner of his and of much other time
overlooking the psychological development of Christ
so explicit in the New Testament,[27] Isaac opts for the
allegorical, the write-it-another-way method. He had a

good excuse: the "books" of creation, written revelation and Incarnation are an accommodation to our condition.[28] In order to discover himself to us the Word has disguised himself. He has become unlike himself, in order that by becoming like us he may tell us about himself, tell us what he is like.

With the balance that is so characteristic, our abbot uses also the reasoned, philosophic methods that, common in some form to all periods of theological reflection, were very much to the fore in the up-and-coming theology of his day; so much so that even St Bernard (supposedly so anti-intellectual) was, on occasion, both willing and able to lapse into metaphysics.[29]

Isaac's technical language would seem to offer no great hurdle to anyone even slightly acquainted with scholastic metaphysics. Yet even such may find it helpful to notice that our Cistercian uses "substance" in three different ways. "First" and "Second Substance" apply, as he puts it, to, say, "man" as an actual individual and to "man" as a class or species, respectively.[30] In the following Sermon,[31] however, "substance" is the equivalent of the great "unshaped" that Plato cheerfully suggested went with all sorts of "shapes" to make the "shaped".

No doubt about it, Isaac goes to a great deal of trouble to tell us that God is neither an individual of a kind nor a kind of individual, no frame fits him. It is no easy thing to talk correctly, or, come to that, to talk at all of God's sheer being; and when the question has to do with God and his creation, well, little wonder so many theologians prefer to talk about theology.

Isaac was keen on theology; keen on what, for him, was the latest "creation" in God-talk fashion; but, if he could not fully escape the Valley of Glory, still less could he escape being dazzled by the glory of God and the God of glory; he was up against the Numinous, the N to infinity. Such being the case, he had to lapse out of his lapse into straight metaphysics and fall back on the slanted, stained-glass-window metaphysics of metaphor;[32] better a puzzling

reflection in a mirror than the stygian darkness of
a syllogism that has blown a fuse.

THE MESSAGE

To complain to or of a novice in a monastic noviciate
that he never puts a foot right is extremely dangerous.
Not that the poor fellow may get discouraged, no
such luck; but that he may be only too delighted to
yield to the temptation of offering cheek with the
meek and humble reply that, of course, he never puts
a foot right, otherwise how explain his putting foot
in a monks' noviciate?

If it is hazardous to condemn a person for doing
his own thing, it is still more so to blame him for not
doing something that would not help him achieve some
desirable result. Take the case of reproaching St Bernard
in his Sermons on the Song of Songs with not inter-
preting the book consistently. It is quite true that he
does not, but then he never intended to. Such a complaint not only spoils enjoyment of the Sermons, it
prevents the reader from noticing that each Sermon is
a complete unity in itself.[33] This is a reminder that the
same is valid for these Sermons of Isaac; each is self-
contained, be it one of a series or not. And such was
his intention. Those promises to treat of something
"in a new beginning"[34] begin to make abundant sense
if each Sermon is, like every man, *pace* Mr Donne,
an island.

Such being the case, it might seem a somewhat
thankless task, a kicking against the goad, to attempt
some sort of synthesis of the doctrine contained in
Sermons One to Twenty-Six inclusive. Even so, even
if what is here offered is slightly off the mark, it may
stimulate careful reading of each and provoke the
synthesis, approach, whatever, that does justice to
them and their author.

The basic principle, thesis, dominant note,
leitmotiv of these Sermons would appear to be
summed up accurately in the words, "He who has

come down is none other than he who has gone up."[35]
There is no need whatsoever to make a fuss as to
whether descent necessarily precedes ascent or the
other way round; the movement is 'vertical', that
is what counts.

In the Beginning there was the "descent" of
Creation. Even the Blessed Trinity itself may be
regarded as a "descent": the Proceedings of the
Divine Society are a "come-down" from Father to
Son in Holy Spirit. Creation is an "e-motion", a
"being-moved", in absolute freedom, of the Immutable; a descent of "gift" through Spirit and Son
"from the Father of all that gives light, with whom
there is no slightest shadow of alteration."[36]
Creatures are because God has "come down" in the
world, since as their cause he is their very being. God
also "goes up" in the world or with the world because
"what was made was life in him,"[37] alive in him;
no-thing has come down from heaven except the
creation planned in heaven.[38]

With the Creator–Sower so sowing himself, it is
not strange that the one visible creature made capable
of recognizing and welcoming the presence of God
should be able to "investigate", to search for God
and find him in the beauties of the visible creation.[39]

Yes, man is able and ought to seek God's footprints in the Garden of Creation. There is a snag, however: Original Sin. Man is not only blind, he is para-
lyzed as well; he is unable to see and incapable of
going on his way to God.[40] Man has gone down from
Jerusalem and fallen.[41] Jack and Jill have come
tumbling down from pride to envy and to all other
vices.[42] Man, half-dead, cleaves to the dust, sticks fast
in the mire of the dregs.[43]

The Sower takes on a new role and becomes the
true surprising[44] Samaritan.[45] Without leaving Jerusalem,[46] he comes to Man and not only puts clay on
his eyes, but bends down and writes himself into the
dust of Man by the Finger of God.[47] The soul and
body of Man have been reunited with God and with
each other by the Spirit of God.[48] To put this another
way, Jesus is the Ladder Jacob saw in his dream; no

wonder he was glad. Communication, ceaseless and effortless, between Heaven and earth has begun.[49]

The early Cistercians, with a professional interest in the Rule of St Benedict, would give no mere nominal, intellectual assent to this. The Ladder of Jacob's dream was, if the Rule was right, supposed to be their dream, a sacrament of what their spiritual life ought to be all about: lowliness in this present world leading to the heights of Heaven hereafter; ever-growing humility that leads to the full blossoming of charity; self-emptying love that brings the freedom of nothingness and the ignorance that is wisdom.[50]

Experience of such ascent–descent makes sense of following Christ in his ascent of the Cross, the plank on and through which he saves us from perishing.[51] Fellowship with the Crucified is a very personal affair, and it is terribly important to keep the Lord awake during the journey across the sea of this world. The three nails, so to say, that keep Christ awake and hold the monk to his profession are reading, meditation and prayer.[52] Hold, yes, but only to promote the relationship. Model and Mediator, the New Moses becomes increasingly the Message and its Meaning; the emphasis changes focus from living to learning, from sight to insight; the Serpent on the standard[53] becomes the Master who leads his disciples up the mountain, and also down; the Lord is both Mountain and Valley.[54]

Jesus not only went up to pray, he went down to preach and be of service. Monks should strive to balance the "direct" search for God and "distracting" service to the neighbour; the "higher" in one way, the "lowlier" in the other.[55] This was no new teaching,[56] yet, somehow, the "sanity" of it was not mad enough for Isaac on Ré. By then, with heart set on an upward journey, he tended to grudge the neighbour the attention he deserved.[57] Increasingly he was concerned with right-ordered love, with that putting deeds under the reason and the reason under God, that is the recovery of Paradise.[58] He would (and he sounds like the ecology-conscious) escape into pure air and limpid, sky-reflecting lake; it was all within, and was all the more real for that.[59] God, the soul, the body, these were the great realities for him;[60] it was enough if in the Spirit and through the Son it was granted him in the End to see the Beginning.[61]

NOTES

1. See, for example, Louis Bouyer, *The Cistercian Heritage*, (London, 1958) 161.
2. PL 157:1269 ff.
3. *Sermon 5.*13; *Sermon 25.*8.
4. PL 194:1896.
5. Is 5,25; 9, 12, 17, 21; 10, 4.
6. E.g., *Sermon 2.*10-11; *Sermon 14.*2,4-10; *Sermon 18.*15.
7. *Sermon 48,* PL 194:1853.
8. For more exact dating, see Bernard McGinn, *Isaac of Stella on the Divine Nature,* pg.52, Analecta Cisterciensis, Rome, 1973.
9. See Bernard McGinn, *The Golden Chain,* pg. 238, Cistercian Studies 15, Washington, 1972.
10. As noted by Gaston Salet, s J, in his Introduction to Dom Hoste's edition of Isaac's Sermons, pg. 14, note 1.
11. Abbot Gilbert, 1163–1167.
12. *Sermon 4.*1 and 16; *Sermon 12.*1; *Sermon 14,*7-9; *Sermon 16.*16.
13. St Bernard, e.g., *Ep 82; Ep 86.*2; *Ep 87.*3.
14. *Sermon 14.*12.
15. *Sermon 21.*18.
16. *Sermon 23.*3; *Sermon 14.*11. The best biographical account of Isaac in English is to be found in McGinn's, *The Golden Chain,* referred to in note 9.
17. *Sermon 7.*6; *Sermon 8.*10; *Sermon 9.*10; *Sermon 16.*15; *Sermon 25.*1.
18. *Sermon 14.*12-14.
19. *Sermon 14.*12.
20. *Sermon 14.*7.
21. See, e.g., St Augustine, *Conf,* 6,3,3; RB ch. 48.
22. Ps 36.30.
23. Extensive discussion of all this subject is found in Jean Leclercq, *The Love of Learning and the Desire for God,* New York, 1961 (1962, paperback), pgs. 18 and ff (23 and ff); 89-90 (78); 153 (127).
24. *Sermon 16.*5; cf. Leclercq, *Love of Learning,* pgs. 188-189 (155).
25. *Sermon 16.*5; *Sermon 18.*3.
26. *Sermon 1.*4.
27. Lk 2.52; Hb 2.17; 4.15; 5.8.
28. *Sermon 9.*3-6.
29. E.g., *Dil,* 12, 35; *Csi,* 7, 16; *SC, 80.*5.
30. *Sermon 19.*12-18.

31. *Sermon 20.5.*
32. *Sermon 24.12-16.*
33. See Jean Leclercq, *Recueil d'Études sur Saint Bernard et ses Écrits,* Vol. I, pg. 203.
34. *Sermon 4.19; Sermon 16.20; Sermon 23.20; Sermon 24.23.*
35. Ep 4.10.
36. Jm 1.17; *Sermon 24.8.21-22; Sermon 9.10.*
37. Jn 1.3-4; *Sermon 22.22-23.*
38. *Sermon 23.1.*
39. *Sermon 22.23.*
40. *Sermon 4.2; Sermon 5.3; Sermon 7.4,12; Sermon 8.13; Sermon 9.4.*
41. *Sermon 6.1-4.*
42. *Sermon 6.7-8.*
43. *Sermon 6.3-4,10; Sermon 7.6,11; Sermon 10.3.*
44. *Sermon 5.1; Sermon 6.20; Sermon 10.11; Sermon 16.14; Sermon 17.6.*
45. *Sermon 6.1,16.*
46. *Sermon 7.3-4,15.*
47. *Sermon 12.2; Sermon 9.12-13; Sermon 16.13.*
48. *Sermon 6.11-12; Sermon 7.8; Sermon 9.12.*
49. *Sermon 9.18; Sermon 12.4; Sermon 13.1-2.*
50. RB ch. 7.
51. *Sermon 15.4-5.*
52. *Sermon 14.7-8, 13-14; Sermon 15.12.*
53. *Sermon 15.12-13.*
54. *Sermon 11.1-2; Sermon 12.2 and ff; Sermon 13.1-2;* cf. *Sermon 16.13.*
55. *Sermon 12.8;* cf. *Sermon 3.19; Sermon 17.18-19.*
56. E.g., St Gregory, *Mor,* 7, 15, 18; PL 75:775.
57. *Sermon 25.5-12.*
58. *Sermon 4.17; Sermon 5.16; Sermon 21.15-17.*
59. *Sermon 4.9; Sermon 25.15.*
60. *Ep an,* PL 194:1875.
61. *Sermon 4.15; Sermon 5.13; Sermon 24.20-23; Sermon 25.7-8.*

ABBREVIATIONS

Ep(p)	Letter(s)
Serm	Sermon(s)

THE WORKS OF PETER ABELARD
Dial   *Dialogus inter Philosophum Judaeum et Christianum*
Epit Th   *Eptimone Theologiae Christianae*
Introd   *Introductio ad theologiam christianam*

THE WORKS OF AELRED OF RIEVAULX
Iesu   *De Iesu puero duodenni*

THE WORKS OF SAINT AMBROSE
Apol David   *Apologia prophetae David*
Bened Patriarch   *De benedictionibus patriarcharum*
Expos Luc   *Expositio evangelii secundum Lucam*
Fide   *De fide*
Hex   *Hexaemeron*
Off   *De officiis ministrorum*
Par   *De paradiso*
Spir   *De Spirito sancto*
Tob   *De Tobia*

THE WORKS OF SAINT ANSELM OF CANTERBURY

Deus H	Cur Deus Homo
Fid Trin	De fide Trinitatis
Mon	Monologium
Praes D	De concordia praescientiae et praedestinationis
Process Spirit	De processione Spiritus sancti
Prosl	Proslogion

THE WORKS OF SAINT AUGUSTINE OF HIPPO

Catech rud	De catechizandis rudibus
Civ Dei	De civitate Dei
Conf	Confessiones
Corr grat	De correptione et gratia
Disc Chr	De disciplina christiana
Doct christ	De doctrina christiana
Don Pers	De dono perseverantiae
Expos Gal	Expositio epistolae ad Galatas
Ep Joan	In epistolam Joannis
Gen litt	De Genesi ad litteram libri duodecim
Gen Man	De Genesi contra Manichaeos
In Joan	In Joannis evangelium
In Ps ...	Enarratio in Psalmum ...
Lib arb	De gratia et libero arbitrio
Mag	De magistro
Musica	De musica
Quan an	De quantitate animae
Serm Mont	De sermone Domini in monte
Sol	Soliloquia
Trin	De Trinitate
Virg	De sancta virginitate

THE WORKS OF BEDE THE VENERABLE

In Joan	In S. Joannis evangelium expositio
In Luc	In Lucae evangelium expositio
In Marc	In Marci evangelium expositio
In Pent	In Pentateuchum commentarii
Hex	Hexaemeron

THE WORK OF SAINT BENEDICT

RB	Regula monachorum

THE WORKS OF SAINT BERNARD OF CLAIRVAUX

Adv	Sermo in adventu domini
Ann	Sermo in annunciatione dominica
Apo	Apologia ad Guillelmum abbatem

Asc	*Sermo in ascensione domini*
Ass	*Sermo in assumptione B. V. M.*
Circ	*Sermo in circumcisione domini*
Conv	*Sermo de conversione ad clericos*
Csi	*De consideratione libri V*
Ded	*Sermo in dedicatione ecclesiae*
Dil	*Liber de diligendo deo*
Div	*Sermones de diversis*
Gra	*De gratia et libero arbitrio*
Hum	*De gradibus humilitatis et superbiae*
Miss	*Homilia super Missus est in laudibus Virginis Matris*
OS	*Sermo in festivitate Omnium Sanctorum*
Pasc	*Sermo in die Paschae*
Praec	*De precepto et dispensatione*
SC	*Sermo super Cantica canticorum*

THE WORKS OF BOETHIUS

Arith	*De arithmetica*
Cat Arist	*In Categorias Aristotelis*
Comment in Porph	*Commentaria in Porphyrium*
Consol Phil	*De consolatione philosophiae*
Diff	*De deffinitione*
Div	*De divisione*
Duab nat	*De duabus naturis*
In Porph D 1	*In Porphyrium dialogus primus*
In Porph D 2	*In Porphyrium dialogus secundus*
Interpret Prim	*Interpretatio Priorum Analiticorum Aristotelis*
Interpret Sec	*Interpretatio Posteriorum Analiticorum Aristotelis*
Quomodo substantiae	*Quomodo substantiae bonae sint*
Trin	*Quomodo Trinitas unus Deus*

THE WORK OF CALCIDIUS

Comment	*Commentarii*

THE WORKS OF SAINT JOHN CASSIAN

Coen Inst	*De coenobiorum institutis*
Coll	*Collatio(nes)*

THE WORKS OF DENIS THE PSEUDO-AREOPAGITE

Cl	*De coelesti ierarchia*
DN	*De divinis nominibus*
MT	*De mystica theologia*

THE WORKS OF ERIUGENA

Div Nat	*De divisione naturae*
Prol Joan	*Homilia in prologum sancti evangelii secundum Joannem*
Comm Joan	*Commentarius in s. evangelii secundum Joannem*
Praed	*De praedestinatione*
Super I C	*Expositiones super Ierarchiam Coelestem*

THE WORKS OF SAINT GREGORY THE GREAT

Dial	*Dialogorum libri IV*
In Evang	*Homiliae in evangelia*
In Ezech	*Homiliarum in Ezechielem liber I et II*
In Ps P	*In septem psalmos poenitentiales expositio*
I Reg	*In regum expositiones*
Mor	*In expositionem beati Job moralia*

THE WORKS OF SAINT HILARY

Trin	*De Trinitate*
In Matt	*Commentarius in evangelium Matthaei*

THE WORKS OF ISAAC OF STELLA

Ep an	*Epistola de anima*
Ep off mis	*Epistola ad Joannem Episcopum Pictaviensem de officio missae*

THE WORKS OF HUGH OF SAINT VICTOR

Arca	*De arca Noe morali*
Arrha an	*De arrha animae*
Erud didasc	*Eruditionis didascalicae libri VII*
In Eccles	*In Salomonis ecclesiasten homiliae XIX*
Sacram	*De sacramentis christianae fidei*
Summ Sent	*Summa sententiarum*

THE WORKS OF SAINT JEROME

Comm Joel	*Commentaria in Joelem*
Expos Job	*Expositio interlinearis in librum Job*
In Matt	*Commentaria in evangelium s. matthaei*
Interpret Did	*Interpretatio libri Didymi de Spiritu sancto*
Nom hebr	*De nominibus hebraicis*

THE WORK OF MACROBIUS

Comment	*Commentarium in somnium Scipionis*

Psalms have been cited according to the Vulgate enumeration.

A cumulative index will appear in the final volume
of the sermons of Isaac of Stella.